Making the Most of the
PENINSULA

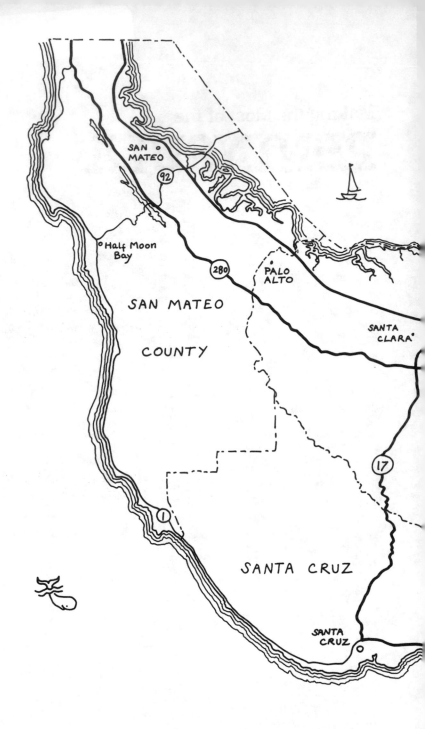

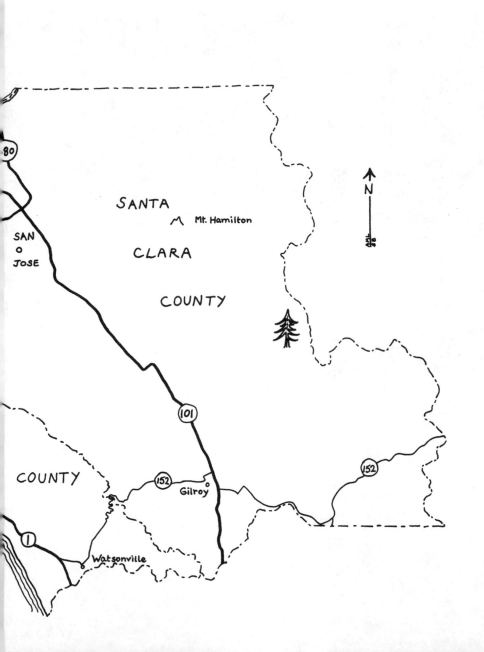

Making the Most of the

PENINSULA

A California Guide to San Mateo, Santa Clara & Santa Cruz Counties

by Lee Foster

PRESIDIO PRESS

Published by Presidio Press 31 Pamaron Way, Novato, California 94947

Library of Congress Cataloging in Publication Data

Foster, Lee, 1943-
    Making the most of the peninsula
    Includes index.
        1. San Mateo County (Calif.)—Description and travel—
Guide-books. 2. Santa Clara County (Calif.)—Description and
travel—Guide-books. 3. Santa Cruz County (Calif.)— Description and
Description and travel—Guide books.
    I. Title.
    F868.S19F66   1983   917.94'7   83-832
    ISBN 0-89141-164-X (pbk.)

Edited by Joan Griffin
Cover by Jon Goodchild
Photographs by Lee Foster
Maps by Shirley Barker and Adair M. Langston
Typeset by Techni-Process/Computer Press
Printed in the United States of America

To Bart, Karin, and Paul

Contents

x

Introduction

This book will guide the native or traveler who wants to become acquainted with the fascinating region south from San Francisco, the *peninsula*, which I define broadly as San Mateo, Santa Clara, and Santa Cruz counties.

The peninsula is a remarkable, vital, and diverse area that proved endlessly intriguing to me during 10 years of my life there. Few experiences focus the spirit more thoroughly than a quiet walk in the cathedral of redwoods at Big Basin Redwoods State Park. And what technical discovery of our time has been more crucial than the Intel chip of 1972 that formed the basis of the computer revolution? The imagination with which we define the prospects of our own lives can't help but be enlarged as we walk through the peninsula, wonderingly, with such visionaries as Gaspar de Portola and his entourage, the first Europeans to set foot on this landscape. For the present-day explorer there is much to celebrate here.

I've organized the book in a manner that an explorer on the peninsula will find handy and logical. The first sections cover the northern peninsula and the bay side through Palo Alto. Then we cross the mountains and encounter the coast from Half Moon Bay through Santa Cruz. Finally, we return to the Santa Clara Valley and wander from the original Mission Santa Clara through the Silicon Valley of today, winding our way south to such pleasures as the Garlic Festival of Gilroy and the lovely south Santa Clara County park, Mt. Madonna.

You can read this guide, perusing it from beginning to end. Or you can go to the Index and Resource List at the back and look up a subject that interests you, such as Stanford or Elephant Seals, and consider just that section. All major topics of interest in the three counties have their own Index headings, including many generic subjects such as Backpacking or Wineries.

The book aims to give you an accurate and engaging write-up on each place of interest, plus the location, and a phone number to call for further information. I avoid the main pitfall of other guidebooks, which insist on freezing volatile information by saying, "The Western Barbed Wire Museum is open on Thursday afternoons only and the admission is $1.79." My experience has led me to conclude that readers are frustrated, after driving 50 miles on a hot Thursday afternoon, to find the museum is now open only on Friday and the price is $4.95, including children. For changeable information in this age of the telephone, simply call ahead for hours open and fees, if they are relevant at a site you plan to explore.

I visited personally each place mentioned in the book while doing research in the year prior to publication, so you can be assured that this volume is a work of fact rather than fiction. I intend to review and update the book every two years or so in the 1980s. (If you wish to insist that I committed grave sins of omission or commission when choosing or covering subjects for this book, you may write me in care of the publisher, and I will weigh changes in future editions.)

Good maps are important tools for exploring this region. The best maps are those provided free to AAA members. The complete set of maps to ask for, from the general to the specific, is: Peninsula Points; San Mateo County; Santa Clara/Santa Cruz Counties; Daly City; San Mateo City; Palo Alto; Greater San Jose North; Greater San Jose South; and Santa Cruz City.

Though everything of interest in the area has been considered, special emphasis has been placed on the thickly textured drama of human history and the abundant pleasures of nature available in the public parks.

The Human Drama

The world of nature on the peninsula is perennial and eternal, with the blue-eyed grass seeds sprouting and flowering each spring and the San Andreas Fault grinding away over an unimaginable time span. Nature can be explained as we encounter it. For example, the Los Trancos earthquake walk offers the best opportunity on the peninsula to discuss the San Andreas Fault. But the story of human history here is more accidental and arbitrary, with people of several epochs contributing to sites we visit. A broad outline is helpful at the outset.

The human story of the peninsula falls into three main eras: the Indian, the Spanish-Mexican, and the American.

Ohlone Indians flourished here from perhaps 7000 B.C. to 1800 A.D. The exact duration of Indian presence is difficult to determine, but clever detective work and carbon dating at shell mounds have suggested the roughly 9,000-year heritage. The Ohlones were a hunting and gathering people, who fed themselves in the salubrious environment without raising crops, seldom going hungry, eating the acorns, shellfish, fish, seeds, and game that were abundant. Because of the relatively benign climate, they required little protective clothing or housing.

Ohlone men mainly hunted and fished, spending much time in sweat houses and gambling games. Women built houses and made baskets, which were used even for carrying water and for cooking. Hot rocks were dropped into a basket full of water and food to boil the contents. Women also gathered the oak acorns and processed them laboriously by pounding the acorns into meal, then leaching out the tannins, before cooking.

The Ohlone population in the greater Bay Area in 1777 has been estimated at about 9,000, one of the densest populations of native Americans anywhere, though the number seems small compared to our daily experience of five million Bay Area residents.

Due to the importation of diseases for which the Indians had little immunity, such as smallpox, measles, and tuberculosis, the Ohlones were doomed by the entry of the Spanish into their world. This was the ultimate effect, regardless of whether different factions in the Spanish system wished to enslave them or to save their immortal souls.

One of the Ohlones' principal legacies, though only recently appreciated, was that they lived here for 9,000 years doing relatively little damage to the life-support system upon which they and all other creatures depended for a sustained existence. Because they neither left pyramids nor fashioned enduring gold jewelry, the humble Ohlones will always remain mere footnotes in the popular imagination, which places little value on preserving a biosystem and living within its means.

The Spanish-Mexican era was brief, 1769–1848, but it

established the names on the landscape, much of the pattern of cattle ranching, and the initial roadways that we still use today on the peninsula. Spain needed a scheme to hold the terrain against the Russians, who were expanding from the north, and the British, who controlled Canada and looked on California with uncertain intentions.

Spain wanted to manage the territory with a minimum investment at this twilight time in her empire's resources, so she used three entities: missions to convert the natives to Christianity and to make them self-sufficient within an agriculturally productive system; pueblos, or farming towns, to support the troops and settlers; and presidios, or forts, to protect the missionaries and the settlers, establishing order in the new territory. Missions were founded on the peninsula at Santa Clara and Santa Cruz.

The peninsula city of San Jose was California's first town. On November 29, 1777, the Spanish governor of California, Felipe de Neve, ordered Lt. Jose Joaquin Moraga to establish the pueblo of San Jose de Guadalupe. This first pueblo had 66 adventuresome people and was located about 1.5 miles north of the present downtown San Jose. De Neve envisioned that this pueblo would supply food to the presidios at San Francisco and Monterey.

Mexico's successful struggle for independence from Spain had widespread implications for the frontier territory of California, including the peninsula. When Mexico became independent in 1822, the government secularized the missions, allowing the cattle and sheep herds, productive agricultural lands, and structured life of the Indians to fall into receivership. The mission system disintegrated quickly as the rich mission lands were granted by the government to prominent families of Californios, as Mexicans in California were called. This ushered in a brief era in which the horse-loving vaqueros dashed across the screen of California history, developing large herds of cattle whose hides could be traded to the Boston ships that came around the Horn.

The American era began in force in 1849, although a steady trickle of Americans had already arrived by sea or migrated overland in the 1840s. A few enterprising American traders had settled earlier in Monterey and on the peninsula. The event that triggered the inrush of Americans, as well as a tide of other nationals, was, of course, the Gold Rush, which started in 1848 after James Marshall discovered flakes of gold in a sawmill race on the American River. Mexico ceded California to the U.S. with the Treaty of Guadalupe Hidalgo in 1848 and California entered the

Union in 1850. San Jose served briefly as the first state capital, but was abandoned as too remote from the center of activity at Sacramento and eastward in the gold country.

The peninsula's history from then on is a tale with chapters as diverse as redwood lumbering and mercury mining. But prominent among these stories is the growth of fruit farming after Louis Pellier introduced the French prune (la petite prune d'Agen) in 1856. Enduring fruit orchards quickly replaced wheat, which had enjoyed a brief dominance in agriculture. Diversified fruit production was aided by advances in drying and canning, as well as by the national network of railroads that allowed distribution of the food to markets in the East. In recent decades, the increasing population's demand for urban land has cut back this food production drastically, until the peninsula's largest agricultural crop is now not even food, but flowers.

Since the fifties, the centrally important business here has been the growth of electronics, especially the manufacture of computer hardware and software. As a sign of the times, this book was written and typeset with Osborne word-processing capabilities developed in the so-called Silicon Valley. Silicon is the element used in wafer-thin computer chips with their numerous circuits.

With this brief overview of the layers of human history in mind, let us proceed on our adventure of discovering the peninsula.

Poppies on Sweeney Ridge

Gaspar de Portola's Discovery 1

The View from Sweeney Ridge

T he fitting place to begin an exploration of the peninsula is Sweeney Ridge, a prominence above Skyline College in San Bruno. There you get a 360-degree view of the Bay Area. It might be argued that this is the most spectacular view on the peninsula. On a clear day you can see everything from San Francisco Bay and Mt. Diablo to the east, the Pacific Ocean and the Farallon Islands to the west, Mt. Tamalpais or even Mt. St. Helena to the north, and the San Andreas Reservoir or deep into the peninsula along the bay to the south.

From Sweeney Ridge, Gaspar de Portola and his party in 1769 became the first Europeans to see San Francisco Bay. When his scouts had explored further, Portola conjectured that he was indeed on a peninsula.

Sweeney Ridge Skyline Preserve

S weeney Ridge is a two-mile-long, 1,200-foot-high ridge of which the Sweeney Ridge Skyline Preserve is a 58-acre parcel, deeded to the public during Richard Nixon's administration as surplus federal land suitable for a park.

The entire Sweeney Ridge beyond the preserve is a subject of controversy because many conservationists and historians would like to see it purchased by the public as the premier historic and nature site on the peninsula. Congress has approved funds to

7

acquire the remaining ridgelands as part of the Golden Gate National Recreation Area, but the current administration has yet to act. If completed, this purchase will further link the chain of trails that may one day make it possible to walk from Sweeney Ridge all the way to Santa Cruz on public lands, following parks, watersheds, and open space holdings.

Access to this splendid ridgeland is from Skyline College off Skyline Boulevard. From Freeway 280, traveling south, turn west on Westborough Boulevard and then south on Skyline. Leave Skyline at College Avenue and enter Skyline College grounds. At the sign indicating the campus layout, turn left and proceed a half mile on the oval road to parking lot B. Park there and look up the hillside, above the maintenance yard, to see a yellow automobile barrier and gate allowing entrance to Sweeney Ridge. A sign indicates the park entrance. Walk down the main road, then up the service road to this gate and enter the preserve. Continue to follow the service road as it winds around the ridge up to a white concrete building, once a Coast Guard radio station.

The walk up Sweeney Ridge can be done in an hour. More ambitious hikers can proceed on dirt paths to the green radio transmitting station on the ridge farther south, where the Portola marker can be found beyond the structures.

As you walk along the road in the preserve, the views unfold before you with dramatic tension, displaying aspects of the scene before the grandeur of the final panorama. First you see the ocean side, Pacifica and the rolling hillsides characteristic of the region. Quail and meadowlark are plentiful. The wind can be vigorous, so come prepared with warm, wind-resistant clothing. The moods of Sweeney Ridge vary dramatically with the seasons, from the pensive, ethereal foggy overcast of summer to the bright, clear afternoons of spring and autumn. Bunches of wildflowers proliferate, especially poppy, lupine, Douglas iris, Indian paintbrush, mustard, and yarrow. The vegetation is diverse, split about evenly between grasslands and chaparral, where the dominant plant is baccharis. Due to the fog, there are some fairly moist pockets, where ferns flourish. The roadside abounds with poison hemlock.

When you reach the promontory near the white concrete bunker, it's time to savor the view. Binoculars can be used to good advantage to search for distant sites or watch the red-tailed hawks swoop over the hillsides in search of ground squirrels.

With a little imagination, it's possible to approximate the feelings of Gaspar de Portola and his 63 men who, having walked all the way from San Diego through the roadless wilderness, were puzzled because they had not found what cartographers said was an impressive Monterey Bay. Now they were confronted with a large body of water never before reported. For 200 years sailors had passed near the Golden Gate without discovering the bay. It was "invisible" because of the proximity of Angel Island, Alcatraz Island, and the even profile of the East Bay hills as seen from the sea through the narrow Golden Gate. Portola was puzzled to account for this large body of water. From Sweeney Ridge he could not see the Golden Gate inlet, which would have told him this was a bay.

Portola's Expedition

The discovery trip of Gaspar de Portola was crucial in peninsula history. In San Mateo County alone there are 11 designated historic spots, some with markers, tracing the camps of his party.

Several of these camps were along the coast, as Portola and his men worked their way north. Eventually the explorers crossed the spine of the mountains above present-day Pacifica and saw, from Sweeney Ridge, the bay. From there the party proceeded south along the bay side of the peninsula, stopping finally at the ancient "tall tree," the *palo alto*, in the present city of that name, before turning back to Monterey.

Here are some of the camps and markers:

South of Pescadero 8.8 miles on Ocean Shore Road, the group camped on October 23 near the mouth of Gazos Creek. Many members of the party were seriously ill, including Portola himself, at times. Berries and vegetable foods eaten at the Waddell Creek area provided enough vitamin C to reduce scurvy, but the connection between the berries and prevention of the disease was not well known. As a further complication, severe diarrhea followed the encounter with these new foods, making the trip life-threatening.

At San Gregorio Beach, one coastal encampment is commemorated with a marker, which says:

> Portola Expedition Camp. On October 24, the Portola Expedition camped at an Indian rancheria on San Gregorio Creek, about one half league from its mouth. Tired and sick, they rested here over the 25th and 26th.

At present Whitehouse Creek they found Indians living in huts

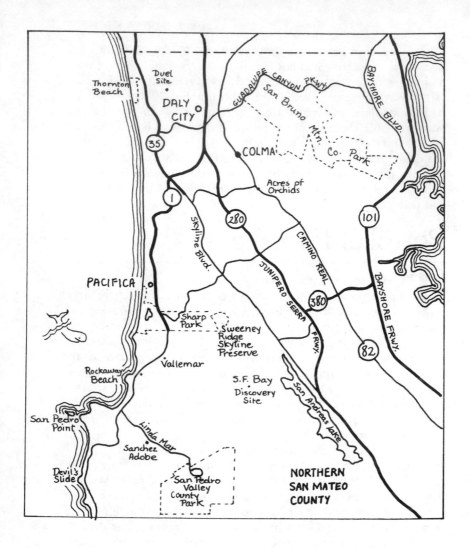

NORTHERN
SAN MATEO
COUNTY

of split pine, with a large circular house in the center that could hold the entire village. The Spaniards were impressed and called the site *La Rancheria de la Casa Grande*, Village of the Big House. At Tunitas Creek, 8 miles south of Half Moon Bay, Portola noted a large Indian village.

South of Half Moon Bay 3.8 miles, he camped on the present Ocean Shore Road, along the south bank of Purisima Creek, on October 27. The Indian village on the north bank of the creek was called *Las Pulgas*, after the fleas that were the bane of the times.

East of Half Moon Bay .7 miles, the party camped close to the mouth of Pilarcitos Creek on October 28th and 29th, when Portola himself was gravely ill.

On October 30 the expedition camped by a stream at the foot of Montara Mountain, which blocked their way. They needed food badly and were fortunate to find here a supply of mussels. They named the camp after the mussels, *El Rincon de las Almejas*.

A marker in Pacifica along the inland side of Coast Highway 1 notes Portola camped here "at San Pedro Creek, where there was an Indian village, from October 31 to November 3. To that camp scouting parties brought news of a body of water to the east." The marker lies treacherously along the high speed road, so park some distance away and walk to it if you wish to read it.

From there the party moved inland to the crests, where the great discovery of San Francisco Bay is recorded and commemorated with a marker. The difficult-to-reach marker on Sweeney Ridge reads:

> Site of the Discovery of San Francisco Bay. On October 13, 1769, Captain Gaspar de Portola was camped by the creek at the south of this valley when scouting parties brought news of a body of water to the east. On November 4 the expedition advanced. Turning inland, the party climbed to the summit of Sweeney Ridge and beheld the Bay of San Francisco for the first time.

The party clambered down the hill to make camp on land now inundated by San Andreas Lake. After the hike up Sweeney Ridge, you may wish to follow Portola's descent. Drive a few miles south along Freeway 280, turn off on Skyline, and stop where Skyline meets Hillcrest in the town of Millbrae to read about this camp:

> First camp after the discovery of San Francisco Bay. On November 4, 1769, the expedition of Captain Gaspar de Portola, after crossing Sweeney Ridge, beheld the Bay of San Francisco for the first time. That night they camped at a small lagoon, now covered by San Andreas Lake. Finding the bay too large to go around and thinking they had bypassed Monterey Bay, the expedition camped here again on November 12, 1769 on their return to San Diego.

At the camp in Palo Alto, the 63 men and some 200 horses and mules rested while scouts were sent around the south tip of the bay to explore further. A scout, Sgt. Jose Francisco Ortega, who had ventured as far as a hilltop in present-day San Leandro, advised that more watery obstacles lay to the north, so Portola and his officers elected to retrace their steps to San Diego.

No one tells the story better than the original three diarists: Portola himself, engineer Miguel Costanso, and chaplain Juan Crespi. Frank Stanger's book gathering these documents, called

Who Discovered the Golden Gate?, is available from the San Mateo County Historical Association (see the Index for a write-up on their museum).

The scout on Sweeney Ridge who happened to be the first to see San Francisco Bay was Lt. Bruno Hecate, naval officer of the King of Spain. He bestowed the name of his patron saint on the other large park in north San Mateo County, San Bruno Mountain.

San Bruno Mountain County Park

Fortunately, much of San Bruno Mountain is now protected as a county park. It is a needed but as yet unimproved amenity for crowded peninsula residents seeking some communion with nature. It is also a place where two endangered species of butterflies, the mission blue and San Francisco silverspot, make their homes. Preserving San Bruno Mountain, in part for the butterflies, is a modest way in which peninsula residents have voted and acted against the worldwide loss of plant and animal species, the expected eradication of an estimated 20 percent of the animal gene pool and 15 percent of the plant gene pool by the year 2000.

The road up San Bruno Mountain, after you leave Bayshore Freeway 101 on Bayshore Boulevard and then turn west on Guadalupe Canyon Parkway, gradually ascends to reveal much of Daly City below. Looking north, the old railroad shops of the Southern Pacific, the phone company staging area for service trucks, and the huge Cow Palace, site of many expositions, stretch out before you. Close-up on Bayshore Boulevard, several huge brick warehouses, such as the Lazarro Coal Company buildings, have a sturdy air about them. One can't help but regret seeing this construction gradually fall into decay, with half the windows broken. The entire setting of San Bruno Mountain would be more picturesque if human litter and graffiti could be reduced. This may come in time, as the park develops more, with trash barrels, appropriate picnic areas, and a greater sense of community pride.

Turn left onto Radio Road, where you can park and climb the mile-long Cable Ravine Trail to the top. You can also park here and hike northwest on April Brook Trail in spring to see good wildflower displays. For a first visit, you may prefer to drive to the top and park amidst the radio and TV signal transmitting installations. There you'll enjoy the sweeping vistas and a hike out the Ridge Trail.

The hillsides of San Bruno Mountain are a lovely sight in springtime, with a profusion of lush wildflowers, such as buttercups. There are also thorny gorse and numerous European broom, whose showy yellow flowers delight the eye, though this foreign plant is so intrusive it has become something of a pest in the California landscape. Eucalyptus from Australia are remnants of past woodlots and windbreaks. It was once thought profitable to farm eucalyptus for wood to burn in railroad engines and in home heating stoves.

At the top of Radio Road and on walks along the ridge beyond the final radio transmitter you get a special view of downtown San Francisco to the north and planes taking off from San Francisco International Airport to the southeast. Looking south you see the sobering graveyards of Colma, where the dead of San Francisco are buried because no graveyards are allowed in the city. Between the graveyards are swatches of color from commercial flower growing, now the most important agricultural crop in San Mateo County. Most of the flower production occurs here and around Half Moon Bay.

The people of San Mateo County have made a substantial long term commitment to their parks and San Bruno is one of the newest in the county chain. Starting in 1924, the citizens voted authorization and funding for the San Mateo County Memorial Park, a redwood park to honor those who served in World War I. This is a fine hiking, camping, and picnicking park, which will be discussed later. Today the county parks host over 2 million people per year.

Though most of the county park mandate concerns the management of nature areas, the same parks and recreation department administers two major historic sites in the county, the Sanchez Adobe and Dr. Tripp's Woodside Store, both well worth a visit, as write-ups later in this book suggest.

The major parks in the county system will be discussed as they appear geographically in our itinerary. For overall park information, including a brochure on the park system, send a stamped, self-addressed envelope to San Mateo County Parks and Recreation Department, County Government Center, 590 Hamilton Street, Redwood City 94063. Their phone is 415/363-4020.

The Cities

Driving west from San Bruno Mountain along Guadalupe Canyon Parkway, you encounter Mission Street, which becomes El Camino Real at East Market Street. This was the original route for traveling south from San Francisco to the peninsula in the days before engineers with modern earth-moving equipment had the audacity to cut through the hillsides next to the bay and create Bayshore Freeway 101.

A little touch of the future can be seen in Daly City at McDonald's restaurants, 505 Serramonte and 2450 Junipero Serra. Both have wind-power machines that contribute about 10 kw of power to their lighting. When the restaurants are closed and the electricity is not being used, it is fed into the PG&E grid system. The owner of these restaurants calculates that the wind generators will pay for themselves in four years. (Interestingly enough, the most common use of solar energy on the peninsula, hot water collectors, would not be feasible here, in the owner's judgment, because Daly City is such a foggy area. Plenty of wind, but not much sun.) At the latter location the decor is old photos showing John Daly, founder of Daly City; the Ocean Shore Railroad, a dream never fully realized for a coastal railroad from San Francisco to Santa Cruz; and numerous boxing matches for which the town of Colma was once famous.

When you plunge into everyday life in Daly City, another expression of the times can be seen at the Westlake Bowling Alley, 99 Southgate Avenue. All the scoring is computerized and automatic, with video readouts above the lanes. Alongside the bowling lanes and also adjacent to a next door fast-food restaurant are video arcades with currently fashionable games, descendants of Pac-Man. Mesmerized teenagers feed in their quarters. At the fast-food restaurant a bean burrito is a good choice as a hunger stopper.

The entire ambiance of the Westlake Bowl tells you two important things about Daly City. First, all the Asian faces indicate the growing Third World populace here. And second, the bowling alley is itself a major social organizer, with its own newsletter, telling of upcoming birthdays and announcing recent scores for teams such as the Morning Glories, Sons in Retirement, and Levin's Chargers.

While exploring the towns here, look at Grand Avenue in South San Francisco, a good example of urban blight forestalled by careful attention to street beautification, which enables the downtown to compete with shopping centers. Nearby Brisbane was so named because the developer felt the terrain resembled the town of that name in Australia.

Acres of Orchids Tour

The Rod McLellan Company's Acres of Orchids presents a fascinating look at commercial flower growing on a large scale. Free tours and orchid-care workshops are available at 1450 El Camino Real, South San Francisco, 415/871-5655.

Orchids are not the only flowering plants here, but McLellan has an international reputation for them. The palette of colors and diversity of types are exquisite.

Flowers bloom here all 365 days of the year. You learn in the Flask House how orchids are cloned from microparts of a parent plant to produce identical offspring. The Orchid Sales House contains the largest collection of orchids in the country. Many orchid-growing hobbyists get their start with plants from here. McLellan also runs an Orchid Boarding House, where thousands of customers' plants are temporarily housed and treated.

During the hour-long tour, you also see how orchids and other flowers are prepared for shipping, especially for air shipments from San Francisco International Airport. The proximity of the nursery to the airport is as important as the closeness of the great Dutch nurseries of Aalsmeer, for example, to the airport shipment point of Schiphol. Air shipment has opened up new national and international flower markets.

Over four million cut flowers leave this nursery every year. In the U.S., McLellan was one of the first to use paper cartons for shipping, cellophane wrapping to keep the flowers fresh, and air freight for rapid national distribution.

Among the other flowers grown here ambitiously are gardenias. One enclosure, the size of three football fields, has about 80,000 budding gardenias and other flowers. Fern sporing is another activity at McLellan's, with over 100 varieties of ferns grown from spores.

Over the decades floral fashions have changed. The tour recalls this aspect of the floral story. From the 1930s to the fifties gardenias were much favored. McLellan's gardenia corsages were then as prominent in the flower marketplace as his orchids are now.

This family-held company began during the Gold Rush.

Grandfather David McLellan started a dairy and produce business on the peninsula. Son Edgar carried on, but displayed a special green thumb, plus the tact of softening the monthly bite of the milk bill with a bouquet of flowers. In the late 1890s he turned his attention full time to the flower business. Edgar's three sons took over the enterprise, and Rod, who specialized in orchids, named his company Acres of Orchids. Today the enterprise has 1.3 million square feet of growing space here and at another nursery in Watsonville.

Broderick-Terry Duel Site

At the northwest corner of Daly City off El Portal Way is a small park that commemorates a famous duel: the duel that ended duels in California.

Two granite markers point out where California U.S. Senator David C. Broderick and California Supreme Court Justice David S. Terry aimed their pistols at each other to settle an affair of honor. The conflict of the times was which side California should join in the impending Civil War. Heated words were thrown all over the state, with these two prominent men among the partisans. Words escalated to personal acrimony and the challenge of a duel resulted.

Looking at the markers today, it seems impossible that either man could have missed. Broderick fired his shot into the ground, but Terry took careful aim and sent a bullet into Broderick's heart, which caused his death three days later. The death so outraged California's citizenry that a state law was soon passed forbidding duels.

Despite these violent beginnings, the park is a pleasant small enclave of greenery, suitable for a picnic.

The Coast

On a sunny day this northwest coast of San Mateo County offers both pleasing vistas and bracing salt air to stimulate the lungs. Winter days are sometimes sunnier than summer afternoons when the phenomenon of fog may reduce the amount of sunlight and the pleasure of an outing. Hot air expands in the inland valleys, reducing pressure, drawing in moist sea air, which forms fog when it hits the hillsides. Condensation from fog, even when there is no "rain," is a major

The pier at Pacifica

coastside moisture source, amounting to 15 inches of drip per year off the redwoods farther south.

Thornton Beach

Thornton Beach, accessible from John Daly Boulevard, offers a good beach walk and prominent bluffs from which to look out to sea. Thornton has been the best beach experience easily accessible to the public in northwest San Mateo County. Hang gliders sometimes drift down to Thornton from their launching site at Fort Funston, to the north. Picnic tables overlook the waves. The sandy beach stretches for some distance. However, Thornton's hillsides and roads, as well as water supply and sewage system, suffered severe damage from slides in the fierce storms of January 1982, closing the park. The future of Thornton in an era of tight budgets was uncertain as of 1983.

Pacifica and Rockaway

As you travel south along Coast Highway 1, the Pacifica Pier is a good stopping place. Park in Pacifica anywhere along Beach Boulevard or on the side streets and then walk out the long, concrete pier, alive with fishermen catching sea perch on grass shrimp or kingfish on anchovies. The ocean also offers up an occasional exotic, such as a sting ray. Crabbing takes place here, using large nets baited with dead fish.

Walking the pier can be recommended as a satisfying, simple entertainment. On a sunny weekend, line-tangling numbers of fishermen stand shoulder to shoulder, but camaraderie runs high, and almost always someone somewhere along the pier pulls in something, which heightens the spirit of hope even if an oddsmaker would sound a note of discouragement.

The concession stand at the beach end of the pier sells food and drink, plus fishing tackle. More importantly for the explorer or the novice fisherman, the store boasts one wall of snapshots showing the huge salmon and striped bass that didn't get away.

Between December 1 and February 1, migrating gray whales can be seen passing south from the Arctic to Scammon's Lagoon and other lagoons in mid-Baja California for birthing and mating. If you ask around at the pier, fishing aficionados may tell you stories of the day a gray whale passed close to or even right under the pier.

Pacifica merits some exploration for its seafood restaurants, such as the Pacifica Seafood Grotto, 1966 Francisco Boulevard,

415/355-1678. Try their rex sole. Other good seafood restaurants can be found with a view of the breakers, two miles south, in Rockaway Beach. Try poached salmon at the Moonraker, 415/359-0303. For a more economical meal, especially if accompanied by an entourage of children, consider the excellent pizza at Romano's, 415/359-0528, in Rockaway Beach.

Ocean Shore Railroad

Along the road from Sharp Park to Rockaway you pass Vallemar Station, now a bar and restaurant. Stop for liquid refreshment here, but save your appetite for the restaurants in Pacifica or Rockaway Beach. Look around at a few pieces of memorabilia here from the Ocean Shore Railroad. This building once served as a station depot for the railroad, which promoters intended as a scenic link between San Francisco and Santa Cruz.

Track-laying began about 1905, slowed because of the 1906 Earthquake, and foundered when the company's finances weakened. Tracks eventually ran down to Tunitas Creek, south of Half Moon Bay, where a Stanley Steamer auto met the train and carried passengers farther south to Swanton. There another train, on the track running north from Santa Cruz, greeted passengers. Surely this was a scenic route, but the train was finally derailed by the age of the automobile and the eventual Coast Highway 1. The last whistle blew in 1920.

The story of the Ocean Shore Railroad is a lore-filled subject. Railroad fans can steep themselves in this absorbing saga by asking at bookstores for Jack Wagner's *The Last Whistle*. Other nostalgic depots of the Ocean Shore appear farther south along the coast. The motto of the railroad was "It reaches the beaches," and ads promised "the most fascinating scenery in California. Cliffs, bluffs, beaches, rocks, redwoods, gardens, and marine scenery." Whole towns, such as El Granada down the coast, were laid out in anticipation of a boom that never came.

San Pedro Point, Devil's Slide

South from Rockaway lies San Pedro Point. Drive down Coast Highway 1 and out Shelter Cove Road for a good look at the point. Peering south you'll see how steeply the rocky coast approaches the sea. In this area, called Devil's Slide, the road narrows and its future can't even be predicted. Voluminous rains severed the narrow road north of Montara in January, 1982, and may do so again. Devil's Slide has a spooky history of accidental deaths as tourists or newlyweds have stopped their cars along the cliffs and then, urging the beloved to back up to get within the snapshot frame, have sent the loved one tumbling to an ugly death over the edge.

A well-known clothing-optional beach can be entered by turning into the parking lot where the road sign says 15 MPH, paying the modest parking fee, and then walking across the highway and down the hillside to the beach.

Rockslides and mudslides on the steep hills of this region had been mainly a theoretical problem until the winter of 1981–82. The unrelenting rains of January, 1982, brought severe slides, property loss, and some loss of life.

Inland from Coast Highway 1, two adventures are worth experiencing here, the Sanchez Adobe and San Pedro Valley County Park.

The Sanchez Adobe

Every appreciator of peninsula history should make a pilgrimage at some time to the Sanchez Adobe on Linda Mar Boulevard near Adobe Lane in Pacifica, 415/359-1462. This simple, dignified structure is a small architectural triumph, a whitewashed adobe completed in 1846 during the Mexican era. It is the only adobe in San Mateo County available for the public to visit.

The Sanchez Adobe presents a pleasing, classic sense of proportion and symmetry. The architectural achievement is noteworthy, considering the spare building resources of the era. Surrounding the adobe are huge old Monterey pine, Monterey cypress, and eucalyptus.

You can visit the site at any time and look through the windows at the three downstairs rooms. A veranda around the building makes it possible to peer also into the upstairs rooms. On some afternoons the adobe is open. This is the preferred time to visit, as you are allowed into the rooms. Call ahead for the appropriate time.

One downstairs room is devoted to saddles, spinning wheels, butter churns, and other domestic artifacts. Another room shows a kitchen table, complete with period plates and utensils, next to the fireplace. These memorabilia are from a somewhat later time than the early Sanchez era, but they reflect the continuity of the property's use. Actually, the site was first an outpost in 1785 that

The Sanchez Adobe

produced food for Mission Dolores in San Francisco. One downstairs room shows many of the artifacts used by Costanoan Indians, as the Spanish people called the Ohlones, thinking of them as "people of the coast."

Upstairs, the central room is furnished as a genteel parlor setting of the 19th century. The two end rooms are re-created bedroom settings. At the windows you can see the 24-inch thickness of the walls.

A historical marker near the house tells its story. The adobe was the home of Francisco Sanchez (1805–62), *alcalde* or "mayor" of San Francisco and commandant of militia under the Mexican Republic, grantee of the 8,962-acre Rancho San Pedro, and later a respected American citizen. His house, built 1842–46, was later owned and remodeled by General Edward Kirkpatrick. The County of San Mateo purchased it in 1947 to preserve the setting as a public museum.

Near the back of the property, logs outline where archeologists have determined there once were additional structures to serve as priest's quarters, kitchen, and foreman's headquarters when the site produced food for the mission.

Benches at this tranquil setting provide a pleasant rest and picnic stop. For a more elaborate picnic, especially with a cluster of children, go to nearby San Pedro Valley County Park.

San Pedro Valley County Park

T his park, off Oddstad Boulevard in Pacifica, 415/355-8289, is an excellent holding in the San Mateo County system. It offers good hiking trails, many picnic tables, and an ample meadow where children can romp. The nature lover will appreciate fine examples of the coastal stream riparian plant community and some drier coastal shrub terrain.

Near the park entrance you'll find the interesting and short Oak Glen Nature Trail. In December–January and again in March–April it is possible to see steelhead spawning in this stream. Most of the fish are 7–8 inches, but there are some 20-inch fish. It takes some patience to spot the steelhead, but the spawning phenomenon is a remarkable expression of nature to behold. This nature walk includes a particularly luxuriant live oak and good examples of different ferns along the stream, where you can compare the leaves of sword fern with those of wood fern.

Get a free trail leaflet as you enter the park. Among the hiking trails consider #4, the old Weiler Ranch Road, if you want a level walk. This trail takes you a mile into the canyon, with opportunities in early morning and late evening to see the abundant game, including deer, fox, coyote, and sometimes bobcat. Steeper trail #5 is the Valley View Trail, 1.6 miles, good for those who don't mind a steady 15 percent grade. This trail has geological significance for its Calera limestone and shale deposits. Trail #3 takes you to an Old Trout Farm, and Trail #2 leads to Brook Falls, which flow in winter.

Look to this park in the future for interesting developments. There will eventually be a trail over the hills from here to Montara Beach. Also, a 35-mile trail will some day begin here and proceed through Crystal Springs watershed to Huddart Park. Closer at hand, new trails will lead through manzanitas that may be the largest specimens in the state. Within the park there are two endangered plant species, both varieties of manzanita. The new trails will also offer good examples of a California tree that few visitors recognize, the chinquapin.

Freda Koblick's *Night Sky* at the North Terminal, San Franciso Airport

Towns from Country Estates 2

William Ralston's Dream

F rom the airport through Belmont, the bay side of central
San Mateo County once was an enclave for the wealthy.
Silver and banking kings of 19th-century San Francisco
established imposing homes. One of those homes, William
Ralston's palace in Belmont, remains intact and open to the public.

For the appreciator of nature, the Coyote Point Museum for
Environmental Education, located next to the bay, is the
peninsula's most sophisticated interpreter of our natural
environment. In this territory the recommended place to
commune with nature is the new Sawyer Camp Historic Trail
along the Crystal Springs watershed.

We'll start with a look at San Francisco airport.

San Francisco International Airport

T he airport occupies a substantial 5,200 acres of bayside
property in northern San Mateo County and continues a
distinguished history of peninsula aviation. Professor
John Joseph Montgomery made the first successful U.S. glider
flight in 1883, on the peninsula, as noted on a plaque now located
at the University of Santa Clara. In 1910 French aviator Louis
Paulhan launched a 10-minute powered flight from the Tanforan
Race Track, no longer in existence, in northern San Mateo
County. In 1911 daring Bob Fowler took off from Mills Field, as
the present San Francisco airport was first called, and flew all the

way across the bay. The same enterprising Fowler made the first
Pacific to Atlantic flight, San Francisco to New York, in 45 days
with 60 landings.

D. O. Mills, the influential citizen for whom Millbrae is named,
owned the land on which the airport stands. Mills Field became
San Francisco Airport in 1931 when the City of San Francisco
purchased land from the D. O. Mills estate. Today the city runs
the airport through an Airport Commission.

From this site Boeing Air Transport made the first
transcontinental commercial flight, in 1931. Pan American
Airways made the first round-the-world commercial flight,
beginning and ending here, in 1937. In 1941 San Mateo County
built another airport for general aviation, in Half Moon Bay, and
in 1964 acquired Howard F. Harper's privately owned airport in
San Carlos. San Carlos is also a busy airport today. In fact, it is the
busiest single-runway airport in the country.

San Francisco International Airport intrigues natives and
visitors alike because large jets take off, one every two minutes on
the average, day and night, carrying over 60,000 passengers daily,
22.4 million per year. This is the fifth busiest airport in the
country.

An interesting public access to the fascinating spectacle of the
airport exists at a parking lot off an airport road where Millbrae
Avenue crosses Bayshore Freeway 101 at the west end of the
airport runways. From this designated lot you can get a close-up
look at jets taxiing for their takeoffs. You may be surprised at the
number of airplane fans who like to stop at this parking lot to
watch the big metallic birds thundering into the sky.

The airport terminals themselves are also worth a visit. You
may want to get the attractive free brochure with a rudimentary
map of the terminals, called the Transit and Parking Guide, by
calling airport public relations, 415/876-2421, or by sending them a
stamped, self-addressed envelope: San Francisco International
Airport, P.O. Box 8097, San Francisco 94128. Ask them also for a
mimeo map showing the terminals in detail.

The terminal to visit is the North Terminal, opened in 1979.
You can get to the airport by Samtrans public bus, 415/871-2200,
or by driving your car and parking at the Close In garage. For
years this garage seemed to be under construction. Now it is
possible to negotiate it without feeling you are lost in a maze. Go
to the Mezzanine level and take the People Mover carpet into the
North Terminal.

The airport also has two other terminals. The Central

Terminal, closed for remodeling, is scheduled to re-open in 1984 with modern facilities for international flights. International and some domestic flights now use the South Terminal, which is somewhat antiquated and of far less inherent interest to the browser than the North Terminal. South Terminal, which will eventually be replaced, is a good example of the functional design favored in 1950s' airport construction. The South Terminal today has an indifferent restaurant, a small bar that sells oysters, and a duty-free shop where canned California almonds can be recommended.

North Terminal

A visit to the airport when you're not under the tension of catching a flight is a wholly refreshing experience. In the North Terminal you'll notice many things you would otherwise overlook in the rush to meet a plane. You can also acquaint yourself with the territory, which can reduce the stress of future trips when you're meeting or catching a flight.

The North Terminal won several well-deserved architectural awards. A lofty acrylic and steel sculpture called *Night Sky*, by San Francisco artist Freda Koblick, hangs in the rotunda midway down the main concourse. Koblick championed plastics as a sculptural medium before others accepted it. A full-scale relief map of San Francisco, with a carved wooden block for each building, is on display in a lounge off the rotunda. This tour-de-force map should not be missed. Historic photos of the region and maps of its early periods can also be seen.

Throughout the main concourse you'll find a changing art exhibit that has included many distinguished shows. On the walls are several permanent art pieces, such as Robert Bechtle's *San Francisco Nova, 1979*, a profoundly lonely painting in devastating photo-realism style of a man watering his lawn at a typical San Francisco–area house. Several of the late sculptor Benny Bufano's endearing, simplified animals are scattered throughout the setting. His *Peace* sculpture greeted you as you entered the airport.

All the while, of course, scurrying people run past you to meet their airplanes, generally oblivious to these pleasures. For a quick meal try the North Beach Deli, which serves a tasty pastrami sandwich as you gaze up at a mural of historic North Beach and other decor, such as old magazine covers or ads for Morton Salt and Butternut Bread. The Espresso Cafe has good cappuccino and tempting desserts. A restaurant simply called the Coffee

House affords good views of planes while you eat. The Terrace Restaurant is the most elaborate setting for a sit-down dinner, while crab dishes and other seafood delicacies are sold at the Crab Pot restaurant.

When shopping at the airport, you'll find T-shirts and books that celebrate the region in the Gift Shop and Book Store. At a dozen locations you can buy sourdough French bread. Frozen crabs are sold at the Flying Crab stand.

Some little-known aspects of the airport environment should be pointed out. On the Mezzanine over the United Airlines counter in the North Terminal you'll find an excellent nursery for small children, something to keep in mind if you are ever delayed and have children in tow. At no expense to the traveler there are even private rooms with a rocker, crib, sink, and toilet for parents with very young children. This airport is also one of the most progressive in providing full access for people with disabilities. Also, of concern to all people who fly, the airport has been selected repeatedly by the Aviation Safety Institute as one of the half dozen safest in the U.S., praised especially for its practiced emergency response plans to cope with a disaster.

When driving south from the airport along the bay, stop at 888 Airport Boulevard in Burlingame for free information on the region. The office is that of the San Mateo County Convention and Visitors Bureau, 415/347-7004. Parallel offices are located in Santa Clara, San Jose, and Santa Cruz.

Coyote Point Museum for Environmental Education

J ust south of the airport, the Peninsula Avenue turnoff toward the bay from Bayshore Freeway 101 takes you to Coyote Point Park, gem of the San Mateo County park system's current expansion program. Despite the era of tight 1980s' budgets and post–Proposition 13 starvation rations for parks, fortunately some money has been found to develop this pleasant bayshore park.

The major achievement in this park is the new Coyote Point Museum for Environmental Education, a facility of national stature for its forward-looking interpretation of man's place in nature. This resource merits the attention of every peninsula resident and visitor. Call 415/342-7755 for current hours and admission fees.

Museum is an inadequate word to describe this undertaking. The Coyote Point Museum amounts to an impassioned song, a poetic statement, linking man to nature, beginning with homage to the sun as the source and generator of life. You enter the museum at the crest of the mountains running along the spine of the peninsula, guided by thoughtful observations about the prudence with which man must manage the environment for long term survival. You then proceed down three levels to the ocean and the bay, through broad-leaved and coniferous forests, past chaparral and grasslands, to the baylands and the coast.

Along with an introduction to these six major biotic communities in the peninsula region, you experience a few fundamental concepts concerning the interlocking web of life, communities and ecosystems, cycles and rhythms in nature, limits and controls in our environment, food systems on which man and all other animals depend, and the diversity needed to make a biological environment stable. The tone of the museum is both celebrative of our link with nature and gently apostolic about the need for clear, long range thinking if we hope to survive.

Some exhibits here are capable of exciting wonder, such as a large jar of water containing waterweed, a sea plant on whose leaves it is possible to see forming bubbles of oxygen, without which we mammals would soon perish. Another captivating exhibit shows the immense vertical tree of creatures needed to support one hawk for one year. Cloth figures of the creatures represent the 1,069 mice, 98 small birds, 20 gophers, 18 rabbits, 15 squirrels, 15 shrews, 2 weasels, 9 game birds, 7 snakes, and 4 rats that make up the average annual diet of just one hawk. The museum has the ability to awaken in a visitor an appreciation of the intricacies of nature and a profound awareness of the consequences for each land-use choice that would pave over or develop additional peninsula lands.

Aside from the museum, Coyote Point has a public marina, picnic areas, biking and walking paths, and a short nature trail with good examples of imported acacias and eucalyptus from Australia. The feel of the park is somewhat urban and bay-oriented rather than rustic. Its only disconcerting aspect is the presence of a rifle range whose volleys tend to impair the aura of tranquility that the rest of the park seeks to achieve.

30

William Ralston's Enclave

An imposing house on the peninsula in the 19th century, that of William Ralston, is now part of the College of Notre Dame in Belmont. Most of the other great houses no longer exist. A marker outside the structure on campus tells the story:

> Ralston Hall. This redwood structure was completed in 1868 by William Chapman Ralston, San Francisco financier. Incorporating Count Cipriani's earlier villa, this enlarged mansion with its mirrored ballroom became the symbol of the extravagance of California's Silver Age. It anticipated features later incorporated into Ralston's Palace Hotel in San Francisco.

Located at 1500 Ralston Avenue, the college can be visited any time for a look at the outside of Ralston Hall, the former Ralston house. You can also look through the windows into the chandeliered, mirrored ballroom, an echo of Versailles. Tours here are informative on the interior detail of the building, but an appointment is required. Phone in advance 415/593-1601.

The campus also has an art gallery with four shows per year and a chamber concert series, which takes place in the Ralston Hall ballroom and has flourished for over 20 years. The Carriage House Theater, in Ralston's old stone carriage house, hosts traveling performances and student productions. Enrichment classes on various subjects are also offered to the community.

William Ralston entertained sumptuously at this 80 room country showplace and put up his guests in the 50 bedrooms. No expense was spared on the parquet floors or silver doorknobs of the Belmont home. When Ralston wasn't focusing his attention here, he was developing his Palace Hotel in San Francisco.

Ralston was a vigorous exerciser who liked to race the train into San Francisco, or from San Francisco to his house, often beating it by remounting relays of horses along the route. In the 1860s Ralston made his fortune as a partner in the fabulously rich Comstock Lode silver mines in Nevada. He then opened a bank in San Francisco that flourished until 1875, when a financial crash in mining stocks caused a run on the bank and forced its closing. Amidst these anxieties, Ralston died while swimming on a hot day in chilly San Francisco Bay, another of his typical physical feats. There was speculation that his death was suicide, but an autopsy found no water in his lungs and the coroner ruled that the

William Ralston's house in Belmont

death was "asphyxia with cerebral congestion." His life insurance was promptly paid.

The San Mateo County Arts Council, 1219 Ralston Avenue, 415/593-1816, uses the 1907 manor of San Francisco banker George Center as galleries for arts and crafts. The council is located in hospitable Twin Pines Park, which has been a pleasant streamside picnic grounds since the late 1800s. Large bay, buckeye, and eucalyptus trees flourish here.

Country Manors

The histories of Belmont, Burlingame, and Hillsborough are intimately linked, all owing their existence to the initial vision of banker William Ralston.

For a detailed account of the early estates of this region and the way each town was formed, look at Frank Stanger's *South From San Francisco*, available from the San Mateo County Historical Association (see write-up on them).

Originally the area was part of a Spanish land grant given by Governor Pio Pico to his secretary, Cayetano Arenas. In the 1860s banker Ralston dreamed of a "sacrosanct colony" for the well-to-do, tucked into the hillsides above the bay in San Mateo County. Burlingame and Hillsborough eventually embodied this ideal, with Burlingame boasting the first country club in California, the Burlingame Country Club, founded in 1893.

Ralston admired the warm, tranquil, oak-covered hillsides of bayside San Mateo County, protected from ocean fog by the crests of the Santa Cruz Mountains. One of the early guests at Ralston's lavish gatherings in Belmont was the minister to China, appointed by Abraham Lincoln, Anson Burlingame. Ralston planned to encourage such men of means to buy adjoining acreage. Impressed by the locale, Burlingame subsequently purchased 1,100 acres as an estate for his retirement after his China service, though he died before he had a chance to live here. In 1908 the town of Burlingame incorporated.

While exploring Burlingame, stop by an art gallery, simply called The Gallery, 329 Primrose Road, to see a range of creations from oil paintings to pottery. There are many interesting antique stores, shops, and restaurants in the vicinity. Try tacos *al carbon* or chimichanga at La Pinata, 1205 Burlingame Avenue, 415/343-0684.

The town of Hillsborough expresses in quintessential form the notion of a retreat for the wealthy. Covering only 6.26 square miles, Hillsborough, by ordinance, permits only residences and excludes all businesses. House prices begin over $300,000. All of San Mateo County, it should be added, is a relatively affluent area compared to national norms, with average household income at $27,249 in the most recent census.

Another of the great estates that you can drive by is the deserted Carolands, 565 Remillard Drive in Hillsborough. Harriet Pullman Carolan, heiress to the Pullman railroad car fortune, built this lavish minipalace in 1915–16 as the focus of a 500-acre estate. Architect Willis Polk supervised construction of the Renaissance-design residence. In the early 1950s Countess Lillian Remillard Dandini acquired the estate and the six remaining acres. Today the abandoned property has a forlorn air, as of dreams and an era passing.

Preserving Peninsula History

To remind future generations of California's heritage, over 900 historical landmarks have been designated throughout the state and 30 sites have been elevated to the status of state historical parks. The peninsula has 29 of these landmarks in San Mateo County, 36 in Santa Clara County, and 6 in Santa Cruz County. Two sites on the peninsula, both in Santa Cruz County, have been elevated further to the status of state historical parks. They are the Santa Cruz Mission and Big Basin Redwoods State Park, where the idea of the state parks began.

Not all the designated historical landmarks are actually marked, however. Those that are will be mentioned when we discuss the area in which they exist.

For example, consider the de Anza expedition. Equally important in early peninsula history to the Portola expedition was the actual settlement-founding party led by Juan Bautista de Anza. Two historic sites, one of which is marked, recall encampments as de Anza and his group of settlers traveled from Monterey to a new home in San Francisco.

The marked camp is two blocks up Arroyo Court off El Camino Real in San Mateo. The marker, on the creek side of the road, reads:

> Historic Camp Site. Here on the banks of San Mateo Creek Captain J. B. de Anza camped March 29, 1776, after exploring the peninsula and selecting the sites for the Mission and Presidio of San Francisco. Here also the party of families, soldiers, and priests on the way to establish San Francisco camped for three days, June 24–27, 1776.

However, more than the stone markers themselves, a network of historically minded citizens keeps the past alive and present. In San Mateo County that group is the San Mateo County Historical Association, which sponsors a fine museum.

San Mateo County Historical Museum

This museum, at 1700 West Hillsdale Boulevard on the College of San Mateo campus, 415/574-6441, offers a free introduction to the history of the northern peninsula. Begin with a careful look at the exhibits. The excellent small bookstore attached to the museum offers many volumes on regional history. After the museum, visit the four major sites in San Mateo County with which the museum shares an affinity. These sites, discussed elsewhere in the book, are the Sanchez Adobe in Pacifica, the Filoli estate and the Tripp Store in Woodside, and the Lathrop House in Redwood City.

The museum has an extensive library of books and documents on San Mateo County history, available for in-library use, plus a collection of photos that can be reproduced for your use at cost. Membership is advisable if you want to receive their newsletter, buy books at a discount, and participate in their activities. Each August the association also sponsors a Victorian Days in the Park celebration at San Mateo's Central Park. This fair features arts and crafts, food booths, costumes, and an emphasis on different ethnic contributions in the county.

The museum illuminates the area's history with presentations from the different eras, as outlined in the introduction to this guide. Some artifacts present additional details from the eras.

A large reed canoe shows how Ohlone Indian fishermen maneuvered in the bay or even in the ocean.

An exhibit on the Californio period details the trading pattern of Boston ships, whose captains sought cattle hides in exchange for finished goods. The leather helped fuel the shoe- and harness-manufacturing industries of New England. Ample herds of cattle enabled the Californios to amass hides, which were called "California banknotes" in those days. Richard Henry Dana recorded the era perceptively in his *Two Years Before the Mast*, listing some items of trade that his ship brought to California to barter for hides: tea, coffee, sugar, spices, raisins, molasses, hardware, crockery, tinware, cutlery, clothing, boots, cotton, crepe, silk, shawls, scarfs, necklaces, combs, and furniture.

In the American period that followed the annexation of California, lumber was a sustaining industry on the peninsula. But other enterprises also flourished, including the harvesting of oysters, which began in the 1870s with John Stillwell Morgan's successful seeding of eastern oysters in 16,000 acres of bay waters. His business lasted for 75 years until pollution destroyed it.

Among specialized crops grown in the 19th century was flax. Alexander Moore farmed 1,500 acres near Pescadero in 1868, drawing linen fibers from the stalks and pressing linseed oil from the seed.

Whaling was another important enterprise along the San Mateo coast, with whaling stations at Pillar and Pigeon points. Among the museum exhibits is an old metal try pot in which whale blubber was reduced to a fine oil useful for soap, candle, and lubricant manufacture.

San Mateo County remained a preserve for wealthy San Franciscans in the latter half of the 19th century. Photographs show the great estates of Darius Mills in Millbrae, William Ralston in Belmont, James Flood in Menlo Park, and William Crocker in Atherton.

With the museum as a starting point, a native or visitor can get a handle on the history of this region.

The Mission Heritage

Interest in the Mission style of architecture has been a strong tradition throughout California history, extending even now into tiled, arched, and stuccoed subdivisions. The Burlingame Railroad Station at Burlingame Avenue and California Drive is an interesting early expression of this style. A marker at the station tells the story:

> Burlingame Railroad Station. This first permanent building in the Mission Revival style of architecture was designed by George H. Howard and J. B. Mathison and financed by local residents and the Southern Pacific Railroad. It opened for service on October 10, 1884. The roof used 18th century tiles from the Mission San Antonio de Padua at Jolon and the Mission Dolores Asistencia at San Mateo.

Today that Mission Dolores Asistencia in San Mateo is nearly forgotten, but the area was an important food supplier and travelers' waystop during the mission era. South of Baywood and El Camino Real in San Mateo rests a marker recalling this contribution. The marker, in a clump of juniper, reads:

> Here stood the hospice, built around 1800 by the Spanish Padres on El Camino Real to break the journey from Santa Clara and to serve the Indians of Mission Dolores, circa 1800.

The Italians

Among ethnic groups who have contributed much to peninsula life, none is more visible than the Italians. Their individual stories are tales of alienation, discrimination, and stress in the late 19th and early 20th centuries, but many Italian families eventually became established and ascendant in the social structure. Today they still maintain a lively identity, apparent to the public at Columbus Day celebrations in October.

Italians were some of the first and certainly among the most skilled produce farmers on the peninsula. They introduced garlic, broccoli, eggplant, zucchini, bell pepper and artichoke. Artichokes

were first planted in Half Moon Bay and in the Pedro Valley of
Pacifica in the 1860s. These plants thrived because they liked
continuous fog and the absence of frost. The crop remains
important today and is controlled by Italian growers.

By 1900, Italian farmers held the lion's share of the California
produce market. But there were also other amenities to consider,
such as flowers. The area around Colma was popular with Italian
flower growers. Bert and Joe Lagomarsino became known as the
"Violet Kings" of Colma; their flowers were sold at the 1904
World's Fair in St. Louis, a 2,000 mile journey made in refrigerated
railroad cars. Carnations later became a popular crop in the same
area. Italians served as the chief gardeners of the great houses on
the peninsula, such as the Filoli estate in Woodside and the Flood
estate in Menlo Park.

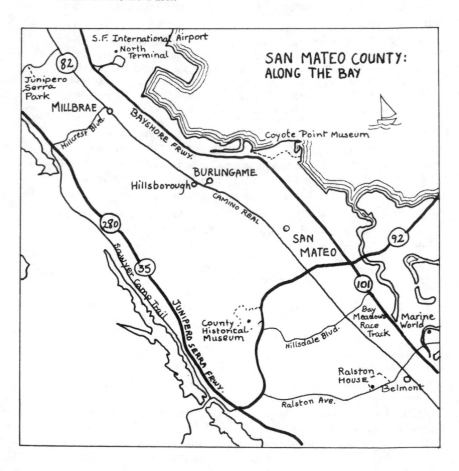

Several vineyards were founded on the peninsula by Italians. In the northern peninsula John Beltramo founded a winery in the 1880s. His descendants still manage the Beltramo Liquor Store on El Camino Real in Menlo Park. Italian grape growers and winemakers continue to be prominent in the southern part of the Santa Clara Valley, where names such as Bonesio, Pedrizzetti, and Filice are well known. The Bargettos, who own a winery of that name in Santa Cruz, are relative newcomers. Because so many Italians were prominent in the saloon and wine trades, they prospered after the repeal of Prohibition.

Italians also were prominent in business and in the hotel trade. The Mosconi Hotel, still doing business today in Half Moon Bay as San Benito House, is the oldest hotel on the coast side.

Among the Italians in business, none was more famous than A. P. Giannini, founder of the Bank of Italy, later called the Bank of America. Giannini pioneered a new style of banking, dependent on the investments of the small shareholder. Giannini would ride his horse long distances to extend credit to Italian farmers and encourage savings. His empire grew, based on his concept of branch banks. Giannini's Seven Oaks house in San Mateo played an important role in his survival at the time of the 1906 Earthquake. As flames snaked their way to his bank in San Francisco, Giannini loaded all the bank's assets into a wagon, hiding the money under crates, then drove it to his home, where he stored the money in the ash trap of his fireplace. From these "secured funds" his bank was back in operation only a week after the quake.

The Italian whose works have touched the greatest number of peninsulans is the sculptor Beniamino Bufano. Diminutive Bufano was a giant in the art world. Two peninsula locations, the Hillsdale Shopping Center/Mall at Hillsdale Boulevard/El Camino Real in San Mateo and the North Terminal of San Francisco International Airport, contain large numbers of his works. Bufano's sculptures are characteristically animals, though he also sculpted St. Francis and various peace figures to express his pacifist sentiments. The animals are his lasting fame. They seem vital, full of soul, quiet and peaceful yet energetic. Their simplified forms and smooth textures appeal to a wide range of people. At the Hillsdale Shopping Center you can see a cat, owl, rabbit, family of bears, and a mouse, as well as a statue of St. Francis. The North Terminal of the airport, which you drive to after passing his *Peace* statue on the entrance road, has a camel, polar bear, and elephant.

The Good Life, Then and Now

For people of the late 19th century on the peninsula, the pleasure of watching fast horses was a major entertainment. A heated dispute among horse-minded gentlemen of the day was whether a trotter ever had four feet off the ground at one time. Leland Stanford, in an effort to settle the argument, hired Eadweard Muybridge to photograph a horse in motion. Muybridge's sequence of images contributed to motion picture development.

At the turn of the century the Tanforan Race Track, opening in 1899 in San Bruno, was an important social center. Large crowds came down from San Francisco on a new electric trolley that ran to San Mateo, stopping alongside the race track. This track also contributed two footnotes to aviation history. The first airplane flight on the Pacific Coast took place here in 1910. In 1911 one Eugene Ely illustrated the concept of the aircraft carrier by taking off from Tanforan and landing on a platform built above the deck of the battleship *Pennsylvania*. In 1963 Tanforan Race Track closed and in 1964 it burned to the ground. The land was then sold to real estate developers who built the Tanforan Shopping Center.

Today Bay Meadows Race Track nurtures the tradition of horse racing. Thoroughbreds, horses bred and trained for distance runs of three-quarters to two miles, race from September into February, with several special races paying $200,000 or more to the winner. Quarterhorses, bred and trained for short runs of up to a quarter mile, compete from February through May, with purses as high as $400,000.

The track is clearly visible at the Hillsdale Boulevard exit from Highway 101. Phone 415/574-7223. Every Saturday morning in autumn horse fans are welcome to visit the stables, talk with jockeys and trainers, and learn about the drama behind the races.

The fine dining so enjoyed by William Ralston continues to flourish in the peninsula's diverse restaurants. Since there is a certain bias in this book for the Mexican contribution to California, then and now, culinary and otherwise, I recommend a chile relleno at La Fiesta, 201 El Camino Real in San Bruno, 415/588-6243, or an enchilada Puerto Vallarta at Casa Maria, 1590 Old Bayshore Highway in Burlingame, 415/692-3113. The

Distillery at 271 El Camino Real in San Bruno, 415/588-7088, offers prime rib and music on weekend nights.

For a night out, you might want to combine theater with a pre-theater meal of classy Chinese cuisine at Kee Joon, 433 Airport Boulevard in Burlingame, 415/348-1122. The waiter can guide you through their artful menu. Kee Joon also provides a view of planes landing. A chateaubriand can be suggested at La Baie, 800 Airport Boulevard in Burlingame, 415/343-2711.

For evening entertainment the Circle Star Theater is the peninsula's main host for musicals and big-name box office attractions, from Willie Nelson to Sammy Davis Jr. The Circle Star, in San Carlos, is reached via the Whipple Exit off Bayshore Freeway 101, 415/364-2550.

The Hillbarn Theater specializes in light comedy theater. Their location is 1285 East Hillsdale Boulevard in Foster City, 415/349-6411.

A little bit of the peninsula's past becomes present six times a year at antique shows on the San Mateo County Fairgrounds. Some of these antique shows draw collectors from all over the country. The fairgrounds host the annual July County Fair and Floral Fiesta and numerous other ethnic and exposition functions during the year. The location is 2495 South Delaware Street in San Mateo, 415/345-3541.

Marine World Africa/USA

Though it may move later in the 1980s, possibly to another Bay Area location, Marine World Africa/USA rested in 1983 on land along the bay in Redwood City. This northern California counterpart of southern California's Sea World or Lion Country Safari can be entered on Marine World Parkway off Bayshore Freeway 101. It is open every day in the summer, but only weekends in winter. Phone 415/591-7676 for hours and current prices.

The 65-acre park has numerous acts featuring animals, such as killer whales. A special forte of the park is the affection training of tigers and other animals so the beasts, accompanied by their trainers, sometimes walk freely among the public. Dolphins, sea lions, whales, lions, African and Indian elephants, chimpanzees, birds of prey and exotic birds are all part of the menagerie you encounter here.

A jungle raft tour through a simulated African veldt floats you past zebras, giraffes, rhinos, ostriches, and other exotics. Like many modern style zoos, Marine World is set up so that animals can roam with relative freedom rather than be restricted in cages. In the Reef Aquarium you see sharks and giant sea turtles. Trick water skiing, including some barefoot skiing, also entertains visitors.

For kids, there's a large waterslide called Tiger Mountain Rapids, a cool treat on hot summer days, and The Whale of a Time World playground, which has innovative play elements. A dolphin show gives children an experience with these endearing creatures.

Junipero Serra County Park

This close-in park, nestled in the San Bruno hills where Highway 280 meets San Bruno Avenue, has pleasures both urban and rustic.

Stop at the ranger's office, 415/589-5708, to admire a large ceanothus bush that blooms profusely in spring. Adjacent to the ceanothus is a California spring wildflower garden that boasts poppies, red flax, and lupines. Ask for the Live Oak Nature Trail guide to the self-guided walk that starts near the park entrance.

The west-facing lowlands of the park preserve a wild habitat with a diverse showing of California plant species. Signposts lettered A to Z, corresponding to the Live Oak guide booklet, alert you to many aspects of the native flora, even though the sound of the freeway and the hum of jets overhead remind you how close you are to an urban area. Some of the plants on the trail can be enjoyed all year long, such as the large oak trees, whose broad limbs sprawl over the hillsides, or the many fine examples of madrone, bay, and buckeye. Other plants flourish only in the spring, such as the delicate blue Douglas iris. Throughout the park in spring there is an abundance of miner's lettuce, an edible green so named because the gold miners favored it as a salad. Be wary of the extensive poison oak, whose shiny three-leaf pattern should be avoided. An unusual feature of this nature trail is a sighting pipe that points you exactly to Mt. Diablo, whose top has been the surveying marker for much of northern California, including the peninsula.

The upper and middle ranges of the park are carefully

landscaped and groomed, including the planting of Australian eucalyptus trees. Mowed meadows near the park entrance also offer attractive picnic areas.

Near the top, at Crows Nest Shelter, you get the peninsula's best look at busy San Francisco International Airport, with clear views of planes taking off and landing. From this vantage point you also see the layout of the flatland and bay terrain on the north peninsula.

At the highest point in the park, in a grove of eucalyptus trees, you'll find many pleasant picnic tables and barbecue pits.

The park's name honors the indefatigable Franciscan who started the chain of missions in California. Historically, the park land was part of Rancho Buri Buri's 15,000 acres, which were parceled off in large chunks among wealthy San Franciscans in the latter half of the 19th century. When these large estates were further subdivided in the 20th century, the county park system had the opportunity to buy this land for the public.

Sawyer Camp Historic Trail

For one of the loveliest walks on the peninsula, enjoyable any time of the year, take the Sawyer Camp Historic Trail. The trail is accessible either where Hillcrest and Skyline boulevards meet in Millbrae, next to Highway 280, or at the trail's other end, where Skyline intersects the trail south of the Hayne/Black Mountain Road turnoff onto Skyline from Highway 280.

The trail is 6 miles long, going gradually downhill from Hillcrest to the end below Hayne Road. That can mean 6 miles back also, if you have no car shuttle. The recommended way to enjoy this trail, actually a paved road, is via bicycle, starting at the Hillcrest end. Bicycling back is not laborious. The walker without a shuttle and with moderate ambition would do well to start at the southern end, walk in 3 miles of relatively level land past Lower Crystal Springs Reservoir, picnic at the Jepson Laurel tree, of which more will be said later, then walk back out.

Connecting with the Sawyer Camp Trail, north from Hillcrest, is the San Andreas Trail, with walkers only on a dirt path to Larkspur Avenue, another access point, and then walkers or bikers on a paved strip from Larkspur to the entrance along Skyline Boulevard south of San Bruno Avenue. This trail is less attractive than the Sawyer Camp Trail because it parallels closely the freeway. There are hopes that this trail will someday strike west across the watershed to reach the Portola discovery site.

When you start the Sawyer Camp Trail at Hillcrest, notice a historical marker commemorating Gaspar de Portola's encampment here. He is the original explorer to whom we are all indebted. (You might want to glance at the write-up on Portola, which came earlier and describes this marker.) The marker rests on a rock of serpentine material, the characteristic geologic outcropping in this area.

Sawyer Camp Trail begins with a gradual downhill slope after

Bikers on the Sawyer Camp Trail

passing through an attractive grove of cypress trees and one outstanding example of Monterey pine. You then cross the San Andreas Dam, built in 1869, as the plaque on the west side reminds you. From the middle of this dam lovely vistas stretch north across the water and south through broad-leaved tree forests to Lower Crystal Springs Lake, your destination. You are walking or biking through a rift created by the San Andreas Fault in its eternal grinding. The trail honors not a lumber sawyer, as you might have guessed, but one Leland Sawyer, who trained performing horses for circuses in the 1870s and managed an inn here for travelers on their way to Half Moon Bay.

The trail then follows the western side of the stream through moist, cool forests of bay, then buckeye. Under the trees there are profusions of red larkspur wildflowers in spring. Whole hillsides of ferns flourish here, plus plenty of poison oak later on, so take care, especially of children running or biking ahead of you. Picnic tables are strategically located, first in a clump of dense, small, moss-covered bay trees and then in another lovely cluster of buckeye trees.

Midway along the 6 mile trail you reach a venerable arboreal statesman, the Jepson Laurel, whose plaque attests that it is the second largest known specimen of California bay laurel in the state. An even larger bay laurel was cut down before the adjacent reservoir could inundate it. Look at the giant, even larger now than its marked dimension in 1923 of 22 feet 4 inches in circumference and 55 feet in height. The tree is now fenced off to protect it from the inadvertent destructive effects of well-wishers, who compact the earth around its roots when walking and scrape the bark off limbs when climbing. The organizers of this trail have provided numerous picnic benches, plus drinking water and restrooms, at this Jepson Laurel site.

The last miles take you along the east side of Lower Crystal Springs Lake, with a view over the water. Be sure to bring binoculars on this trip to see the bird life, which may be as close to you as an Anna's hummingbird sitting on the fence along the trail or as far away as Canada geese resting on the reservoir in the midst of their migration flight.

The only slightly disconcerting experience on this trail is the chain link and barbed wire fence that entraps somewhat the spirit, creating a caged sensation. The fence has been necessary in this drinking-water watershed, but as modern water-purification techniques are introduced by the water district, the argument for the fence becomes more tenuous.

Historic Lathrop House, Redwood City

Cities along the Bay

3

Redwood City to Palo Alto

F rom Redwood City, a town named during the first lumbering boom, to Palo Alto, the city of the "tall tree," this section of the peninsula offers much to the explorer. Several of the fine old Victorian houses in the region have been preserved, starting with historic Lathrop House in Redwood City. This area includes the best remaining place to see bay plant and bird life, the Baylands Interpretive Center near the end of Embarcadero Road in Palo Alto. Downtown Palo Alto today is a vibrant center for restaurants and art galleries.

Lathrop House

R ight in the middle of developed Redwood City, across from the Hall of Records, stands one of the four notable historic landmarks you can visit in San Mateo County. This is the Lathrop House, at 627 Hamilton Street. (The other three are the Sanchez Adobe in Pacifica, the Tripp Store in Woodside, and the San Mateo County Historical Museum in San Mateo, all discussed elsewhere.)

The Lathrop House, also called the Lathrop-Connor-Mansfield House, is an ornamented Gothic creation, painted gray with white trim, complete with stylish fish-scale shingles on its steep roof. The house was moved here in 1905 from its earlier location on Broadway. Before visiting, call 415/365-5564 to check on hours. Restoration began in 1968, spurred by the city's centennial.

The story of the house goes back to 1858, when Mary C. Lathrop bought the lots on which the Fox Theater now stands from the earliest landowners, the Arguello and Mezes families. The house, as first constructed there, included 11 rooms, plus a kitchen and servants' quarters. It was called "Lora Mondi," which translates roughly as "beauty spot of the world."

The house is sturdy, having survived both the Earthquake of 1906 and two moves of the structure to new locations. Architecturally, the house is an interesting California expression of the revived interest in Gothic style architecture as applied to residences. The tall gables and graceful arches are not encumbered by the ornate lacework of later Victorian structures.

Benjamin Lathrop, husband of Mary, built the house in 1863. He was an astute businessman with many successful ventures. Lathrop arrived in California in 1854, age 39, after a career that began in South Carolina as an Indian relations and linguistics expert. From South Carolina he moved his family to New Orleans, where he was appointed to a judgeship. When gold fever swept the country, he journeyed from Louisiana to California. Lathrop opposed a "vested interest" clique in the county elections of 1856 and sided with the reform movement. He served in various public offices and was also an active founder of the Southern Pacific Railroad.

Later owners of the house were also prominent. General Patrick Edward Connor, who purchased it in 1870, was a Civil War commander who later had responsibility for keeping open the Overland Trail. The wife of Joel Mansfield, the sheriff, purchased the house in 1904. Historic photos of all these owners are on display, including an 1858 daguerreotype of the Lathrop family.

Once inside, try to find one of the enthusiastic local supporters of the Lathrop House to lead you around. Downstairs you'll find a study and parlor, complete with a piano that belonged to the Lathrop family. Benjamin Lathrop's niece, Jane Lathrop, married Leland Stanford.

Other ground-floor rooms include a dining room and kitchen, with butter churn, oak table, and wood-burning stove. The house's original pine floor and some of its early redwood paneling are still in good repair.

Upstairs you'll find a child's bedroom with period dolls and the adults' bedroom with bath chamber. Walls throughout the house are covered with careful reproductions of Victorian era wallpaper. The authenticity of the restoration can be assured if you look at wallpaper in the closet of the bath-chamber room, where three layers have been carefully peeled back. The outer layer is from about 1900, so the earlier layers must be from previous decades. The exact same designs can be seen on the repapered walls today, faithfully reproducing the taste of that era.

Sales from a small antique shop in an upstairs room contribute funds to the restoration.

Lathrop House is only the first of several historic sites that can be reached on foot from here. From Lathrop House volunteers sometimes lead walks to acquaint visitors with Redwood City. These are worth attending if your schedule allows.

Historic Redwood City

At Lathrop House you can obtain free a one-page walking map of historic Redwood City with some of the main buildings indicated. The *Redwood City Historical Trail Booklet* is also available for a modest fee and is worth the investment.

With a little imagination you can place yourself back in Redwood City between 1850 and 1880, when this settlement was the most substantial town between San Francisco and San Jose. Redwood City boomed as a lumber, tanning, and shipbuilding town in the 19th century.

The lumber trade served the appetite for building in burgeoning San Francisco. From the embarcadero a lively trade flourished in redwood boards, posts, and shingles. The lumber came from the hills of Woodside, down Kings Mountain Road near the Tripp Store, and from other areas, such as Searsville.

Bark from the tan oak, which contains large amounts of natural tannin, was used to tan hides. Frank's Tannery in Redwood City enjoyed an unsurpassed reputation as a provider of leather for shoes, harnesses, and aprons.

Ships as large as the 75-foot, two-masted *Perseverance* (1883) were built here. Redwood Creek ran wide and deep through the town then, with ships plying their way right up to present-day Broadway. The names of McLeod, Bell, Tyler, and Littlejohn were respected as shipbuilders who launched numerous vessels in the maritime trade lanes. Today, as the only deep-water port in the South Bay, the Port of Redwood City hosts some ocean trade.

Following the walking map, you see the grand, copper, county courthouse roof from 1903. Several modest 1860–80 houses survive where Middlefield Road and Stambaugh Street cross Beech Street.

Charming photos and drawings in the *Redwood City Historical Trail Booklet* re-create in your mind the rustic hospitality of the Grand Hotel, now a mere memory. One of the earliest buildings, Chamberlain's Store, remains today as the Quong Lee Laundry, on Main Street between Broadway and Marshall. The building is

little changed from the day in 1859 when contractor Richard
Driscoll completed the store for John Diller. Known successively
as the Old Pioneer Store, then the Chamberlain Store, the edifice
and warehouse behind served as a sale point for general
merchandise and at times as a courthouse, jail, and Wells Fargo &
Co. express office. After John Diller returned to Pennsylvania, the
store was eventually taken over by a man with perhaps the most
unusual name in the county, Philander Peregrine Chamberlain.

Originally the land on which Redwood City rested was part of
the grant of Rancho de las Pulgas, given to the Arguello family.
The Arguellos hired a capable attorney named S. M. Mezes to
represent them in the courts that decided land titles after the
American takeover. Squatters on the Arguello land were forced to
pay when the courts decided that the property did indeed belong
to the Arguellos. Mezes himself received the land of Redwood
City from the Arguello family as partial payment. He proposed
the name Mezesville for the settlement, but the local population
rejected that appellation over time. After Redwood City became
the county seat, there were a couple of determined efforts by San
Mateo to wrest away the honor, but they were unsuccessful.

October 1863 was a major milestone in the life of Redwood
City because the San Francisco and San Jose Railroad link was
then completed. An opulent picnic at the palo alto (the tall tree
where the railroad trestle crosses San Francisquito Creek near El
Camino and Alma Street in Palo Alto) marked this event. The
railroad shook Redwood City out of its overland isolation in the
rainy, muddy winter months and eventually caused the port to
decline because it was cheaper to ship lumber by rail to nearby San
Francisco.

Marine Ecological Institute

A s a complement to the land-based experience of bay flora
and bird life at the Baylands Interpretive Center off
Embarcadero Road in Palo Alto (discussed later in this
chapter), consider also the one opportunity available along the bay
to get out on the water in a boat with naturalists. That is the
Marine Ecological Institute, 811 Seaport Boulevard, Redwood
City, 415/364-2760.

The tour takes you aboard an 85-foot research vessel, *Inland
Seas*, and introduces you to the bay's fragile ecology. A core
sample of the bay bottom is usually taken during the trip, showing

the tube worms and mollusks that live in the mud. It's discouraging to see that it takes 39 inches of core sample in some areas to get past the mud deposited by hydraulic mining in the post-Gold Rush era. The fortieth inch of core sample reaches the oyster-shell bottom that was the original environment. Trawl nets lowered during the trip reveal fish, plankton, and algal life in bay waters. Water samples are tested for dissolved oxygen, temperature, and salinity, all parameters that determine which organisms will thrive.

Atherton

During the first decades of the 20th century, Atherton was known as Fair Oaks. Families used their homes here as summer retreats in the benign and sunny peninsula climate while San Francisco was chilly and foggy. The railroad, with a stop at what is now Atherton and another at what was and still is Menlo Park, made it easy for the man of the family to commute to San Francisco to work. Automobiles were little used for commuting in the early days of the horseless carriage because of the frequent tire changes needed.

Many of the Atherton homes were fairly self-sufficient, with large vegetable and fruit gardens. Butchers, bakers, and produce carts from Redwood City made daily rounds through the estates.

In 1923 Fair Oaks incorporated, but because the name was already in use for a town near Sacramento, the name was changed to Atherton, after early landowner Faxon Dean Atherton. The population in 1923 was 650.

Atherton has always been seen as a preserve for the well-to-do. The 7,000 residents of Atherton today continue to restrict business and excessive growth that would infringe on the quiet, tree-lined exclusivity of the area. This is as Faxon D. Atherton envisioned. He was an aristocrat who migrated here from Chile with his large family. Atherton purchased 500 acres along El Camino Real in 1860 with plans to build a summer home. He constructed a modest home in the present area of the Menlo Circus Club and became a leading area citizen. His daughter-in-law, Gertrude Atherton, was the famous and prolific novelist.

When Menlo Park wished to incorporate in 1923, the people of Atherton decided not to join in that new community, but to found their own town, named after the Chilean who had set the pattern.

Among the many interesting, large Atherton estates to drive by is the Joseph Frank house at 402 Middlefield Road, corner of

Glenwood and Middlefield. This Greek-revival house was built for Joseph Frank, who operated Frank's Tannery, a business of consequence in Redwood City. Architecturally, the house has a wood Colonial Revival style once popular on the East Coast. The present owners have taken some pains to restore and preserve it.

Royal Oaks, the house easily visible on the corner of Middlefield and Fair Oaks, was built in 1908 for E. J. and Miriam Moore Pringle. The Georgian-style house has 7,000 square feet of living space and originally included 3.3 acres of surrounding land. Tastefully restored in 1981, the house served in 1982 as the Decorator Show House, giving the public a glimpse of its fine interior detail.

The opulent, historic houses of Atherton are rarely open for public viewing, but an exception occurs each spring when the Decorators' Show House features one of these structures. Proceeds go to the the Coyote Point Museum for Environmental Education. Phone 415/342-7755 for details.

Menlo Park

Named by two Irishmen for their home region of Menlough, a town in county Galway, Menlo Park is a prosperous suburban commuter town for professionals working in San Francisco or in the Silicon Valley industries. D. J. Oliver and D. C. McGlynn were the early Irish ranchers here.

Allied Arts, the old train station, Stanford Research Institute, the United States Geological Survey, and *Sunset* magazine are some of the major places of interest.

Allied Arts Guild

A peninsula romance with the Spanish Mission style of architecture and garden setting can be seen at the Allied Arts Guild, Arbor Road and Creek Drive, in Menlo Park.

This low-slung cluster of Spanish-style buildings from the 1920s houses art, craft, and gift stores, run as a benefit for the Children's Hospital at Stanford University. Lunches and an afternoon tea are served, with reservations recommended, 415/324-2588.

The grounds are a small portion of the large Rancho de las Pulgas (fleas were the bane of early peninsula life), a land grant from the Spanish king to Don Jose Arguello, commandant of the

Presidio of San Francisco. In 1929 Mr. and Mrs. Garfield Merner purchased the 3.5 acres of the present guild and gardens. Their idea was to establish a crafts guild similar to what they had known in Europe.

The Merners collaborated with architect Gardiner Dailey and artist Pedro de Lemos. They restored an original barn and sheep shed on the property and added new buildings conforming to a Colonial Spanish motif of thick walls, courtyards, archways, white stucco walls, and red tile roofs. The Merners patterned the grounds and gardens after those they had seen in the Granada province of Spain, importing various tiles and art objects from Spain, Tunisia, and Morocco. The three main gardens are named the Court of Abundance, Garden of Delight, and Cervantes Court.

Among the interesting shops here are those run by artisans, such as Custom Handweavers for textiles, The Barn Wood Shop for handmade furniture, and The Glassblower for ornate and practical glass artifacts.

Menlo Park's Historic Buildings

There is much to discover in downtown Menlo Park, heart of a community established in 1854.

The Menlo Park Train Station, a yellow and white building at the foot of Santa Cruz Avenue, is one of the preserved gems of the Southern Pacific Railroad line from the era when the railroad was more encouraging to passengers. Leland Stanford, Mark Hopkins, and James Flood were among the 19th-century titans who used this stop as their embarking point. The railroad station building is now the home of the Menlo Park Chamber of Commerce, so if you have a question on directions they can help you.

Appropriately enough, the green building south of the railroad depot is home for the West Bay Model Railroad Association, which is open to the public at 8 P.M. the third Friday and fourth Wednesday of each month. Their collection of miniature rolling stock is one of the largest in the Bay Area.

The peninsula's major paperback bookstore, Kepler's, is a few blocks south at Victoria Lane on the 800 block of El Camino Real. Coffee, scones, and omelets are excellent at a cleverly named restaurant, Late For The Train, at 561 Oak Grove, open only for breakfast and lunch, 415/321-6124. The British Bankers Club, 1019 El Camino Real, is a stylish meeting place for lunch, dinner, or socializing. Try their cannelloni or fresh petrale meuniere, 415/327-8769.

The Edgar Mills House in Menlo Park

   Cross the railroad tracks toward the bay to see one of the
attractive and enduring architectural classics in the area, the former
Edgar Mills mansion, now law offices at 1940 Noel Street, off
Ravenswood. Turning south on Noel and crossing Ravenswood,
you see the main cultural center of Menlo Park: the library, the
Burgess Theater, and a large swimming pool. The grassy playing
fields are a spot of greenery where many urban office workers eat
their lunches. Lovely old live oak trees grace the landscape.
   At the corner of Ravenswood and Laurel stands historic Gate
House, a carriage house that withstood the 1906 Earthquake while
the grander home of the Mark Hopkins family, Sherwood Hall,
perished. The rooms of Gate House are now used by various
community organizations.

Stanford Research Institute

This large research institute, occupying 70 acres along Ravenswood Road in Menlo Park, maintains a low profile. Its branch offices in places such as Saudi Arabia or Tokyo are as vigorous as the home offices here. The organization will research anything it is paid to consider.

Founded in 1946, SRI now employs 3,000 people full time. They range over dozens of academic disciplines, such as the physical sciences, mathematics, and the behavioral sciences. The eight divisions of research at SRI are Urban and Social Systems, Engineering Systems, Electronics and Radio Sciences, Information Science and Engineering, Physical Sciences, Life Sciences, Economics, and Management Systems.

SRI conducts about $165 million in research contracts each year. The organization is not a think tank, but a solutions-to-problems institute that depends for its survival on getting contracts. During the Vietnam War years, the institute's president and his car were severely pummeled with rocks because the institute seemed to symbolize research without any concern for its effects. Formal ties with Stanford University were severed in 1969 to remove the university from the military effort. Cancer cures, environmental cleanup, and solutions to the energy crisis have been as much a part of the SRI agenda as military research.

The public has little contact with SRI. No public tours are available.

United States Geological Survey

The USGS map sales office in Menlo Park at 345 Middlefield Road, Building 3, is intriguing to visit. Here you can buy a detailed topographical map for any area of the peninsula, California, or the West. The USGS maps have long been a resource for hikers and backpackers. However, when an area changes frequently, the maps may be slightly out of date. Besides topo maps, USGS also sells thematic maps, one of which shows where mineral resources, including gold, have been found. A hazards map outlines earthquake faults, potential landslide areas, and flood plains at risk. A complete directory of the maps is available.

Aside from maps, USGS also provides extensive free literature on subjects ranging from the historic voyage of John Wesley Powell down the Colorado River to the procedures for mapmaking, which grow increasingly refined with satellite information. Priced literature available here entices people with special historical or geologic interests. Consider titles such as *Principal Gold Producing Districts of the United States*. The building's lobby contains interpretive displays on historic mapmaking techniques and on geologic subjects of interest, such as the massive landslides in 1982. Call 415/323-8111 for further information.

Sunset/Lane Publishers

Sunset/Lane Magazine and Book Company, so influential in forming western styles and tastes, have their headquarters at Middlefield and Willow roads. The facilities can be toured, giving the reader a glimpse of the editorial offices, gardens, photo studios, and food testing kitchens that produce material for *Sunset*, the monthly magazine. *Sunset* boasts a circulation well over a million in only the western states, its self-determined territory.

Tours are Monday through Friday, 10–3. Call 415/321-3600 for details.

The astute editorial guiders of Sunset/Lane have developed an enduring mix of four subjects for their magazine and books: travel, gardening, food preparation, and home improvement. As a small index of *Sunset's* influence, the prominence of wine as the beverage of choice in so many California homes owes much to the appearance of people enjoying wine in almost every issue of the magazine for the last 25 years. While other magazines have been founded and buried, *Sunset* has managed to achieve a special sustainable formula of "good news," life-enhancing practical suggestions. For its readers the magazine serves as an antidote to the "problems" and controversies with which almost every other magazine or newspaper is filled. No other magazine in the West enjoys as wide an advertising base as *Sunset*, even though several categories of ads are not permitted, such as cigarettes, hard liquor, and women's hygienic products.

Sunset began in 1898 as a promotional magazine for the Southern Pacific Railroad to encourage travel/settlement in the West. After 1914 it was, for 15 years, a literary magazine. In 1928 the Laurence Lane family bought the magazine and fashioned their successful editorial mix, focused on the westerners-only audience.

A tour of the grounds demonstrates the western orientation of Sunset/Lane and shows you where many of the article ideas for the magazine originate. The headquarters buildings, designed by Cliff May, reflect several aspects of western history and the western lifestyle. The buildings themselves are of simulated-adobe construction, about two feet thick, with wide overhangs and interior courtyards, creating an informal yet productive work environment. Construction material for the walls was a 30-pound, handmade brick. The floors are, similarly, a handmade desert tile. Some western living ideas, obvious in the construction, are the close blend of outdoor and indoor space, the use of all-year gardening strategies, and the low, rambling, one-story style, typical both of the Spanish missions and the ranch houses of the West.

Over the years the Lane family has purchased an extensive collection of Navajo rugs, which are on display. Furniture in the offices tends to be of sturdy western style.

Palo Alto: The Baylands

Few peninsulans appreciate fully the bay's physical presence or the importance of its diverse flora and fauna. The expanse of the open, shallow south bay does not have the spectacular appeal of a redwood forest, though its absence of man-made structures adds an important spatial dimension to human feeling in the region, especially for the seeker of solitude. Beyond this spatial presence, the plant, animal, and bird life of the south bay are extraordinary when studied intently. Abundant plant life contributes favorably to the oxygen replenishment cycle so needed to freshen the air we breathe in our polluted urbanized environment.

Protected baylands at the end of Embarcadero Road in Palo Alto offer the best opportunity peninsulans have to encounter the riches of bay plant and bird communities.

Palo Alto Baylands is at 2775 Embarcadero, Palo Alto. Call 415/329-2506 to learn of current hours open and when naturalist-led tours are available. The 120-acre salt marsh and surrounding property is owned and operated by the city of Palo Alto.

Here you can make the acquaintance of salt marsh flora and birds. A trail system of boardwalks and levees allows you the unique experience of "walking in the marsh," even during high tide. The main boardwalk leads out from the interpretive center to an observation deck near the water's edge. Connecting boardwalks installed originally for maintaining utility towers add to the potential walking territory.

The Lucy Evans Baylands Nature Interpretive Center was built in 1969 to express growing awareness of the important biosystems in the bay. It was named after an active conservationist from Palo Alto, Lucy Evans, whose lifelong interest in history and natural history earned her the title "Baylands Lucy."

At this center, on the fringe of the salt marsh, there is a room for lectures, a library, exhibits, and an observation deck. The mounted birds, from a great blue heron to sandpipers, are a few examples of the many species found here. Trained naturalists guide the operation. Programs during the week usually require reservations, but the center welcomes drop-in visitors on weekends. Guided bird and plant walks, slide shows, movies, and ecology workshops are some of the activities here. Programs emphasize seasonal migration patterns and the interdependence of plants and animals.

Sandpipers and Clapper Rails

The 1,500 total acres of preserve along a 2.5 mile frontage allow for a sufficiently large habitat to maintain a range of species. Marsh hawks, white-tailed kites, canvasback ducks, goldeneye ducks, and burrowing owls are just some of the winged residents. Migrating, overwintering, and permanent resident birds can be seen. For birdwatchers, this is an excellent place to see secretive California clapper rails at high tide.

Even the most casual observer of the bay will notice the bird life,

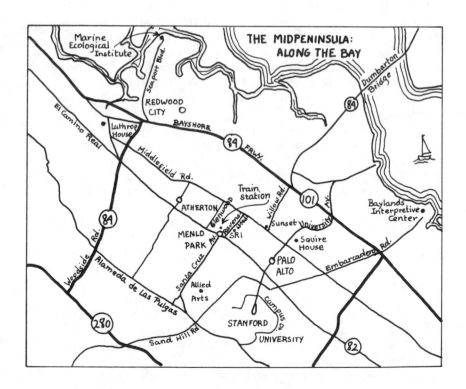

which is diverse and bountiful. About half of the 200 species of birds common to the peninsula can be seen in the shallow waters and marshes of the bay. Students of bird migration patterns have concluded that about 70 percent of all the birds migrating down the Pacific Flyway stop in the southern arm of San Francisco Bay. Many species of birds exist and feed side by side because they seek different kinds of food in the same area, perhaps determined by the lengths of their beaks or legs, their penchants for algae or insects, or their relative abilities to float on the water.

Ranger-naturalists at the Baylands Center estimate that over one million birds depend on this Palo Alto habitat either during their migration or all year-round for food, water, rest, and protection from the elements. Ten thousand western sandpipers have been counted here on a single day. At the Baylands Interpretive Center, the ranger-naturalists can help you make the acquaintance of feathered citizens of our region by teaching you to distinguish a dowitcher from an avocet, a pintail from a mallard, and a linnet from a Brewer's blackbird.

Pickleweed and Cord Grass

To the initiated the plant life of the salt marsh is as absorbing as the birds. Microscopic algae serve as the cornerstone of an ascending food chain, creating the base of the feeding pyramid needed for bay brine shrimp and fingerling striped bass. The plants, of course, ultimately control what birds will be present.

Over 100 species of plants have been found at Baylands, but three are dominant in the salt marsh: salt grass, cord grass, and pickleweed. One of the most important limiting factors is salt concentration. Most plants die when exposed to a water solution of more than two percent salt. The salt causes water to flow out of, rather than into, the plant. But here salt concentrations often reach six percent. Plants that have adapted successfully to this salt concentration are called halophytes.

Salt grass (*Districhlis spicata*) thrives at and above the extreme high tide zone. This short, coarse grass grows in dense mats and resembles Bermuda grass. Its leaves excrete salt. The zone in which this grass grows may be quite narrow if the bank is steep.

Pickleweed (*Salicornia virginica*) grows in the mid-tide range. This is a pale green succulent plant whose common name comes from the ends of its stems, which are thick, juicy, and consist of small segments. The stems are green and produce food because the leaves are very small and scalelike.

Cord grass (*Spartina foliosa*) lives along the edge of the bay and in the lower ranges of the tide zones. This dark green perennial grass looks somewhat like a small corn plant, growing to a height of four feet, topped in autumn with plumes of golden grass flowers. This plant is one of the most productive on earth, yielding 10 tons of food per acre, higher than the productivity of a wheat field. Most of the animals of the salt marsh depend on cord grass for their subsistence.

Mussels and Harvest Mice

Animal life in the Palo Alto baylands is sometimes secretive, though abundant. Mussels can be seen exposed at low tides, but the legendary oyster beds that provided such abundant food for the Indians have yet to be reestablished. Butterflies are among the most noticeable of creatures here, ranging from the tiger swallowtail to the pigmy blue. The salt marsh harvest mouse exists only in bay marshes and has a mortal stake in the preservation of refuges. The size of the habitat near Palo Alto, at least, has now been stabilized.

Brine Shrimp

If you have ever driven across the Dumbarton Bridge and noticed what look like one-man barges with nets, chances are you're seeing brine shrimp harvesting. Brine shrimp are one of the exotic small crustaceans in the bay. The water turns bright red with the color of the shrimp at the time the 3/8-inch crustaceans are harvested for use as aquarium fish food. Eggs of brine shrimp are also harvested and sold as fresh eggs to be hatched later.

About six fishermen ply the 2,000 acres of Leslie Salt Co. ponds on motorized rafts to make the harvest. The rafters look for red water that suggests high concentrations of the shrimp. Harvesting is a backbreaking activity. Each man lifts out some 300–400 buckets of shrimp and water per day, with each bucket weighing 40–50 pounds. The shrimp are then cooked and dried for sale.

Palo Alto

This middle- and upper-income community of predominantly white professional families began historically with the founding of Stanford University. The main employers who support this prosperity today are the university, the large range of specialized electronics companies in the region, and the medical-legal-financial apparatus thriving on affluence.

The Squire House

Entering Palo Alto from Bayshore Freeway 101, you pass the imposing house of John Adams Squire at 900 University Avenue. This Georgian Classical Revival structure with its Greek columns reflects Squire's Boston upbringing more than the rustic, Spanish world of California. Son of a wealthy meatpacker, Squire came west with his wife Georgiana in 1888. She taught Latin and Greek at what was then the State Normal School in San Jose, now San Jose State University. Squire himself pursued the study of classics at Stanford and indulged his interest in meteorology.

As their family grew, the Squires decided to move from a house on Emerson Street to the present location. They hired architect T. Patterson Ross to construct their dream home. Squire died at the house in 1930, but his wife remained there until 1959. Today the house is a private residence, though for years it lingered before the wrecker's ball until interested citizens rescued it in 1971 and established its historic status with a plaque in front.

The Squire House in Palo Alto

Downtown Palo Alto

The heart of this mid-peninsula city is a pleasant and rewarding place to browse. A stroll here should begin with paying homage to the giant tree for which the city was named.

From University Avenue, walk up Alma Street north to its end, four blocks. In a quiet, shaded grove of younger redwoods you'll find a bronze marker on a granite stone. The marker refers to the still standing single trunk of the "tall tree," the palo alto, that played such an important role as a landmark in early peninsula history. The tree originally had two trunks, as noted in several early visual records, such as the celebrated topographical map of 1776 drawn by Padre Pedro Font. Subsequently, one of the trunks has fallen and lightning has lopped off the top of the other. The best view of the tree can be obtained by walking over the railroad trestle crossing San Francisquito Creek and looking at the tree from the Menlo Park side. Here, incidentally, you'll find a Vita Course, one version of the parcourse exercising stations so popular now in urban environments.

The marker describes one of the most important moments in the history of this tree:

> Under this giant redwood, the Palo Alto, November 6 to 11, 1769, camped Portola and his band on the expedition that discovered San Francisco Bay. This was the assembling point for their reconnoitering parties. Here in 1774 Padre Palou erected a cross to mark the site of a proposed mission (which was later built at Santa Clara).

(The story of Portola's expeditions, so central to an appreciation of peninsula history, is told earlier in this volume.)

If you visit the marker in winter, when San Francisquito Creek is flowing strongly, you may see steelhead fighting their way up the waters to spawn. The creek was famous earlier for running one of the first water-powered sawmills in California.

Aside from the palo alto, the city is justifiably proud of its total arboreal heritage. The trees of Palo Alto can be studied with much delight. Excellent specimens of a wide range of varieties grow here. From the Revenue Collections Office at City Hall, 210 Hamilton, 415/329-2317, you can buy a special small book, *Trees of Palo Alto*, and then locate the specimens by street address. For example, the book tells you that a handsome buckeye tree, over 70 years old, can be seen at 690 California Street. A good example of the most characteristic tree of the region, coast live oak, with its spiny evergreen serrated leaves, remains at 410 Churchill Street. A 400-year-old valley oak, whose deciduous leaves are heavily lobed, exists at 450 Sequoia Street.

Within downtown Palo Alto, stroll the handsome brick-lined sidewalks of University Avenue and parallel Hamilton Avenue. Take in all the side streets between Alma and Waverley streets. Allow an unstructured afternoon for rambling here because there is much to see. Some of the main attractions are bookstores, art galleries, and eateries.

Palo Alto Bookstores

Palo Alto is a bookish community, perhaps because of Stanford's presence. In downtown Palo Alto you can find a wide selection of bookstores. Shirley Cobb Bookstore, 452 University, has been a fixture on the street for over 40 years and has probably put more books in the hands of peninsulans than any other single store. Stacey's, at 219 University, has books of all kinds, but as a sign of the times you might browse a 50-foot wall devoted solely to books on computers, a subject central to the region's recent history. Down the block at 135 University is the Stanford Bookstore's technical division, with a range of medical and engineering texts. Across the street, the Plowshare, 162 University, stocks many volumes on mystical and religious subjects. At 200 Hamilton is Wreden's Books, a dealer in rare and out-of-print books.

Two miles south of this downtown area, around California Avenue, you'll find a second cluster of bookstores important in peninsula cultural life. At 310 California Avenue is Printer's Inc, an attractive bookstore and coffee house combination. The Palo Alto Conservation Center, 2253 Park Boulevard, has a bookstore and extensive library on conservation, nature, and food gardening subjects. The same building provides space for eight other environmental groups, ranging from the Sierra Club to the Committee for Green Foothills. Bulletin boards assist the peninsulan who wants better access to nature by listing upcoming hikes with like-minded persons. An attractive garden shows how drought-resistant landscape plantings can beautify a yard and yet save water. The crucial book and materials store for people interested in food gardening and more energy-efficient living is Ecology Action, 2225 El Camino Real, where you can get books as well as seeds, tools, and organic gardening supplies.

Wall Murals and Galleries

Wall murals provide an unusual decor for downtown Palo Alto. Artist Greg Brown received several commissions, which range from the cheerful spaceman at a grocery store parking lot on the 200 block of Lytton to the *trompe l'oeil* walls of a wine shop, 574 Emerson. Be sure to see the nun firing a windup airplane off a balcony at 436 University Avenue.

Art galleries and antique stores also abound in downtown Palo Alto. Gallery House, at 538 Ramona, is a longstanding juried co-op where you can see paintings, ceramics, graphics, and sculpture of local artists in changing shows. Down the street is Blue Willow Antiques, at 520 Ramona.

Ramona between University and Hamilton has two 1920s neo-Mission-style buildings by artist-craftsman Pedro de Lemos, at 530 and 535 Ramona. These buildings form a small world of shops and restaurants, which preserve in the setting the original live oak trees. The structures set the style of the block and were echoed in other buildings by architect Birge Clark, emphasizing archways and iron balconies. Mission-revival architecture, using tile roofs and thick, simulated-adobe walls with stucco surfaces, intrigued Californians in the 1920s.

The Artifactory at 226 Hamilton houses a dozen craftspeople, who do their work at the site, such as UpRise Leather. University Arts at 267 Hamilton offers a wide selection of lithographs as well as framing and art supplies. At Los Robles Gallery, 167 Hamilton, you can see Roman glass as well as modern wood furniture. The Bentwood Rocker Antiques, 201 Hamilton, deals mainly in massive wood chests and dressers, plus stained glass. Just when you think you've seen everything here, you stumble on a new store, such as the Great American Framing Factory at 525 Alma.

Restaurants

Downtown Palo Alto comes alive at lunchtime with an outpouring of people. One eatery to try is the Good Earth, 185 University, 415/321-9449. Good Earth caught the cresting wave of demand for natural, wholesome, yet attractive food and rode that breaker to a chain with national ambitions. Try their garden patch salad, which has nine seasonal vegetables. Liddicoat's, at 340 University, was formerly a select grocery store, but now houses a dozen specialized fast food booths, from Japanese fish tempura to Filipino sweet and sour pork. There are plenty of chairs and tables upstairs for seating. Caffe Santa Maddalena at 233 University, 415/322-1846, is a lively Italian trattoria with a cafeteria style. Try the osso bucco.

The most historic restaurant is delightful MacArthur Park, 27 University Avenue, 415/321-9990. You can miss the restaurant entirely if its secretive location is not pointed out. Continue on University Avenue from Palo Alto toward Stanford and turn right after you pass under the railroad trestle. The restaurant is located next to the train station. The ample, white-painted structure was a World War I hostess house, designed by Julia Morgan in 1918 for Camp Fremont, in Menlo Park. The structure was later moved to this site in Palo Alto, where it served community recreational needs. A bronze marker in the front tells the story, adding that this is the only building remaining from that World War I training camp. Try the mesquite charcoaled swordfish or the fish of the day.

The Hoover Tower and Libraries, Stanford University

Leland Stanford's University 4

Professorville Yesterday and Today

On October 1, 1881, Senator Leland Stanford and his wife officially opened Leland Stanford Jr. University, an educational establishment that would eventually win international fame. After the tragic death from typhoid fever of their 16-year-old son in Florence, Italy, the Stanfords decided to turn their 8,200-acre stock farm into the Leland Stanford Jr. University so that "the children of California may be our children." Years later the cerebral establishment was still called "The Farm" because Stanford had used the grounds first to raise prize racehorses, orchard crops, and wine grapes. The early faculty built homes in Palo Alto, one neighborhood of which was dubbed Professorville.

Today this campus for 13,000 students is well worth an afternoon of exploring. You can guide yourself with a free map available from Visitor Information at the top of the stairs as you approach the main quadrangle. You can also participate in student-led tours by calling 415/497-2862. The university is adjacent to Palo Alto, accessible by turning onto Palm Drive or Embarcadero Road from El Camino Real.

For the explorer, the first places to visit on the Stanford University grounds are: the main quadrangle and Memorial Church; the Hoover Tower with the Hoover Institution of War, Revolution, and Peace; the Stanford University Museum of Art; then the University Bookstore, the Meyer and Green libraries, and Tresidder Union.

Stanford's Legacy

The name of Leland Stanford recalls an era in the history of the peninsula, which had a profound influence on California and the nation. An engaging and careful historical study by Dorothy Regnery, called *An Enduring Heritage*, describes the life and architectural legacy of Stanford and other substantial early builders of estates on the peninsula.

Starting modestly during the Gold Rush as a merchant in Sacramento, Stanford managed to accumulate enough capital to become a partner in building the transcontinental railroad over the Sierra Nevada. The success of the railroad brought Stanford prodigious wealth. While still a merchant, Stanford rose in Republican Party circles and was elected governor of California.

The Main Quadrangle

The most historic section of the Stanford campus is the original sandstone quadrangle with its thick Romanesque features and Memorial Church. Distinctive in the university architecture are the enclosed courtyard, archways, red tile roofs, thick walls, and buff sandstone from which the buildings are constructed. The dominant architectural model was the Romanesque style. There is a general feeling of unity, especially in the earlier buildings.

The primary architect for Stanford University was Charles Coolidge, but the client, Leland Stanford, was far from passive. Because the Stanfords liked a certain Swiss hotel they visited, a copy of that hotel was made to appear on campus as Encina Hall. Stanford hired the greatest landscape architect of the day, Frederick Law Olmstead, but made it clear that Olmstead was his employee. Stanford liked to participate in all details of the campus development.

Leland Stanford conceived of the university as a physical plan more than as an intellectual monument. At his death in 1893 there was no clear allotment of the developing space for different faculties. His wife, Jane, and her brother, Ariel Lathrop, proceeded with the building, but without the dominant force of the senator.

Memorial Church, dedicated in 1903, was Mrs. Stanford's memorial to her husband. The mosaics on the front were made in the Salviati Studio in Venice, Italy, and shipped to California. The church's tower toppled in the 1906 Earthquake and was never rebuilt.

Hoover Tower

Hoover Tower, the 285-foot landmark on the campus, offers a panoramic view of the surrounding region if you take the elevator ride to the top. Hours open vary with school schedules, so call for current times, 415/497-2053. Concerts using the 35-bell carillon of Hoover Tower ring out at noon, 5 P.M., and on special occasions.

The tower houses part of the Hoover Institution on War, Revolution, and Peace, which has millions of papers and books related to world conflict. Included in the collection are the presidential papers of Herbert Hoover, Stanford's most celebrated graduate. Some of the holdings are on permanent display in two rooms at the base of the tower.

The Herbert Hoover Room contains many documents from Hoover's boyhood, professional mining days, and presidency. Hoover wrote technical books on mining and directed mining operations in such distant locations as China. This son of a Quaker blacksmith was also an avid fisherman who wrote, "All men are equal before fish." Hoover's reputation eventually went into decline when he was perceived as either the cause of or scapegoat for the Depression. The other room, dedicated to Hoover's wife, Lou Henry, contains artifacts such as Belgian lace, Oriental vases, and South American/Mexican silver either given to the Hoovers as political gifts or collected by them in their itinerant life.

The institution now serves as an international teaching and research center on economic, social, and political change in the 20th century. Its political bias has generally been toward the right.

At the lobby you can obtain maps and literature about the Stanford campus, including a handout on several outdoor sculptures added to the university landscape in the 1970s.

Stanford Museum of Art

The Leland Stanford Jr. University Museum of Art, on Museum Way off Palm Drive, has an eclectic collection that includes much Stanford family memorabilia and the gold spike that united the first transcontinental railroad. Call 415/497-4177 for hours open.

Built in 1892, this is the oldest museum west of the Mississippi. Architecturally, the building was the first to use reinforced concrete structural techniques. Railroad rails served as the reinforcers in the concrete.

The museum has an outstanding collection of Auguste Rodin

sculptures. Other collections include Oriental jade and ceramics, California landscape paintings, western Indian basketry and ceramics, ancient Near Eastern ceramic vessels, and an Egyptian mummy. One of the intriguing California contributions to the museum is a 19th-century Yurok Indian canoe carved from a single redwood log. Yuroks used these canoes on the Klamath River and in ocean trips to hunt for sea lions.

The Stanford family collection includes many artifacts from the young Stanford boy's brief life. He possessed the same eclectic collector's mentality that characterizes the holdings of the museum. Items include a rock from a castle and a hair from Napoleon's chair, gathered while visiting Europe with his parents. His bicycle, an early velocipide, stands in the middle of the family memorabilia, below large paintings of the family.

The Student Campus

Student libraries can also be a resource for peninsula residents, who may read books there but not take them out. The newer Meyer Undergraduate Library has elaborate computerized listings of its books and periodicals. The older main library, the Cecil H. Green Library, is primarily a resource for graduate students.

The Student Bookstore has a wide range of books, including volumes on California history and natural history. Tresidder Union houses a pleasant restaurant with cafeteria service.

The Stables

The original Stanford stables, approachable on Fremont Road from Junipero Serra Boulevard, played an important role in settling a hotly debated issue among gentlemen of Stanford's day. Look for the red barn from 1870 a few hundred yards down Fremont Road.

The issue was: Did a trotting horse at some point in its gait have all four hooves off the ground at the same time? Stanford hired photographer Eadweard Muybridge to set up a battery of cameras that could record a horse in motion. Muybridge's photos showed that the horse was indeed airborne at one moment. This sequence of 24 images in motion was made in 1878–79, and in addition to settling the dispute, it also fostered an advance in the history of motion pictures.

A bronze marker at the site recalls these experiments. The plaque reads:

In commemoration of the motion picture research conducted in 1878 and 1879 at the Palo Alto Farm, now the site of Stanford University. This extensive photographic experiment portraying the attitudes of men and animals in motion was conceived by and executed under the direction and patronage of Leland Stanford. Consecutive instantaneous exposures were provided for by a battery of twenty-four cameras fitted with electro-shutters. Eadweard J. Muybridge, photographer, carried out the investigation and showed that the photographs could be combined in projection to give the true appearance of motion.

The main purpose of Leland Stanford's Palo Alto Farm was the breeding and training of blooded trotting horses. Using his own theories of breeding and training, Stanford proved highly

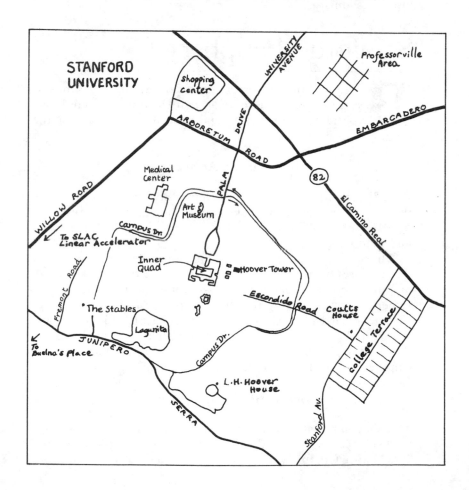

70

successful. His trotters set 19 world records. The bronze statue of a horse, standing on a marble pedestal, carries this inscription:

> This monument, the gift of Mr. Timothy Hopkins, marks the location of the Palo Alto Stock Farm established by Leland Stanford 1876, discontinued 1903. The names and records of some of its famous trotters are inscribed hereon.

The list begins with Electioneer 125, world champion and sire of nine world champions.

Beyond these markers stands the aging red barn, built in 1870 and still used today for boarding horses. Some interested alumni and corporate leaders would like to see the barn restored as a historic landmark.

Stanford's Periphery

Because of the mammoth size of the Stanford campus, several interesting entities that the outsider would consider almost parts of another town are actually on the fringes of the university's property.

The Linear Accelerator

At 2575 Sandhill Road, behind the university, you can visit one of the costliest research tools ever built, the Stanford Linear Accelerator (SLAC). Phone 415/854-3300, ext 2204 for tour information.

The linear accelerator is a two-mile long electron accelerator that explores the properties of small atomic particles with the aid of a pulse-powered beam of 20–45 billion electron volts. Experiments here during the 1970s on the nature of elementary particles earned a Nobel Prize for Burton Richter. SLAC is the largest tool man has ever created. A 90-minute tour includes a slide/lecture presentation and bus ride around the 480-acre center. Children under 11 must be accompanied by an adult.

Stanford Shopping Center

This shopping center, on the north edge of the campus, has a good bookstore, Books Inc, and an interesting access-to-nature store, The Nature Company. Bravo Fono is a cafe that raises pastry making to a high art, 415/322-4664. Try also the ragout and peasant bread of the Hungarian proprietors.

One building in the shopping center is from Stanford's time. The Old Stanford Barn on Quarry Road, actually a winery built in 1883, now houses several offices, an ice cream shop, and the Golden Spike restaurant, 415/321-8304, a good lunch stop for a steak sandwich.

Lou Henry Hoover House

On the campus you can drive by the Lou Henry Hoover House, the former residence of the Herbert Hoovers. Here Hoover received the news in 1928 that he had won the presidential election. The Hoovers always considered the house and Stanford campus their home. This house, at 623 Mirada Avenue, now serves as the residence of the president of the university.

Herbert Hoover and his wife, Lou Henry, led a somewhat itinerant life until after World War I, when they asked Professor A. B. Clark and his son, Birge, under the watchful guidance of Mrs. Hoover, to design the house. This structure, from 1919, is a unique blend of American pueblo–cliff dwelling exterior and English country manor interior style elements. In the evening light the white stucco walls of the facade catch the sun in the manner of a southwestern cliff dwelling. The house served as the Hoover family residence from 1920 to 1944. At the time of Mrs. Hoover's death the house was given to Stanford University.

The Frenchman's Ayrshire Farm

An interesting structure in the Escondido Village housing complex on the Stanford campus has its own tale to tell.

This was the cottage, originally a single story, that one Peter Coutts and his family built after their sudden arrival in 1875. Coutts bought 1,200 acres of land and hired a hundred men to put up some 19 buildings, including barns, a windmill, and a brick-floored stable.

Coutts apparently had much wealth and ambitious intentions to turn the property into a small agricultural empire. Fine riding horses and Ayrshire cattle were among his prize holdings.

Many local residents speculated about where Coutts had come from and how he had made his money. Coutts was generally genial, but not informative on these points. Occasional visits from the French consul in San Francisco did little to illuminate the situation, but fueled speculation.

Suddenly one morning in 1880, with scarcely a word said, Coutts and his family departed, never to return. Through agents he sold the property the next year to Leland Stanford for $140,000.

Only years later, because of information from a granddaughter, did the full story become known. Peter Coutts was actually one Jean-Baptiste Paulin Caperon, a wealthy banker and publisher of the anti-Royalist newspaper, *La Liberte*, who had left France in 1874 to escape harassment by supporters of Napoleon III. Caperon fled to Switzerland and borrowed the passport of a Swiss cousin, Peter Coutts. In 1880 an unexpected shift in the French political scene gave Caperon a chance to return and regain his properties if he did so at once. Shortly after the French consul informed him of this, Caperon left. He lived out the rest of his days in France, enjoying peace and prosperity, until his death in 1889.

The house has served various functions over the years. It was the residence of David Starr Jordan, first president of Stanford. The tan-painted board-and-batten construction, with green trim, has been well maintained. Today it serves as the administration building for the housing complex, which overwhelms the historic structure. With an act of the imagination you can re-create what Coutts' bucolic setting must have been like. For an engaging, anecdotal account of the lives of many residents in the early substantial houses of Palo Alto and southward, including the Coutts' house, see Phyllis Butler's *The Valley of Santa Clara*, available in local bookstores.

Stanford Computer Music

Like all great institutions, Stanford has developed many subinstitutions that are on the cutting edges of their fields. One to which the public has some access is the Stanford University Center for Computer Research in Music and Acoustics.

The public is invited to a monthly program and tour, usually every third Wednesday night at 7:30. Call for details, 415/497-4971. Concerts sometimes mix computer and human performers, exploring combinations that may stretch your musical sensibilities. You can get on the mailing list alerting you to the three or four concerts given each year.

During the 1970s John Chowning and others did much interesting research here, using the computer as both a generator of sounds and a tool for composition. The subtlety with which a

computer can create a richness of sounds has been greatly
advanced since Robert Moog developed his electronic-music
analog-synthesizer in 1964. Today's composer using a computer
creates digital signals that activate oscillators, electronic machines.
The oscillators produce pure tones. A computer can be used to
analyze sounds by reducing the sound to numbers that describe
the length, pitch, tone, color, and loudness. Such digital numbers
are then filed, recombined, and turned back into sounds by a
digital-to-analog converter. The sounds are put through a
loudspeaker. In this way a range of new sounds, never before
produced by conventional instruments, is possible. A computer
can be used to simulate traditional instruments or create new
ranges of sound. A composer mixes mastery of the new computer
technology with a knowledge of traditional musical language, the
do-re-mi scale that Guido d'Arezzo devised in the 11th century.

It's fitting that Stanford has emerged as one of the leading
centers in the world for this new kind of music because the
university is located in the heart of Silicon Valley, where so much
computer development of other kinds has taken place. Certainly
this is a type of musical experience that is bound to become more
important in the future as modern composers take advantage of
this new technology.

Another of the "new music" groups is Alea II, which takes its
name from the philosophical position of creating aliatory or
chance music, such as John Cage's rolling of the dice to determine .
the structural parameters of a musical piece.

An equally energetic computer world at Stanford is the
Stanford University Artificial Intelligence Project, headed by John
McCarthy. This is a leading center in the U.S. for development of
robotics and "thinking" computers, which can make new
inferences based on their past experience. However, it is difficult
for the public to interract with this group.

Professorville and Early Palo Alto

I n 1876 Leland Stanford established his Palo Alto Farm, as he
called it, on Rancho San Francisquito. As the idea of founding
a university took shape in his mind, the railroad magnate

wanted to have a town site nearby for the professors to live in. He first considered Mayfield, a town already bustling along as a lumber and trade point in the vicinity of the present California Avenue. The Stanfords favored a "dry" town, however, and Mayfield already had established saloons. Stanford decided instead to encourage Mark Hopkins' son, Timothy, to buy 700 acres of the Soto Ranch and subdivide it.

Stanford could not call this town Palo Alto, however, because an enterprising developer in what is now called College Terrace, south of the campus, had filed for that name to describe his 120 acre subdivision. Stanford sued in court over the name and won it with an out-of-court settlement. Hopkins' University Park was rechristened Palo Alto and flourished after the university opened in 1881.

The original Stanford faculty and first core of Palo Alto residents lived in a snug little area called Professorville, still very much intact today and interesting to walk around. The indispensable guides for this walk are the pamphlets, *Professorville* and *Exploring Palo Alto's Past.*

(The pamphlets go in and out of print, but either the pamphlets or xeroxes are available from the Palo Alto Historical Association, whose historian, Ruth Wilson, has an office at the main Palo Alto Library, 1213 Newell Road, 415/329-2664. The association has other publications, plus photos and elaborate files, at the library and sells collections of postcards showing historic buildings. Membership in the organization assists in carrying on their valuable and methodical historical work.)

Professorville is a compact area bounded by Ramona, Addison, Waverley, and Kingsley, with Lincoln Avenue and Bryant Street running through it. By walking these streets you can see the houses, mostly from 1890 to 1910, that served as residences for the first faculty at Stanford. The *Professorville* pamphlet is a great aid to your investigation because it pinpoints 29 houses and gives a brief sketch of their occupants. Here is one typical entry:

> 356 Lincoln Avenue- 1896: Professor Guido Marx designed his unique house in 1896 with the aid of his friend, Professor Albert B. Clark, a member of the Stanford Art Department from 1892 to 1931. Built in a U-shape, one story high, with redwood paneling, the house reflects the Japanese feeling which Professor Marx admired. A member of the Mechanical Engineering Faculty from 1895 to 1936, he and Mrs. Marx served Palo Alto generously in its community life, progressive politics, and musical circles, having underwritten the first concert of Fritz Kreisler at Stanford. Mrs. Marx served as a trustee of the Palo Alto

Library for 21 years, a record at the time of her retirement. Their daughter Barbara Marx Givan and Mr. Givan reside there now.

Most of the early professors chose to build their houses in this area, south of University Avenue near Embarcadero Road, rather than on university property. Embarcadero Road was the most substantial early road into the university. People were allowed to buy land in Palo Alto, rather than lease land, as is required on the university property itself. Most of the early professors favored purchasing their land.

The dominant architecture here is the brown cedar shingle style favored by gifted architects such as Bernard Maybeck. His "Sunbonnet" house at 1061 Bryant is a good example. 1005 Bryant, the house of Professor Frank Angell, is another attractive residence.

Exploring Palo Alto's Past

Some citizens of Palo Alto have a strong feeling for the historical status of buildings from this earlier era of Professorville. Not all the landmarks have been well maintained, however, as demographics changed, with business and residential areas mixing. Many historically interesting houses here date mainly from the period 1890–1935 and extend beyond the earlier Professorville confines.

The *Exploring Palo Alto's Past* pamphlet concentrates on three architectural styles defined in early Palo Alto houses. Besides Shingle, there are also Victorian and Early California–style homes.

The Victorian style was winding down just as Palo Alto was starting up, but the circa 1889 Ashby House at 1145 Forest Avenue, once the home of an orchardist, is a lovely example of a Victorian cottage with shiplap board siding. 1023 Forest is a stately Queen Anne-style house from 1896. 1009 Forest shows how tasteful restoration and remodeling need not harm the historic or aesthetic character of a structure.

Elsewhere, as you explore Palo Alto, take a look at the Downing house, 706 Cowper, a lovely old landmark from 1894. This residence has been restored to serve as professional offices, giving the run-down structure a new life as one of Palo Alto's most handsome house restorations. The building is a good example of Victorian architecture, with its fancy fish-scale shingle work and Queen Anne corner tower, plus ornate railings, moldings, and gables that suggest the term gingerbread.

About 1910 a new style of house, called Early California, emerged. These houses were characterized by low foundations, thick walls, deeply recessed main entrances, wrought iron and plaster grillwork, balconies, and tile roofs. Good examples of this style can be seen in the 1900 block on Cowper, with the purest examples at 1990 and 1950, both built in 1932. Birge Clark was the architect who designed these houses.

Another interesting house is at 1247 Cowper, built in 1927 for novelists Charles and Kathleen Norris, who spent the then-large sum of $100,000 on it. The approach to the house, typical of the Early California architectural style, is through a wrought iron gate, with the house opening onto a central courtyard.

College Terrace

Another interesting architectural area and small community within the bounds of Palo Alto is College Terrace, a tongue of land that extended into Leland Stanford's property from El Camino Real. Stanford sought to buy the 120 acres from Alexander Gordon, who had other ideas. Gordon saw the university developing and reasoned that the land would be valuable for housing. He subdivided the acreage into small parcels for modest-sized houses of professors, local tradesmen, merchants, the whole web of 19th century life. These are not the grand homes of Atherton, but the more modest homes of a community of people from all walks of life. Today College Terrace retains this small town feeling. Gordon named the streets after eastern colleges and briefly called the project Palo Alto, but yielded the name to Leland Stanford for the downtown "professorville" area when Stanford became litigious.

To walk or drive through College Terrace with a knowledgeable introduction, get the pamphlet *College Terrace and Evergreen Park Historical Tour*, put out by the Palo Alto Historical Association. You can get it from historian Ruth Wilson at her office in the Palo Alto Library, 1213 Newell Road, 415/329-2664.

This small brochure is a wonderful guide as you thread your way through the area, looking at the well-turned small cottages and more ambitious, large Queen Anne-style houses with their turrets. 1531 College, now somewhat run down, is a good example of an ornamented cottage built in the 1890s. 1487 College, where I lived during my own student days at Stanford, is a handsome Queen Anne-style house still in fairly good repair. 2124 Oberlin displays the rustic shinglework and stone fireplaces favored in earlier cottages.

Across El Camino Real lies Evergreen Park. 250 Leland is an excellent example of Queen Anne style, unchanged since it was built in 1905. Lovely rose gardens adorn this well-maintained house. 1795 Park Boulevard, dating from 1908, is a good example of a larger Georgian-revival house with much classical detail.

The tour pamphlet is fascinating also for the comments by Birge Clark, who was born in College Terrace in 1893. He recalls how all travel was by horse or horse-drawn vehicle and how almost every house had its own well, water tank, and windmill. The grocer, dairyman, iceman, meatman, and fish seller all came to the house with their carts. Since there was no ever-ready hot water in those days, the Saturday night bath was an important weekly ritual.

Today you might make front-page news if you find even the most modest cottage among Palo Alto's 24,000 houses selling for less than an astronomical sum.

Community Gardens

Beyond the downtown, modern Palo Alto has a touch of the early Professorville era in its community gardens. The first and largest of these food gardens is behind the main library at 1213 Newell Road. This garden site was begun in 1970 and provides plots for about 120 citizens.

All the produce is grown with organic gardening techniques, such as planting fava beans in winter and then turning them under as a "green manure" source of nitrogen. Six other community gardens have been started for about 500 local food gardeners who don't have the space or inclination to food garden at their own home sites. Some participants simply prefer the camaraderie afforded by a community garden. For information call 415/329-2475.

Another interesting community garden is one of the most recent, at the north end of Eleanor Pardee Park, corners of Center and Channing streets. Besides the food garden plots, this site also has a wild garden, which becomes a wildflower meadow in spring. Native plants are seeded here, but otherwise the plot is left to itself, re-creating the plant, insect, bird, and animal life that flourished here before the white man arrived. Aside from its beauty, this wild meadow is an important philosophic concept in parks, offering the visitor the mental refreshment of the unexpected in a wild environment rather than the predictability of a groomed park. The meadow may serve as a model as more

Community Gardens near the Main Library, Palo Alto

people see parks with less of an anthropocentric focus, suggesting that parks should exist not only for man but as a suitable habitat for the region's native flora and fauna. The wild meadow functions in Palo Alto like unkempt hedgerows in the otherwise cultivated English countryside.

Peninsula Music, Theater, Other Cultural Events

Stimulated partly by Stanford University, the peninsula supports a vigorous musical and cultural community, with numerous performers, plus a large and appreciative audience.

To become acquainted with what can be heard and seen, get on the mailing list of the Palo Alto Council for the Arts (CAPA), 617 Ramona #17, Palo Alto 94301, 415/326-8008. They list upcoming performances for a broad range of musical and other cultural events. Stanford University will also send you a free brochure on its Lively Arts Performances, many of which are free, 415/497-2551. For a thorough listing of all cultural activities at Stanford, subscribe to the weekly Campus Calendar of Events, 415/497-2558. The regional junior colleges, De Anza and Foothill, have their own programs, whose dates can be learned by subscribing to their calendar of upcoming events, 408/996-4671. The Palo Alto Cultural Center at 1313 Newell Road is another good local information source, 415/329-2366. Their sculpture gardens and art gallery host changing shows.

The peninsula supports a wide range of musical groups, including four symphony orchestras, of which the most prominent is the San Jose Symphony, conducted by George Cleve. The San Mateo Symphony performs at the College of San Mateo. Two West Bay opera companies and three youth orchestras also flourish.

Old Buelna's Roadhouse

A peninsula eating and drinking institution worth visiting is Old Buelna's Roadhouse in the hills behind Stanford University. Now called the Alpine Inn, located at 3915 Alpine Road, this structure has served as a roadhouse since the 1850s.

The place has a special aura. Wooden tabletops have been so

thoroughly carved with initials that they have passed beyond mere defacement into the realm of folk art. Some mute inglorious local carver has cut a complete set of railroad tracks into one tabletop.

This is a good stop for a beer, a hamburger, and a bit of history. The bronze marker outside tells the story in brief. The building is said to be the only extant roadhouse from the first decade of American control of California.

Around 1850, when some of the gold rushers took up farming in the Santa Clara Valley to the south, they displaced the earlier settlers, Spanish-speaking Californios, people of Mexican descent born in California. Felix Buelna was one of these victims who needed new employment. The son of the poet and teacher, Joaquin Buelna, Felix had taught school at Mission Santa Clara and had served for three terms as mayor of San Jose.

When Felix Buelna left San Jose, he proceeded northwest into the foothills. He failed at cattle ranching and finally decided to start a roadhouse at which he could water the horses and quench with whiskey the thirst of drivers crossing from the bay side of the peninsula to the coastal settlements of San Gregorio and Pescadero. Buelna chose a favorable location. His roadhouse also served as a social refuge for his fellow Californios, whose Sunday entertainments had been outlawed in San Jose. The new city

Generations of carvings at the Alpine Inn

fathers passed ordinances forbidding such Sabbath-desecrating activities as gambling (the game was monte) and bull-or-bear baiting.

Felix prospered, until one day he lost his property in a poker game. Then began a parade of owners and proprietors who lent their names to the present Alpine Inn. Together they form an international crazy quilt of names that suggests the peninsula's diverse ethnic origins: Buelna's Roadhouse (the Mexican proprietor) became Fernando's Place (after an Italian), then Stanton's Saloon (an Irishman), then Black Chapete's (nickname of the Portuguese proprietor, Corvello), then The Wunder (under a German), then Schenkel's Picnic Park (the German under Prohibition), and finally Rossotti's (an Italian). Some people still call the place Rossotti's, or Zott's.

The continuing existence of the roadhouse has always been in doubt, but its future appears more assured today than ever before because of new status as a registered historic landmark. A dangerous early challenge came in the person of Jane Lathrop Stanford, wife of the senator and founder of Stanford University. Jane Stanford had a distinct preference for nonalcoholic beverages. Moreover, she knew how to employ the gentle suasion of the law to ensure that her preference was widely emulated. Unfortunately for her, Buelna's Roadhouse was one of the few establishments trafficking in liquor that was beyond her long legal reach.

In 1907 the president of Stanford, David Starr Jordan, thrust a complaint about Buelna's Roadhouse before the San Mateo County Board of Supervisors, who controlled licensing. He felt that the moral tone of the place was pernicious and that it had a "reputation of being vile, even for a roadhouse." But the San Mateo supervisors were wet in sentiment, partly because they were themselves involved in the liquor trade, and President Jordan's plea did not move them.

The assortment of people you find at the Alpine Inn today reflects the thick tapestry of life on the peninsula. You can eat and drink outdoors on aging picnic tables alongside the bay laurel and live oak trees that line the creekbed. Generations of beer drinkers have enriched the soil with their peanut shells.

William Bourn's Filoli Estate

The Bayside Foothills

5

Filoli to Los Trancos

T he bayside foothills offer an attractive mix of interesting historic stops, such as water baron William Bourn's Filoli estate or Dr. Tripp's Store, where the earlier redwood loggers bought their supplies. The foothills are also rich in parks, with excellent hiking, picnicking, and nature viewing at diverse sites such as Edgewood Park, a relatively new park with profuse spring wildflowers, or the Los Trancos Open Space, whose San Andreas Fault Trail is the best introduction to the awesome forces of geology that influence life on the peninsula.

Filoli

W ithout imported water, the population level of San Francisco and the peninsula would be sharply curtailed. Water is brought overland by pipeline from the Hetch Hetchy Reservoir in Yosemite National Park and stored in the mid-peninsula lakes, where it is supplemented by the natural runoff, and then fed into the intricate piping system that supplies part of the peninsula and San Francisco.

(Along Cañada Road just south of Upper Crystal Springs Reservoir, there is an appropriate shrine where you can see this life-sustaining water rush forth into the system. Stop at this shrine, the Pulgas Water Temple, and linger a few moments before its Greek-columned tribute to water.)

As always in the affairs of men, individuals emerge who are shrewd enough to make these major arrangements of supply, such as water, for the society and then profit therefrom. The water baron of the peninsula was one William B. Bourn II, though his

83

family money came earlier from the Empire Gold Mine in Grass Valley. His great estate, Filoli, is now a historic monument open for tours, reservations required. Phone 415/366-4640 for details. The estate is in Woodside on Cañada Road, 1.3 miles north of Edgewood Road.

Bourn, whose full name was William Bowers Bourn II, was an intriguing man. He was a seventh generation American, descendant of Jared Bourn, who came to New England in 1630. The Bourn family prospered through the generations in the mercantile trades and, in California, in gold mining. Bourn attended Cambridge University in England and fell in love with the Anglo-Irish-European style of life and architecture. He rented Muckross House in Ireland for many summers and bought it for his daughter, Maud, when she married in 1910. It is said that Bourn chose his own home site because it reminded him of the Killarney Lakes region. The ballroom is decorated with scenes from that part of Ireland.

Today the National Trust for Historic Preservation owns Bourn's estate. Filoli Center, a nonprofit corporation, administers the 16 landscaped acres and the 43-room mansion, one of the few grand houses that remains intact from the days of the nabobs from late 19th- and early 20th-century peninsula life. The preserved gardens and undeveloped space around the estate make Filoli a special resource. Though other country estates were equally grand in California, none was preserved in its original setting as well as Filoli. This was largely due to the fact that Bourn, as head of the Spring Valley Water Company, arranged a prohibition of all housing in the watershed, except for his own house, to preserve the purity of the drinking water.

Filoli was built 1916–19 for Mr. and Mrs. Bourn. They engaged eminent architect Willis Polk to do the design and landscapist Bruce Porter to lay out the gardens. The Bourns lived at Filoli until his death in 1936, at which time it was acquired by Mr. and Mrs. William P. Roth. In 1975 Lurline Roth deeded it to the National Trust for Historic Preservation.

The house is a large, eclectic, Georgian-Stuart-American-style affair, built in the grand manner, large enough to be a hotel. It has 36,000 square feet of floor space. Acres of formal and informal gardens, well maintained, gird the house. At one time 18 gardeners tended a meticulous 32 acres surrounding the house. Bourn had the house built for $109,000, a large sum in 1916. He gilded the ballroom with 200 pounds of gold from his own mines.

The two-hour tour begins in the house, which is filled with exquisite detail work, such as oak or walnut floors, walls, and ceilings. Handsome marble mantelpieces focus attention in rooms of stately proportion. An adjacent carriage house, seen on the tour, holds a collection of horse-drawn carriages owned by the San Mateo County Historical Association.

The word Filoli originally came from the words fight, love, and live. When the William P. Roth family bought the estate in 1937, Lurline Matson Roth, heiress of the Matson Shipping Lines fortune, changed the meaning to fidelity, love, and live.

Mrs. Roth's Gardens

The gardens visible today express the careful and attentive work of Mrs. Roth, who nurtured them for almost four decades. The tour covers both the house and gardens, which lie along a north-south axis that rises as you walk away from the house. From the garden setting vistas of the wild mountain hillsides appear. Diverse flowering plants bloom at all times of the year, with azaleas, for example, in flower from December through May and roses from May to November. Along one fence a chronological display traces rose development from early Gallica to the most recent hybrid.

A walled garden exhibits fairly formal, French, garden-pattern strategies, but as you depart from the walled garden the degree of formality decreases and a more natural appearance dominates.

The garden plants are of mixed geographic origin. Two hundred ten Irish yew trees were grown from seedlings taken from Muckross Abbey. Magnolias, rhododendrons, nemesias, and irises are some of the prominent flowering plants. Two dawn redwoods were planted by Mrs. Roth after their discovery in China in the late 1940s. The dawn redwood is a relative of the coast and inland redwoods of California, but was known only in fossils until the momentous discovery of living trees. The original coastal redwoods on the Filoli property were logged off in the 1860s, but lovely oak trees were spared because they were not commercially useful. Some oak trees around the house are known to be over 500 years old.

Indian Middens

One benefit of the undisturbed quality of the Filoli estate has been the opportunity for archeologists to dig a Penutian Indian midden site at their leisure. Indians lived here off and on for 1,000 years up to about 1400 A.D. When the dig has been completed, the artifacts will be displayed, probably at Filoli or at nearby Cañada College.

The Penutian branch of the Costanoan, or Coast Indians, as the Spanish called them, lived basically on shellfish, acorns, and seeds, plus small and big game, ranging from gophers to deer and elk, gathering and hunting their food rather than farming. They imported obsidian to make arrowheads.

About 70–100 Indians in several extended families occupied this site at any given time. The men were 5 feet 6 inches to 5 feet 8 inches in height and were extremely muscular. They attained a maximum life span of 40 years, short by our standards, but consistent with other aboriginal cultures. Their main physical ailment and a contributor to early death was tooth wear, probably resulting from grinding down of the teeth by sand in their acorn meal. Arthritis and other bone and joint disorders were the second main class of ailments suffered by the Filoli Indians.

Though most burials among Bay Area Indians have been egalitarian in their simplicity, one interesting find of this dig was the burial of a male figure with female appearance, an apparent shaman, who was interred with over 200 special artifacts, ranging from bird whistles to quartz amulets.

The watershed west of Filoli supports a diverse wildlife, ranging from red-tailed hawks to beavers, coyotes to Canada geese. The watershed is a swath of green stretching from San Bruno nearly to Woodside and from ridge to ridge along the large geologic fault of the San Andreas. As urban folk seek more and more recreational opportunities, this formerly sacrosanct acreage of the watershed has been viewed with envy. New trails have opened up. The best of these walks is the Sawyer Camp Trail, discussed earlier.

Edgewood County Park

On the hills east of Filoli lies the newest San Mateo County park, Edgewood. The soil in this park is an inhospitable serpentine material that has worn from the rock outcropping. Such soil does not support the imported grasses that tend to grow quickly in spring elsewhere and smother the California annual plants. Native California spring wildflowers flourish here as nowhere else.

Getting into Edgewood requires some detective work because the entrances to this undeveloped park are not well marked. The

At Edgewood Park in spring

entry that puts you closest to the best wildflower area is in the hills above Redwood City. With a good street map make your way to Hillcrest and Sunset. From that intersection turn west down Robertson Way, a gravel road that takes you into the park. Leave your car near the gate by the PG&E substation and proceed on foot.

As you walk in from this entrance during the spring, the meadow floors present a luscious spectrum of wildflowers, from blue-eyed grass to red flax, cream cups to owl's clover. A cluster of oak trees on the ridge above the first sloping meadow is as fair a picnic spot as the peninsula offers, with excellent views of the bay from the San Mateo to Dumbarton bridges. To the west stretches the Crystal Springs watershed. Throughout Edgewood there are fire roads maintained to reduce the summer threat of inadvertent conflagration. The roads are also a boon for the hiker, keeping people on trails so the vegetation is relatively undisturbed. Meadowlarks can be seen sitting on the serpentine rocks, singing their alternately fluting and gurgling songs. Chaparral highlands and oak canyons offer further diversity to the explorer.

Appreciators of Edgewood as a natural environment will need to make their voices heard because golfers are pressuring to turn part of this 477-acre site into yet another course.

Huddart County Park

Huddart Park is 973 lovely acres of forested slopes and deep cool canyons 3.5 miles west of Highway 280 via Highway 84 (Woodside Road) and Kings Mountain Road. The address is 1100 Kings Mountain Road, 415/851-0326. Huddart is best known as a wilderness park close in to the urban area.

The park offers good self-guided nature trails, picnic areas, and 18 miles of hiking trails, often favored by joggers or marathoners in training.

The terrain is forested with tanoaks, whose bark was once used in the hide-tanning trade. Huddart also contains second growth redwoods that have sprouted since the area was logged out in the 1860s. There are fine examples of Douglas fir, the tree species that is the most prominent single source of lumber products in the world.

Extensive equestrian trails are popular here, but the 3/4-mile, self-guided Redwood and Chickadee nature trails, the recommended walks, are for hikers only. The Redwood Trail requires no brochure because sturdy wooden markers identify flora, such as big-leaf maple, California hazelnut, and wood rose. This trail offers the fullest expression of the park's plants. Brodiaea, wild strawberry, and yellow violets are plentiful.

Chickadee Trail requires a booklet, available from the ranger at the entrance to the park. Chickadees are one species of the birds you can see here. Redwood forests, mixed forests of oak, madrone, and bay, chaparral, and grasslands with abundant wildflowers in spring are some of the pleasures.

The San Andreas Fault passes through the park, adding a geological aspect to your experience. Also of special interest are the spaces that opened up when the logging roads were cut. In the eternal battle for light, several species of plants have been given a chance to compete with the redwoods along these roads. One is the sticky monkey flower, a bush known for its prominent yellow flowers, which curl up if the stamens are touched.

In the 1840s this land was part of Rancho Cañada de Raymundo that the Spanish governor granted to John Coppinger, an Irishman who had become a naturalized Mexican citizen. Five sawmills operated near the present park borders in the 1850s. Wagons loaded with lumber rolled down the grade, called Richard's Road, to Dr. Tripp's Store. Richard's Road Trail follows that old logging road. The elevation in the park ranges from 500 to 2,000 feet, so the trails leading up to ridges will send your blood pounding. A relatively rare tree, the chinquapin, can be seen at the 1,800-foot level along the Archery Trail.

Networks of hiking trails link Huddart with more northerly trails, such as Sawyer Camp, and with Wunderlich Park to the south. Consider the rigorous trail to Wunderlich if you have a second car as a shuttle.

Dr. Tripp's Store

The old Tripp Store, now a museum, is one of the most satisfying links on the peninsula with the region's history. A visit is highly recommended, but call ahead 415/851-7615 to check current visiting hours at the site, corner of Kings Mountain and Tripp roads.

The store was originally called the Woodside Store or Woodside Family Grocery when it opened in 1854. Today the building houses many artifacts from the era.

The history of this area rests on lumber. As early as the 1780s, oxen dragged a few downed redwood trees from here through the San Andreas Valley to the mission in San Francisco. At the time of the Gold Rush, the area swarmed with loggers who supplied board lumber, shingles, and dock pilings to the building trades in San Francisco.

Two men on the scene in 1849 became partners. Mathias Parkhurst pooled resources with Dr. Robert Orville Tripp, a trained dentist who had practiced in Massachusetts before the lure of gold brought him to California. A third partner in the original scheme, named Ellis, quickly faded from the picture, but Parkhurst and Tripp remained partners until Parkhurst died in 1863 at the age of 34.

Tripp ended up on the peninsula rather than in the gold fields because the rigors of mining were too arduous for him. He didn't like San Francisco either, because of the damp climate. Parkhurst and Tripp first made a living cutting shingles in Woodside. Later they dragged logs down to the bay and floated them on high tides to San Francisco.

But the growing number of lumbermen in the region suggested to Tripp another line of business, that of storekeeper. There were plenty of potential customers. Charles Brown and Dennis Martin had built lumber mills in Woodside in 1849. Tripp and Parkhurst finally opened their store in 1854. As might be expected, the store offered a wide spectrum of services. Parkhurst became the U.S. postmaster. A circulating library began at the store in 1859 with the name Woodside Library Association. The store also became a bank because it had the only steel safe in the region and Tripp was willing to extend credit. Tripp fixed the lumber workers' teeth. The store was also a meeting place where liquor could be purchased and imbibed.

In 1856 Tripp advertised for a housemaid to take care of the place. He married the applicant, Miss Emmeline Skelton, and built a house for the two of them opposite the store. By 1870 most of the redwood trees on the bay side of the mountains had been felled, but the store prospered because lumber from the coast side still had to be dragged past here to Redwood City's embarcadero.

Inside the board-and-batten constructed store you'll find an interesting assortment of artifacts, starting with the lumbering saws and oxen harnesses used when these draft animals pulled logs down the mountain via Kings Mountain Road. A photo of Tripp shows him as an intent and prosperous businessman. The Tripp

Dr. Tripp's Store in Woodside

Store museum is meant to be a hands-on experience, so you may examine closely the bean sorter, apple press, scales, blacksmith tools, large-wheel bicycle, traps, furs, and harnessings. One corner of the store has the pigeonholes that were the early post office. Tripp actually constructed eight buildings on the grounds near here, but only two remain today. The exterior looks as it did in the 19th century. The interior consolidates a number of activities from Tripp's several buildings, but the clutter is inviting. Major renovations are planned for the store in the 1980s, starting with structural work and then improvements in the range and accessibility of the exhibits.

Agriculture and ranching became prominent in the area in the late 19th century. Tripp himself had five acres of grapes and sold wine under the San Mateo County Pioneer brand. By 1864 there were 800 acres of grapes in the area, though Count Agoston Haraszthy, often called the father of California viticulture, became discouraged with the region and moved to Sonoma for his ambitious plantings.

Tripp died in 1909 and the store was eventually purchased in the late 1940s by the county as a historical museum.

Village of Woodside

Woodside is indeed a village, though the folk are among the most privileged in our society. The environs are now carved into ranchettes and long-lived estates of wealthy and established northern California families. As the name implies, there was wood here at one time, huge redwoods, which were all logged off.

Logging and farming no longer occur here in any magnitude, but keeping horses for pleasure is a popular sport, especially with the network of trails available in the hills above Woodside.

The commercial center of this pleasant, sylvan retreat flourishes at the corner of Woodside and Cañada roads. On the bulletin board outside Roberts Market you can take the pulse of the community, with ads selling horses and offering horse boarding. Pick up a copy of the *Country Almanac* newspaper to get a feel for the place, including an occasional real estate ad for an expensive estate. Roberts Market is a countrified gourmet supermarket with hardwood floors, offering the finest meat cuts and the most luxurious produce money can buy. At the deli in the store, try one of their takeout sandwiches. The wine department is also well stocked.

In the rustic village shopping center, across from Roberts, you can pause for a cup of coffee and superb pastries at La Confisserie bakery or take a full-course lunch at the Stagecoach, 415/851-8010. Try their three egg omelet or Stagecoach hamburger. Walk a half mile down Woodside Road toward the hills and you'll notice on the left the whitewashed town hall, Independence Hall, from 1884.

The first white person in Woodside was a sawyer named Bill Smith, who arrived in 1833 to cut redwood lumber. The first substantial European with a long-term history here was the Irishman mentioned earlier, John Coppinger, who flourished here beginning in 1836. It is probable that Coppinger jumped ship in San Francisco to live in California, aided by Juana Briones Miranda, a Californio woman.

The enterprising Coppinger took to lumbering, probably in the area where Kings Mountain Road meets Woodside Road. His influence grew because he supported Juan Alvarado, collector of customs at Monterey and early governor, in a dispute with the Mexican authorities. Alvarado won and Coppinger received a land grant of about 8,200 acres.

In 1838 Coppinger married Maria Luisa Soto, whose well-established Californio family had come from Horcacitos, Mexico, with the de Anza expedition in 1775-76. Unfortunately, Coppinger died eight years later at the age of 35.

John Greer, captain of the *Wild Duck*, a boat that plied the trade lanes from Chile to California, found upon his arrival in 1849 that gold fever struck the crew. He was left alone with a cripple on board while all able-bodied men went to try their luck in the gold fields, which was called "seeing the elephant." Greer made his way down the peninsula, where he met and married John Coppinger's widow, Maria. Today the Greer family continues to live in Woodside.

In the first decade of the American period the Greer family reached the lowest point in their fortunes, nearly losing their property to the maze of litigation surrounding land titles. At one point, Dr. Tripp of the Woodside Store levied a lien on their rancho for an unpaid grocery bill of $394.61.

A lumberman's village now rests at the bottom of nearby Searsville Lake off Sandhill Road. The historical marker at the corner of Sandhill and Portola roads, partially hidden in a clump of baccharis bushes, tells the story:

> Town of Searsville. Here stood the lumberman's village of Searsville, whose first settler, John Sears, came in 1854. Across the road westerly from this monument stood a hotel. The school, store, blacksmith shop, and dwellings were to the southeast, some on the site of the present lake and others overlooking it. Buildings were removed in 1891 as water rose behind the new dam.

The county's first sawmill was built near Woodside on the banks of Alambique Creek by Charles Brown in 1847. About the same time Dennis Martin was building a second mill, also run by water power, on San Francisquito Creek. These water-powered mills were similar to the famous Sutter's Mill at Coloma, site of James Marshall's 1848 gold discovery.

Whiskey Hill Road, passing near Woodside, suggests the importance of this site as a stopping point for refreshment when bullwhackers and loggers carted redwood logs or lumber from the ridges to Redwood City. The original provider of spirits here was one John Hadler, who ran the Hadler Exchange from a modest shack. In 1889 John Hanson erected the Pioneer Hotel, parts of which are still standing in today's Pioneer Hotel, which now houses a Wells Fargo Bank office.

Wunderlich Ranch County Park

The Wunderlich Ranch is a 942-acre park two miles southwest of the town of Woodside, with a marked entrance on Woodside Road. Phone 415/851-7570. This is a hilly area of mixed forests and meadowlands. Trees here include second-growth redwoods, plus oaks, madrones, and bays. From higher elevations in the park, at 2,000 feet, the vistas are superb.

The ranch was first part of John Coppinger's Rancho Cañada de Raymundo. In 1846 it was deeded to Charles Brown as part of his 2,880 acres of timbered slopes and rangeland. Simon Jones then bought the land in 1872 and developed extensive vineyards and orchards. The coffee-fortune Folgers, who had come to California in 1850, bought the property in 1902. Of historical interest is the fact that James Folger, in 1904, developed one of the state's first hydroelectric plants here, damming a small stream and using the waterfall to turn a turbine. The ranch was deeded to the county by the most recent owner, Martin Wunderlich, in 1974.

Today Wunderlich Ranch Park is largely undeveloped, but there are 25 miles of hiking trails and good opportunities to enjoy nature. Magnificent old oak trees and thick elderberry growth can be found at the lower levels on trails near the parking lot. The park is used mainly by horsemen and hikers. Hawks, quail, bobcat, coyote, and deer abound.

The Meadow Trail, which takes you to high meadows and vistas, is a good beginning hike. Eventually the old ranch buildings, now used for horse boarding, may be restored. First priority is the ranger's headquarters, the building now marked Park Office, once an old carriage house. Inside you'll find an old wood-barrel water cart and several two-seater horse carriages, nucleus for a future small museum interpreting the property's history.

Skyline Boulevard

Traveling Skyline Boulevard from Highway 92 to Alpine Road takes you along the crest of the mountains. The road is sometimes quite windy and foggy, but the vistas can be superb.

Starting at Highway 92, a scenic turnout allows you to see from Skyline the Upper Crystal Springs Reservoir and surrounding watershed, now called the San Francisco State Fish and Game Refuge.

The road south passes through cypress forests, with numerous red larkspur along the road in spring. Farther south you enter redwood forest, all second growth. If there is fog, driving can be high drama with a moorlike feeling similar to northern Scotland. If you have any doubt about the ability of redwood trees to collect fog moisture on their leaves and drip the water to the ground, drive your car along here and watch the trees splash your windshield with droplets.

On the left, driving south, you pass the Bella Vista restaurant, 13451 Skyline, 415/851-1229, which certainly has a remarkable view east toward the bay. The bar is cordial and the continental cuisine elegant. Try their veal oscar or fillet of salmon.

Skeggs Point is the next vista turnout as you journey south. The view is rewarding, but shards of broken glass lead a traveler to suspect that smashing bottles is the favored pastime of the area's teenagers.

Just south of Skeggs Point there is a methusaleh of a redwood tree. This impressive old statesman is about 1,500 years of age and 55 feet in circumference.

Another vista point, just north of Alpine Road, offers the best panorama available from these heights. You can see all the way from Moffett Field to the San Mateo Bridge, with Palo Alto and Stanford University directly below you.

Los Trancos Open Space

T his preserve along Page Mill Road in the foothills behind Palo Alto offers the peninsula's best opportunity to comprehend the geologic forces affecting the region. An excellent Fault Trail has 14 marked stops with a trail guide, available at the parking lot, to explain movement along the San Andreas Fault.

To get to the park, drive 5 miles west along Page Mill Road from Highway 280, past Foothill Park, or else drive a mile east from Skyline Boulevard. A parking lot, the only facility, alerts you to the preserve.

Along the Fault Trail, marked posts show exactly where the fault lines run. But more subtle expressions of the fault are sag ponds and springs, where water is trapped on the surface or percolates to the surface because of constant earth fracturing by fault movement. While walking here you will see boulders that have been carried slowly north from Loma Prieta, a high peninsula peak, 23 miles to the south and visible from here on clear days. A fence, pulled apart along the trail, demonstrates how the land on the west side of the break slipped northward six feet during the 1906 Earthquake. Geologists call the western side of the earth movement the Pacific Plate and the eastern side the American Plate.

Many large, old oak trees in the region show stumps where limbs shook off in the tremors of 1906. These two plates have continued to slide past each other for an unimaginable period of time, impeded in their flow by the friction that builds up for periodic violent release in the springlike action of earthquakes.

Earthquakes have been a dominating fact of life since recorded history began on the peninsula. They figured in the legends of Ohlone Indians. Quakes have caused major damage to life and

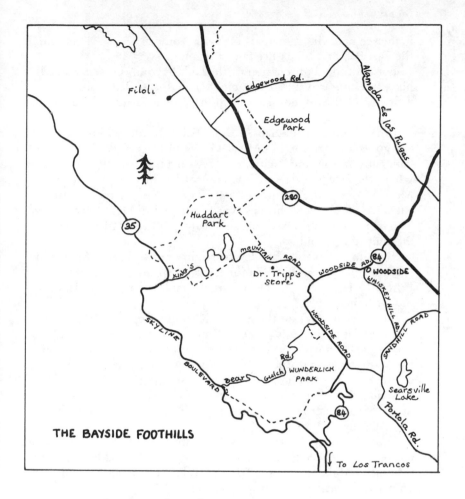

THE BAYSIDE FOOTHILLS

property on the peninsula in the 18th and 19th centuries as well as on April 18, 1906. In the 19th century they played havoc with the buildings of the missions and with the adobes of secular settlers. The 1906 Earthquake sent statues at Stanford, for example, toppling from their pedestals and crashing through concrete walkways.

While walking the trail you can't help but feel the wonder and danger inevitable in the next major quake. Geology students and their professor at nearby Foothill College merit high praise for organizing this trail, an introduction to one of the longest and most active earthquake faults in the world.

At Los Trancos, from a high point at the start of the hike, your eye can follow the San Andreas Fault all the way north past San

Francisco and Mt. Tamalpais beyond. You can see Mt. Diablo in the East Bay and Loma Prieta to the south.

For a thorough discussion of the fault beyond this self-guided hike, you might want to participate in a docent-led walk at Los Trancos. Call Midpeninsula Regional Open Space District at 415/965-4717 for times.

(To see more of the San Andreas Fault on the peninsula, you can go to its beginning at Mussel Rock in Daly City. Here the fault runs in from the Pacific, roughly on a line from Point Reyes, where the largest earth shift was recorded in 1906. Out from Mussel Rock, the epicenter of a 1957 quake reached 5.3 on the Richter scale. Several homes were damaged in Daly City. At Mussel Rock you can see a large V cut out of the cliffside, where the fault runs inland.

To follow the fault, take Coast Highway 1 to Pacific Manor in Pacifica and exit on West Manor Drive, then turn north on Palmetto. There you can see where the fault runs, though landfill obscures the path.

Then drive south on the peninsula along Highway 280, which runs parallel to the fault at the bottom of the San Andreas Valley. That valley is now filled with water. For a good viewpoint, stop by the lugubrious statue of Junipero Serra at the scenic overlook on the east side of Highway 280. Unfortunately, this artwork, now ridiculed by graffiti, does little justice to a great man, but the finger of the mission padre does appear to point, inadvertently, to the fault line.

Foothill College's Electronics Museum at 12345 El Monte Road in Los Altos, 415/948-8590, includes an exhibit explaining plate tectonics and the idea of the Richter scale. You activate the display with a foot pedal and measure the results.)

Geology is only the first pleasure of Los Trancos, however. This 274-acre holding with five miles of trails in the eastern foothills of the Santa Cruz Mountains has much to offer the hiker and nature lover. It is located at the 2,000-foot level. The air is fresh, pungent with the scent of bay leaves. Forests, with especially good specimens of black oak, share the countryside with meadows that invite picnickers.

Several plant communities can be seen here, from chaparral to oak woodlands. Trails in the live oak and bay forests are cool, even in summer. Try the Franciscan Trail after you finish the Fault Trail. More ambitious hikers can connect this preserve with an adjacent open space, Monte Bello. Winter after the rains is an ideal time for a walk here in the bracing air.

The abundance of wildlife ranges from rabbits in the meadow to their predators, foxes and bobcats, whose fur-filled scat can be seen along the trails.

Los Trancos adjoins Foothill Park, a handsome park with excellent nature interpretive displays. However, since the park excludes all people but Palo Alto residents, there is little incentive to describe it in this volume.

The Johnston House, Half Moon Bay

The Half Moon Bay Region 6

Montara to Pescadero

T he broad marine terraces around Half Moon Bay present unique agricultural benchlands, a kind of front porch of California facing the sea. Valuable farmlands here can grow specialized crops. The land is not always exceedingly rich, but the climate is unusual, providing a long, cool, fog-moistened growing season ideal for artichokes, brussels sprouts, and commercial flowers. In the warmer, sunnier inland canyons pumpkins ripen optimally.

The original Mexican settlers came here to escape harassment from Americans and other early adventurers on the bay side of the mountains. They lived in relative isolation because there were no good roads over the mountains until the last decade of the 19th century. Candelario Miramontes brought his family in the 1840s. His land grant lay south of Pilarcitos Creek and was called Rancho Miramontes. Within a few years another family arrived, that of Tiburcio Vasquez, whose property was on the north side of Pilarcitos Creek. Their main interest was cattle ranching. San Benito and, later, Spanishtown were the historic names of the Half Moon Bay community. The town's post office name was changed to Half Moon Bay in 1872, but Spanishtown lasted unofficially well into the 20th century. Produce farming began in the 1870s with migrants from other nations, especially Portuguese and Italians, who shipped out their vegetables from precarious wharves and chutes along this harborless coast.

Today half of the coast's 16,000 people live in Half Moon Bay, but their numbers swell dramatically when outsiders come for the three main annual festivals: the Portuguese Chamarita Festival in May; the Coastside Country Fair over the Fourth of July week; and the Pumpkin and Art Festival in October.

Entering Half Moon Bay Via Highway 92

Most visitors drive into Half Moon Bay along Highway 92. The road crosses foggy, wind-swept chaparral highlands, with much yellow bush lupine, blue blossom ceanothus, and sturdy evergreen baccharis bushes. You later enter fertile coastside creekbeds, where eucalyptus and oak trees grow in the narrow upper reaches and commercial flower-raising operations cluster in the lowlands. Several interesting stops offer pleasures beyond the scenery.

Flower Growers

Stop at a commercial nursery for a look at diversified flower growing. The Half Moon Bay Nursery, 415/726-5392, is 3.5 miles from town. A. Repetto Nursery, 415/573-0732, is next as you approach town. The flower growers are not set up for elaborate public tours, but their shops display flowers and, if traffic is light, a knowledgeable flower seller can sometimes describe the operation for you.

Flower growing is a $108 million per year industry in San Mateo County, actually dwarfing the $24-million vegetable harvest. Flower growers now face stiff competition from Central and South American growers who can air-ship their flowers to San Francisco and other U.S. destinations. Air transport has had a profound effect globally on flower distribution, which is one reason why the Netherlands has become such a great flower exporter in Europe.

Carnations can be raised effectively in Colombia, where a laborer earns two dollars per day, and air-shipped to California, where field hands receive $30 or more per day. Modest transporation costs working in favor of Bay Area producers must be accompanied by ever more skilled production methods to retain price competitiveness, given the difference in labor costs. Climate is another variable, of course.

At Half Moon Bay both greenhouse and open field
flower-growing operations thrive. The spectrum of what grows
here includes iris, sweet william, tulip, azalea, poinsettia,
ranunculus, Easter lily, rose, and mum, among others. (You can
also see commercial flower growing in Colma-South San
Francisco at the Acres of Orchids tour, discussed in Chapter 1.)

Obester Winery

The Obester Winery, two miles from Half Moon Bay on
Highway 92, is an intimate, small, family-run operation with a
sales and tasting room open on weekends. Phone ahead
415/726-WINE. Chances are the traveler will meet the proprietors
themselves, Paul and Sandy Obester, or their sons David and
Doug. The Obesters buy their grapes from Monterey, Mendocino,
and Sonoma counties rather than plant here in a climate they
consider too cool. They are planting some acreage, however, in
Mendocino County's Anderson Valley. The Obesters' skill and
care in selecting grapes has produced some excellent wines, such as
their Johannisberg Riesling, and some appealing experiments.
Their White Cabernet, created by removing the skins as quickly as
possible when the grapes are crushed, is a salmon-colored wine.
An abundance of available red wine grapes at reasonable prices in
this white wine–boom era ensures that their experiment with
White Cabernet will continue.

The Obesters have strong roots in wine production on the
peninsula. Sandy Obester's grandfather is John Gemello, who
operated the Gemello Winery in Mountain View starting in 1934.
Soon the Obesters will manage that operation, taking over from
Sandy's uncle, Mario Gemello, who plans to retire. They hope to
expand and revitalize the winery, at 2003 El Camino Real in
Mountain View, reinstating an annual crush and continuing the
line of Cabernets and Zinfandels for which the Gemellos are well
known.

Spanishtown

Another roadside stop, just beyond the Obester Winery, is
Spanishtown, a cluster of a dozen arts and crafts shops. Galleries
here display the works of local artists, and gift shops include some
imaginative objects. For example, Sea Fantasies offers Black Lace
Sea Fans, sea coral from the Philippines, flattened to make a
unique wall hanging. Pot City has a range of attractive ceramics.

Half Moon Bay

T he town of Half Moon Bay is compact and easy to walk around, so park your car close to the white concrete bridge that crosses Pilarcitos Creek and explore. The bridge, built in 1900, was the first reinforced-concrete span in the state.

On the north side of the bridge you'll see at 270 Main a modest, straightforward Greek Revival–style house from the 1860s. This faded yellow house with blue trim and a pleasant flower garden around it belonged to Tiburcio Vasquez, son of the original land grant owner.

The appeal of Half Moon Bay is that it is both a working town and a travel destination, setting Marnie's Custom T-Shirts, 309 Main near the bridge, alongside Half Moon Bay Feed and Fuel, where you can still buy coal.

As you walk down Main Street from the bridge, good examples show how careful preservation of historic buildings can enhance a community. Next to a lavish flower garden stands the blue Zaballa House, 326 Main. This house ranks as one of the oldest houses still standing here. Today professional offices fill the rooms.

Next you come to the San Benito House, the premier restoration in Half Moon Bay, at 356 Main, 415/726-3425. San Benito House maintains the attractive gardens between it and the Zaballa House. Years ago the building was the Hotel Mosconi. Proprietress Carol Regan-Mickelson has restored this structure to serve as an intimate small hotel, saloon, and restaurant. The restoration has been completed with taste and style. The friendly bar has a decor of light-stained wood. In the restaurant, partly indoors and partly on a deck outside, a menu of continental cuisine changes weekly, emphasizing fresh seafood and produce of the region. A meal here might begin with artichoke soup and be followed by veal piccata or bouillabaisse. The 12 rooms upstairs have been individually decorated with period photos, antiques such as brass beds, and art objects that make them one-of-a-kind lodgings. Throughout there are splashes of bright flowers from the adjacent gardens.

In the same building is the Garden Deli Cafe, good for a short order lunch or snack. Try a burrito.

One block farther, at 448 Main, stands Cunha's general store and grocery, a place not to be missed. Chances are Portuguese or

Italian farmers and fishermen will be gathered there, passing the time. Cunha's is a general store in the old sense, selling every food from meats to deli takeout salads, plus a range of dry goods that you'll find upstairs. This is a good place to get cowboy boots or a straw cowboy hat.

You begin to get a feel for old family, small town ties when you step out of Cunha's and look down Kelly Avenue to see the Manuel Cunha Intermediate School. Many vignettes from life here, especially in the 19th century, are presented in June Morrall's delightful book, *Half Moon Bay Memories*, available in local bookstores. A well-preserved Victorian at 520 Kelly, the Alves House, contains shops with handcrafted items.

Farther down Main Street, the large building on the left in the 700 block puzzles travelers because of the letters I.D.E.S. on it. That is the fraternal lodge and meeting rooms of the Portuguese society, Irmandade de Divino Espirito Santo.

The Half Moon Bay Bakery at 514 Main still uses a brick oven from the 19th century. Ask to see the oven and the wooden paddles used to place loaves of bread inside. Ricci's Corner at 547 Main is a friendly coffee shop favored by the locals.

For a further exploratory look at the older houses of Half Moon Bay, ask at the chamber of commerce for the *Spanishtown Walking Tour* leaflet, put out by the local historical society. The chamber office is in a red railroad caboose at Shoreline Station shopping center, 415/726-5202.

Most visitors to Half Moon Bay arrive by car, but you can also fly into the small airport or boat into the man-made harbor. Half Moon Bay's proximity to San Francisco and its secure harbor made it a favorite rum and whiskey running site during Prohibition. The alcohol came in by boat from Canada.

The White Johnston House

Just outside Half Moon Bay, as you enter town from the south on Higgins Purisima Road, stands the white Johnston House, midway up a long, gradually sloping hill. This house is a major historical and architectural landmark. Its stark position on the hill creates all the feeling of country loneliness that one might experience by viewing Andrew Wyeth's painting, *Christina's World*. Historically, the house was painted white and stood against a background of golden wheat, briefly an important crop.

The remarkable fact about the Johnston House is that this New England–style "saltbox" was built in 1853 when there weren't even roads into the area. Hand-hewn redwood timbers were brought in by ship and floated ashore at high tide. In the 20th century the house sadly declined and was abandoned, but recent efforts to save it have stabilized the exterior. The gathering movement for historic preservation will undoubtedly result in restoration of the interior as the 1980s progress.

Today a historical marker on the road 100 yards from the house tells part of the story. James Johnston was a 49er from Ohio who struck it rich and then homesteaded here in 1853. For his California-born bride, Petra Maria de Jara, he built this saltbox house, whose architectural roots go back to East Anglia. However, there were California touches in the plan, such as a chapel on the second floor and a separate cookhouse, as was the custom in houses of the Spanish Catholic Californios.

In 1970 the citizens of Half Moon Bay inaugurated the Johnston House Foundation to acquire the dilapidated historic building and use it as the centerpiece of a 32-acre recreation area. When the deed was transferred in 1975 to the city of Half Moon Bay, one of those who attended the festivities was Petra Johnston Cooper, then 83 years old, the great granddaughter of James Johnston. Petra Cooper retained in her possession some of the original furnishings of the house.

Higgins Purisima Road can be highly recommended as a back country drive, taking you inland for a look at grassy hillside grazing lands and redwood-forested slopes before returning to the coast.

Half Moon Bay Beaches

Half Moon Bay has several miles of good beaches, plus the headquarters of the San Mateo County Beaches State Park at 95 Kelly Avenue, 415/726-6238. Sunning, walking, and beachcombing are delightful here, but swimming is not encouraged because of cold water, dangerous sleeper waves that overwhelm the unwary with their size, and severe riptides that can carry a swimmer quickly out to sea.

The main and most developed beach access is at the end of Kelly Avenue, where you enter Francis Beach. You'll find picnic tables, barbecue pits, toilets, and dressing rooms for day use. The beach is extensive and clean. All the Half Moon Bay beaches are excellent for kite flying. The trick for sunbathing on clear but windy days, which can be cool, is to tuck yourself behind a sand dune.

Beaches at Half Moon Bay

North of the day use area is a complete state campground, with 51 attractive sites for tents or RVs, set amidst thick clusters of seaside daisies and bi-color lupines. In spring the fragrance of these flowers is delicious as the wind blows inland. A display at the campground explains how winter storms erode away the beach and summer waves build up the sand again in an eternal seasonal interplay. In summer, reservations are advised and are available only through Ticketron. Call the park headquarters for information on the nearest Ticketron.

Other beach accesses are Venice Beach via Venice Avenue and Dunes Beach or Roosevelt Beach via Young Avenue. Roosevelt boasts the highest dunes, something to consider if you need protection from the wind. Roosevelt is also favored by surf fishermen and enjoys the least disturbed seaside vegetation in the fields behind the dunes. The flowers include various yellow and purple examples of the Compositae family, with daisylike heads of many rays coming from a center, and wild radish, with its purple and white flowers in cross-shaped arrangement. Bird life at Roosevelt is also extensive, with numerous red-winged blackbirds.

Horses can be rented for riding on the plateau behind all of these beaches. The largest stable is at the Young Avenue turnoff from the Coast Highway 1.

Coastal Development

The local debate in Half Moon Bay for the last 20 years has been development versus restrictions on growth. A sizable local element would like to spread the word on summer fogs to discourage more permanent residents. The debate could probably be traced back to the first locals, the Costanoan Indians, who made the mistake of welcoming Gaspar de Portola as he made his expedition through here in 1769. The last of these Half Moon Bay Indians, Andres Osorio, died in 1946 at the claimed age of 113.

The modern debate goes back to the turn of the century, when the 1905 Ocean Shore "Reaches the Beaches" Railroad scheme heated up. At that time of railroad building, however, the locals were all for development. The Ocean Shore Railroad never quite made it, plagued by destruction caused by the 1906 Earthquake as well as by foundering management and finances. Only in retrospect have problems associated with an influx of population been understood.

Problems of inadequate water supply and insufficient sewage capacity have helped keep the Half Moon Bay population in check, preserving the flower growing, brussels sprouts farming, and hay ranching on its perimeter. The California Coastal Commission has put pressure on unrestricted growth that would ruin the coastline or destroy the agricultural base of the region.

Festivals at Half Moon Bay

Of the three annual festivals, the Chamarita has the deepest historical roots. This May Portuguese festival on Pentecostal Sunday comes complete with dances, an auction, parades, carnival rides, and the crowning of a queen. Small girls assemble as queens or the retinue of a queen. Chamarita has been held in Half Moon Bay for over 110 years because Portuguese farmers have been an important segment of the community since its early decades.

Chamarita recalls a 14th century time of troubles in the Azores, when earthquakes rocked the area, especially the island of Pico. Drought, crop failure, and famine plagued the people, who prayed to the Holy Ghost for help. When the people had almost perished, a ship is said to have appeared on the horizon, filled with the necessities of life. Queen Isabel heard of this miraculous good fortune and paraded through Lisbon, leaving her crown on the altar of the cathedral as an offering of thanksgiving for the favors of the Holy Ghost.

The newest Half Moon Bay festival may become the most prominent. The Coastside Country Fair is a popular event held from late June through the Fourth of July weekend. A rodeo, showing of quilts and ceramics, display of antiques, and judging of cattle, horses, goats, rabbits, poultry, and swine are just some of the activities that absorb all the townspeople.

On an October weekend the Pumpkin and Art Festival is a major event. The warm, narrow canyons around Half Moon Bay ripen a sea of pumpkins, as many as 4,000 tons annually, in this self-proclaimed Pumpkin Capital of California. When the pumpkins are trucked from the inland canyons to roadside for ready sale, the size of the crop depends on such factors as early autumn rains.

Over 100,000 people come to sample pumpkin foods and see pumpkin carvings. A contest for the biggest pumpkin of all sometimes gets national media attention. Additionally, about 225 juried artists or crafters of fine things show their wares. Proceeds from the fair go to Main Street beautification programs, such as tree planting.

For the changing dates on these festivals, call the Half Moon Bay Chamber of Commerce, 415/726-5202, in the caboose at Shoreline Station shopping center. This caboose is a good local information source for maps and regional brochures when you are in the area.

Coastal Agriculture

An interesting brochure called *Agriculture in San Mateo County* can be picked up at the Half Moon Bay Chamber of Commerce. The brochure alerts you to 33 area farms that sell direct to the public everything from olallieberries to kiwi fruit, with emphasis on pumpkins, artichokes, and Christmas trees. Many of these farms have roadside stands that are seasonal or relatively permanent, such as the produce barn on Kelly Avenue as you turn toward the beaches from Coast Highway 1. The special climate, direct selling to nearby markets, good transport systems by highway and air, and the special resource of skilled Portuguese and Italian farmers have contributed to the region's agricultural prosperity.

Coast Highway 1 to Half Moon Bay

The identity of the Half Moon Bay area as a separate coastside geographic entity was reasserted in the winter storms of January 1982. Raging Martini Creek severed the road a half mile north of the Chart House restaurant in Montara. The rocky stretch of coast north of the creek, called Devil's Slide, belongs to the north county, as road washouts periodically remind residents.

The Chart House, 415/728-7366, above Montara Beach, specializing in seafood and beef, is the first of several good places to dine as you approach Half Moon Bay from the north. Dan's, 415/728-3343, in Moss Beach, offers good Italian dinners. Ethnic enclaves include Tillie's, 415/728-5744, German cooking in Moss Beach, offering bratwurst and gemutlichkeit. In nearby El Granada the Village Green, 415/726-3690, serves tea and scones as members of the British royal family peer down reassuringly from wall portraits. The largest cluster of seafood restaurants is at Princeton near the breakwater. Standard favorites here are The Shorebird, 415/728-5541, or the elegant and historic Princeton Inn, 415/728-7311, now a restaurant only, rather than an inn. Like so many other substantial architectural efforts on the coast, the Princeton Inn, built in 1908, was projected for a dream that was never realized, the flourishing beach trade that was bound to come with the ill-fated Ocean Shore Railroad.

You can also buy fresh seafood at Princeton direct from fishermen on the pier or in shops. Ketch Joanne, 415/728-3747, is a restaurant on the pier selling tasty sandwiches.

Montara

As you drive south, Montara's main points of interest are its beach, a rail station from the Ocean Shore days, and the Point Montara Fog Signal Station and Lighthouse, now a hostel.

The beach at the north end of town is a broad, half-mile expanse of golden sand. One block from the beach parking lot, at Second and Main, stands a brown-shingled private house tucked amidst the trees. This was another of the Ocean Shore rail depots.

The Point Montara Lighthouse lies near the south end of town, at 16th Street, accessible where you see a hostel sign. The site is worth a stop just to see the historic buildings, now in the slow process of renovation. The lighthouse and fog signal building are set on a bluff overlooking the sea. You can call the hostel at 415/728-7177.

The need for some ship-warning system became apparent when the *Colorado*, a side-wheel steamer, ran aground at Montara in 1868. In 1872 the *Aculeo*, a Liverpool sailing ship, met the same fate. Finally, in March 1875, a fog signal station was installed with a deep whistle run by coal-generated steam power. In 1900 an oil lantern was added and in 1912 a Fresnel lens, which allows light to be magnified, completed the lighthouse capability. As technology improved, however, with a light and sounding device located on an offshore buoy, the Coast Guard abandoned the site. The buildings fell into disrepair.

In recent years the American Youth Hostel (AYH) movement has leased the buildings, started restoration, and created a friendly atmosphere about the place. The Coast Guard blessed the arrangement because it eliminates vandalism at the site. In the old fog

The Montara Lighthouse

signal building AYH now has a common room. The 1875 officers' quarters, a handsome Victorian house done in Stick-Eastlake style, will take considerable energy and funds to restore. However, the AYH people are determined to do so and also to provide historical displays interpreting the site. Anyone can visit or stay at the hostel, which is housed in buildings of later construction next to the officers' quarters. Unlike the hostels of Europe, this one is open to individuals and families of all ages. The hostel style requires that all overnight guests participate in cleanup chores.

From the bluffs here you can watch gray whales migrating in December and January, sometimes swimming only 50 yards beyond the rocks. Hostel leaders are experts about hiking trails on Montara Mountain across the road and can offer suggestions. Another hostel awaits travelers 28 miles south at the Pigeon Point Lighthouse.

Moss Beach's Fitzgerald Marine Reserve

Moss Beach has a major attraction, the James V. Fitzgerald Marine Reserve. This ocean front resource, established in 1969, is one of the richest intertidal regions in the state and unquestionably the finest place on the peninsula coast to become acquainted with intertidal ecology. An interpretive center at the office of on-duty naturalist Bob Breen aids in showing you what to look for and points out interesting facts. For example, during the ice age, 15,000 years ago, the sea level was fully 400 feet lower than today. Naturalist-led hikes for the weekend drop-in visitor (for times call 415/728-3584) focus on understanding animal relationships, adaptation techniques, habitats, and the food web of the reserve. Flora and fauna are characteristic of the tidal reefs that stretch between Moss Beach and Pillar Point.

The reserve is accessible from Highway 1 at Moss Beach, driving west on California Street. A small picnic area makes this a pleasant rest stop.

An informative booklet, available at the reserve, indicates that four major areas of intertidal life thrive here. Area 1 includes the beach and the protected inner reef, where black turban snails flourish in populations as dense as 1,800 per square meter. In Area 2, deeper into the water, underrock crabs populate the cobblestone lagoons. Area 3 is the exposed side of the reef, where plants and animals must hold on to avoid being swept away. There you become acquainted with seaweed, such as rockweed and nailbrush, and with animals such as mossy chitons, sea urchins, and giant green anemones. Area 4 is the subtidal zone, accessible only if you have a wet suit. Here are red abalone, huge bullwhip kelp known to every beachcomber, and the permanent rockfish.

Princeton and Pillar Point

Princeton's Pillar Point Harbor is the major breakwater that allows a fleet of commercial and pleasure boats to flourish here. Nowhere along the coast between San Francisco and Monterey is there an adequate harbor, which was a grave problem historically, but the man-made rock breakwater here has done the job. Constructed in 1962, the breakwater provides protection from the great storms that formerly splintered so many boats on the beaches. The breakwater stretches some 7,000 feet, and is composed of 800,000 tons of rock brought up from Davenport. Four hundred acres of protected water surface have been created. A further diagonal, called a "dogleg," was built across the mouth of the breakwater in 1966 to cut incoming swells.

The 1970s saw the addition of boat launching ramps, plus commercial and recreational fishing support facilities, including an extension of the pier. It's interesting to walk the pier to see both commercial operations and pier anglers fishing the bottom. Commercial fishing is a big business out of Princeton, with boats bringing in salmon, crab, and some 80 species of rockfish.

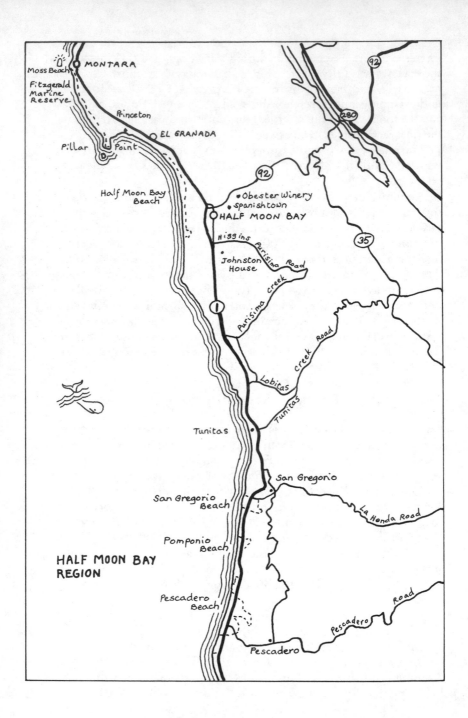

92

280

Moss Beach
MONTARA
Fitzgerald
Marine
Reserve

Princeton

EL GRANADA

Pillar   Point

Half Moon Bay
Beach

92

Obester Winery
Spanishtown
HALF MOON BAY

35

Higgins   Purisima   Road

Johnston
House

Purisima   creek

1

Purisima Creek

Creek   Road

Lobitas

Tunitas

Tunitas

San Gregorio

San Gregorio
Beach

La Honda Road

Pomponio
Beach

HALF MOON BAY
REGION

Pescadero Beach

Pescadero   Road

Pescadero

Pescadero

Establishment of a 200-mile offshore fishing limit on foreign vessels has left a larger take for local fishermen. Formerly, there were as many as 60 foreign vessels fishing off Half Moon Bay, some over 300 feet long, and some taking fish of all sizes.

Pillar Point is the main embarkation for deep sea fishing trips, plus whale sighting jaunts, birdwatching expeditions, and even burials at sea. If you want to try your luck at big-boat, open-sea fishing, this is the place, complete with boats that can rent you all the necessary paraphernalia and a captain who will instruct you on fishing technique.

Three companies operate fishing trips. Huck Finn II, 415/728-5677, uses one 60 foot boat. Captain John, 415/726-2913, has five boats, ranging from 45 to 65 feet. Pillar Point Fishing Trips, 415/728-3377, has six boats from 55 to 85 feet. Reservations are advised, especially on weekends.

Rock cod fishing takes place every day of the year except Christmas, with boats leaving at 7 A.M. and returning at 2:30 P.M. Bait and tackle are available for rent or purchase; licenses can be purchased. Longer trips go overnight fishing for albacore July through September. The salmon season from March through October is especially popular. All the fishing seasons are subject to changes of dates annually as determined by Fish and Game authorities. Some of the boats offer galley service; others specialize in no-frills fishing. You can also fish free from the pier. Fish can be cleaned at provided facilities. It's a pleasure just to see the skilled fillet knives of local fishermen in operation at the cleaning area around mid-afternoon.

To see more of the working fishing boat area of Half Moon Bay, walk down Prospect, left on Broadway, and out Princeton Avenue, past the boat repair and boat selling businesses. While browsing, visit the Merrie Asper antique store, opposite the Princeton Inn on Capistrano Road. The store is strong in cookware and china.

El Granada

This charming little town was laid out by the Ocean Shore Railroad Company. The streets are halves of concentric circles. Climate is sunny and warm. If the dreams of the railroad had materialized, El Granada would now be a select suburb. Lane Realty and Coastside Bakery now occupy the tile-roofed railroad station depot. This is a good stop for coffee and perhaps a slice of fresh-baked raisin nut bread.

South from Half Moon Bay

As you drive south, there are interesting back-country roads to explore, starting with the already recommended Higgins Purisima Road. Indian paintbrush and yellow bush lupine wildflowers greet you in spring as you drive this lonesome, partly gravel road. Old ranches stand near modern houses of confirmed exurbanites as you zigzag to some surprisingly high vistas of chaparral and cattle-grazing grasslands before descending to a short stretch of redwood stream-bank terrain.

You can continue on back roads south by taking Verde Road, where artichokes are farmed, and then the Lobitos Creek Cutoff and Tunitas Road, at the end of which are large open fields for commercial flowers. A short stretch on Coast Highway 1 follows, but the back roads continue with Stage Road to the small communities of San Gregorio and Pescadero. The dominant impression on these back roads is of extensive cattle grazing on the hillsides, but there are always private dramas for the traveler, such as a covey of scurrying quail, a red-tailed hawk sitting on a telephone pole, or a eucalyptus forest planted around the turn of the century.

Tunitas Creek Road and La Honda Road are interesting alternatives to the main roads back over the mountains.

San Gregorio Beach

Without doubt the beaches are a major attraction as you continue south.

San Gregorio is both a one-store village and a beach. The Peterson & Alsford General Store, built in 1889 and rebuilt after a fire in 1930, is now run by Clay and Ellen Miller, plus other partners. They sell everything from Levis to nature books, kerosene lamps to vegetable seeds, but mainly they create a friendly ambiance around their bar, located in the store, where the local populace carries on social life.

San Gregorio State Beach, carved from the cliffs by San Gregorio Creek, is a favorite for sunning. It has restrooms and picnic tables. Lifeguards are on duty during summer, but swimming can be dangerous. Private Martin's Beach, which charges a fee per car, lies just north of San Gregorio and is popular with clothing-optional sunbathers.

San Gregorio was the site of one of Portola's camps, as a marker indicates. One diarist of the expedition, Padre Crespi, reported an extensive Indian population. By 1839 four square leagues of land were called Rancho San Gregorio and had been granted to Don Antonio Buelna. Buelna built a road connecting this property with another land grant at the present Stanford University. His road, La Honda Road, was the first connecting route across the mountains. There was once extensive logging in the canyons in back of San Gregorio as virgin redwoods were cut for lumber and shingles. At San Gregorio a famous resort flourished, called Swanton House, and the fishing was reported excellent for chinook and king salmon.

Pomponio Beach

Pomponio State Beach is named for an Indian who made a last desperate stand as disease and encroachment wiped out his people. For over a decade the wily Pomponio attacked Spanish settlers and the missions. He had an uncanny ability to escape, even if captured. The Pomponio Beach setting is lovely, with a broad swath of beach and bluffs on the north side, plus several picnic tables.

Pescadero Beach and Marsh

Pescadero State Beach is sparsely developed, though there are toilets. This is a diverse beach. Its tide pools are excellent for viewing marine life. A 210-acre wildlife refuge across the road provides opportunities to see great blue herons, kites, egrets, deer, and raccoons. Pescadero Marsh property includes two large saltwater ponds and lush flowing creeks in season as Butano and Pescadero creeks meet and empty into the sea.

Today this marsh is a valuable remnant of a formerly rich coastal habitat for fish and wildlife. In the creek each winter there is a spawning run of about 1500 steelhead, a fraction of what old timers recall in years before the bridge was erected over the creek in 1938. Today the waters are only knee-deep, but then the stream ran strong and deep to eight or nine feet. Seventeen-pound steelheads, 25-pound chinook salmon, and summer runs of blueback trout were said to be almost thick enough here for anglers to walk across the creek on finny backs.

The marshland has been reduced to 500 acres, but that acreage at least is stabilized. Many species of wildlife that can exist nowhere else but in a marshland have made their last coastside stand here. The Fish and Game Department has catalogued 180 species of birds, 50 species of mammals, 33 species of amphibians, and 380 species of plants here, though this listing is not meant to be exhaustive.

Town of Pescadero

Not far from the bridge, two miles upstream, is the town of Pescadero, a charming community to visit. The name means "the fisherman" in Spanish, but at this distance from the sea you won't find many fishermen. You will find skilled farmers, mostly of Italian and Portuguese descent, who grow artichokes and brussels sprouts in topsoil that, in some places, goes down eight feet. A constant fog and an occasional slight frost benefit these two crops, making agricultural opportunities here unique. Beans, lettuce, and strawflowers are other crops.

For many years the color of most buildings in the town was white, partly because in 1896 the freighter S.S. *Columbia* broke up on the rocks nearby. The freighter carried a cargo of coffee and white paint, both of which were salvaged.

Pescadero is a one-street town. Visit the Arcangeli Grocery with its old-fashioned butcher shop. Williamson's Country Store, dating from 1885, is another of the coastside general stores. Here you can get everything from hayforks to fishing rods. The Pescadero Store is a more modern version, with a variety of goods for travelers rather than local people. Molly Ramolla's art studios feature highly original work with casein painting materials and papyrus paper made by the artist. Pescadero is also the home of writer Charles Jones, who has done sensitive literary writing on the region, such as his *A Separate Place*, about La Honda. The last house on the way to the ocean is Oliveira's Antiques, a yard and barn cornucopia of Americana ranging from stuffed foxes to old carriages.

Be sure to walk down the main street beyond the immense flagpole, which stands like an exclamation point behind local patriotism and pride. Beyond the flag you'll see a collection of 19th century California houses that looks almost like a movie set. The power of this honest, simple architecture is moving in the setting of Pescadero. The houses are never far from sight of the vegetable fields or grazing cattle that have always sustained life here. The buildings include an 1860 Methodist meeting place now owned by the Native Sons and Daughters of the Golden West.

A landmark restaurant on Pescadero's main street is worth a stop. That is Duarte's Tavern, 415/879-0464, run by Emma Duarte, her son Ron, and daughter-in-law Lynn. For lunch try the seafood quiche. At dinner start with their artichoke soup, made from local artichoke hearts that have been creamed. The specialty is grilled fresh fish, appropriate in a town called Pescadero, with perhaps grilled artichokes as the side vegetable. For dessert try their homemade olallieberry pie.

An important annual celebration here is the Portuguese Chamarita Festival held every year on the weekend before Pentecost (the fifth Sunday after Easter). The festival dates are coordinated with the same celebration on another date in Half Moon Bay so there is no conflict. Food is served free to all who come, though donations are welcome. A morning parade and an auction of local produce and handicrafts, with proceeds going to local charitable causes, follow through Sunday afternoon and into Monday.

Late in summer Pescadero celebrates again with an Artichoke Festival.

Backpacker at Castle Rock Park

The Central
Peninsula Coast

Redwood Parks and
Año Nuevo

T he appreciator of nature in its redwood forest splendor
and coastal beauty should encounter southern San Mateo
County, both in the inland parks and the accessible coastal
beaches. In this rugged area the hills were harvested for redwood
lumber, especially in the 1880s. Historically, the area remained
quite isolated to the end of the 19th century because of the lack of
roads. Coastal shelves above the sea are field-cropped for
artichokes, and the gentler hillsides are grazed by dairy and beef
cattle.

Information on any of the county parks or beaches can be
obtained directly from the phone number listed for each park.
Overall information comes from Parks and Recreation, County
Government Center, Redwood City 94063, 415/363-4021.

Each state park and some of the state beaches have their own
phone numbers. The state park overall information source is
Department of Parks and Recreation, P.O. Box 2390, Sacramento
95811, 916/445-6477.

Ranger Tom Lindsey of Butano State Park offers some sound
advice for users of any parks. Call ahead to make sure you
understand the park rules, especially about bringing in dogs, use
of park grounds for such things as baseball games, and gathering
or not gathering downed wood for fires. Of course, no gathering
of live plants or animals is allowed in any park. But other rules
may differ from park to park.

(Whether a park is state or county run depends mainly on the
accidents of acquisition, the disposition of the donor, and the

eagerness with which the government entity sought the acquisition, plus, of course, what resources could be offered by the government entity for a parcel of land.)

La Honda

The road to La Honda leaves Skyline Boulevard from the small community of Skylonda, where friendly Alice's Restaurant is a good rest stop for coffee or perhaps a sandwich. The road then parallels the steep plunging bed of La Honda Creek, where there are already large, second-growth redwoods, before smoothing out to more pastoral rolling hills with cattle grazing. Buckeye trees and blue blossom ceanothus are plentiful. Blue lupines and Indian paintbrush adorn the road in spring.

Though the mountain retreat of La Honda was a destination for 19th century campers in the redwoods, most travelers today are just passing through. La Honda is on Highway 84 roughly midway between Skyline Boulevard and the sea. It serves as the access point to the major redwood parks nearby.

La Honda has its own character. At no time was it more renowned than when Ken Kesey and his Merry Pranksters, complete with their well-outfitted bus, used La Honda as a base of countercultural operations in the late 1960s. Today the traveler can sample the local social scene with a stop at the bars and restaurants, such as Apple Jack's or Roger's Back Yard.

Bar is too harsh a word to describe Apple Jack's, where urban cowboys and even some real cowboys get together. The place has a collection of hats that is unsurpassed. On warm days you can sit on the front porch in redwood chairs made from whole logs. On chilly days the fireplace inside is a welcome source of warmth. Apple Jack's was first a blacksmith shop serving the lumber trade in the 1880s. Roger's Back Yard restaurant features La Honda stack pancakes and La Honda chili.

The Pioneer Market is an old time purveyor, from 1877. For decades an adjacent store carried the designation of "the Bandit-Built Store," but the structure has since been torn down. It was proclaimed that the Younger Brothers of the Jesse James gang helped build the store.

La Honda Days in mid-July is the big annual celebration.

If, instead of entering the parks, you drive down to San Gregorio, the road from La Honda follows San Gregorio Creek as the valley becomes ever wider. Cattle and sheep graze the soft hillsides as you approach the ocean. Chr.stmas trees, commercial flowers, and pumpkins are planted on the bottomlands.

Backpacking the Peninsula

The peninsula region offers excellent opportunities for backpacking, which puts you beyond the 95 percent of all outdoor enthusiasts who remain within a mile of their cars. Below is a summary of backpacking opportunities in the relevant parks. Refer to the Index for the complete section on each park elsewhere in this book. Call ahead to learn of current fees and reservation arrangements at each park for backpack camps.

San Mateo County Memorial Park serves as the access point to backpack camps and a hikers' overnight hut in Sam McDonald/Pescadero Creek county parks. (They are discussed in the next sections in detail.) Two new backpacking camps in Pescadero Creek Park have recently been opened.

Butano State Park provides a lovely trail camp 5 miles from the visitor parking lot, starting up Goat Hill Trail. The camp is in a stand of first growth redwoods, 1,400 feet above where you start, so this is a rigorous climb. Butano at its lower elevations is a fern-strewn, rain-forest environment with lush vegetation. Phone for reservations, 415/879-0173.

Portola State Park has a backpack camp an easy 3 miles from the parking lot. Take Summit and Slate Creek trails to the redwoods near Slate Creek and the once-flourishing Page Mill. The vegetation here is mixed hardwood forests with deep huckleberry vines along the trails. Phone for campsite information, 415/948-9098.

Castle Rock State Park offers camping for backpackers only. In fact, the ranger's trailer is located 3.5 miles from the trailhead. Park your car at a barely marked parking lot on Skyline Boulevard, 3 miles south of the junction of Skyline/Highway 9. Though this camp is only for backpackers, it is relatively luxurious, with the rangers giving nature talks and selling firewood. Views of the Santa Cruz Mountains are stunning.

You can make an interesting loop trip in from the parking lot and then back, taking alternate trails, or you can continue from this camp farther on the Skyline-to-the-Sea Trail. You camp next at Waterman Gap, 12 miles down the trail. The exceptional experience of the Skyline-to-the-Sea Trail is discussed in the

Castle Rock write-up. Call ahead to Castle Rock for reservations, 408/867-2952.

Big Basin Redwoods State Park has a number of backpack camps. Try the Sunset Camp near the western side of the park and hike there on the Berry Creek Trail, which takes you past Berry Creek Falls and cascades of water. From here you can also connect to other trail camps on the route to the ocean. Phone for reservations, 408/338-6132.

Forest of Nisene Marks State Park has substantial size, 10,200 acres, and has been minimally developed. The backpack camp is near Sand Point Overlook, 6 miles from the parking lot above Aptos. The area was clearcut of redwoods 1875–1925, but an attractive second-growth mixed forest has arisen. Part of the trail system takes you over old logging tracks to Hoffman's Historic Site. Phone for reservations, 408/335-4598.

Henry Coe State Park, east of Gilroy, offers a fine springtime backpacking experience when the wildflowers burst forth on the grassy hillsides of this former ranch. Several camps are located at spaced intervals from the ranger station. This park can become quite hot and dry by summer. Phone 408/779-2728.

All the mentioned redwood parks on the spine of the peninsula or in the extensive Santa Cruz Mountains provide attractive summer backpacking outings in their cooler, tree-shaded depths.

Sam McDonald/Pescadero Creek County Parks

Sam McDonald Park is steep and rugged, from 400 feet at Alpine Creek to over 1,300 feet on Towne Ridge. The range of elevation makes possible a variety of plant life in different climatic conditions. Headquarters are at 13435 Pescadero Road, near La Honda. Phone 415/747-0403.

The park's 870 acres split about evenly between redwood forest and ridge terrain with grasslands and mixed evergreen trees.

Through this park you can also gain access to Pescadero Creek Park, another 6,000 acres open for daytime hiking. The Towne Trail takes you to Pescadero. Interconnected trails in these parks, plus Memorial and Portola parks, provide the long-distance hiker with plenty of options. Fully 50 miles of trails and old logging roads in the four-park complex are open to hikers and backpackers. Rangers are developing the last mile of trail needed to connect with Big Basin Park. Eventually a system of trails through the Santa Cruz Mountains will allow you to start at Henry Cowell Redwoods and walk all the way to Thornton Beach over public lands. (In 1850 Bayard Taylor walked from San Francisco to Santa Cruz, reporting that it took him three days.)

Hiking to a ridge in Sam McDonald and gazing at the ocean or communing with a cluster of sorrel in a clump of redwoods are among the main pleasures at Sam McDonald Park. The 4-mile Ridge Trail gives you good views of the Pacific.

Within Sam McDonald there is a hikers' hut that can be reserved for overnight stays, reducing the need for backpacking equipment. Sponsored by the Sierra Club, the hut kit was imported from Denmark in 1977 and assembled at its present site, along Towne Trail, a 1.5 mile walk from park headquarters. Modest fees per night are charged. The hut can accommodate up to 14 people and is open to the public, with families welcome. Reservations must be made by calling 415/327-8111.

Under this hut plan, which may be duplicated in future years at other places in the Santa Cruz Mountains, you bring a sleeping bag, food, and personal articles. The hut provides a mattress, electric hotplate, pots and utensils, limited water (it's hauled in), electric lights, and a wood burning stove for warmth. With a plastic garbage bag you take out anything you've brought in. Each hut user operates as a self-policeman to keep the area clean.

Photos on display at park headquarters tell the story of Sam McDonald (1884–1957). The son of slaves, he worked as a groundskeeper and jack-of-all-trades at Stanford University and eventually became superintendent of grounds. He was known at Stanford Children's Hospital for the vegetable gardens he planted and the barbecues he hosted. Sam McDonald worked for the university for 50 years, starting in 1903, and began acquiring the La Honda property in 1917 with the purchase of a two-room cabin and some land along Alpine Creek in the northern portion of the present park. When he died in 1957, McDonald left his 400-acre property to Stanford with the request that the land be used as a park for young people. Today camping in the park, aside from the mentioned hut, is limited to youth groups, fulfilling the donor's bequest. The county purchased adjacent land in 1976, giving the park its present 870-acre size.

Pescadero Creek County Park is a large undeveloped area approached through Sam McDonald County Park, San Mateo County Memorial Park, or Portola State Park. Pescadero's attraction is the primitive setting amidst some giant redwood trees and second growth forests. Hiking trails are the main pleasure while communing with nature far, far from the roadways.

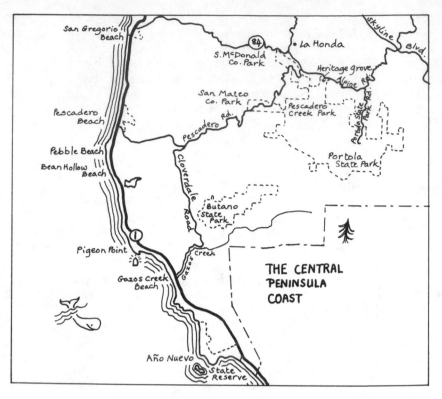

The following text labels appear on the map:

San Gregorio Beach
84
La Honda
Skyline Blvd
S. McDonald Co. Park
Heritage grove
Alpine Rd
San Mateo Co. Park
Pescadero Rd
Pescadero Creek Park
Pescadero Beach
Portola State Park Rd
Pebble Beach
Cloverdale Road
Portola State Park
Bean Hollow Beach
Butano State Park
Pigeon Point
Creek
THE CENTRAL PENINSULA COAST
Gazos Creek Beach
Gazos Creek
Año Nuevo State Reserve

Pescadero Creek Park's redwood forest had a long logging history, which ceased in September 1971, and much of the land is now returning to natural forest, aided by the rangers' scientific management strategies.

For a permit to enter the park, consult the ranger at Sam McDonald or Memorial parks. Backpacking camps have recently been opened in Pescadero Creek Park at Shaw Flat and Tarwater Flat.

San Mateo County Memorial Park

This 327-acre redwood park offers good hiking, nature trails, picnicking, and camping. Overnight camping at its 105 drive-in sites is on a first-come, no-reservation basis. The park is at 9500 Pescadero Road, 5.5 miles from La Honda, 415/879-0212.

Memorial, which honors World War I soldiers, is the oldest

park in the county system and provides a view of first growth redwoods. Besides two interesting nature trails, the park has a fine interpretive center explaining both nature and logging history. Before the Gold Rush the Spanish did little or no logging, but in the 1860s and 1870s there were 30 sawmills operating in San Mateo County, four of which were immediately adjacent to this park. Lumbering was important here for both redwood and the bark of the tanoak tree, whose tannin was used in curing hides. By the early 1900s most of the accessible trees of usable size had been logged.

The two nature trails are the mile-long Mt. Ellen Nature Trail and the shorter Tanoak Nature Trail, with its easy wheelchair access for the disabled. On these trails you see the coniferous forest environment of redwood and Douglas fir trees. In the campground the forest floor has been restored to its rustic flora. One stately redwood tree has been measured at 225 feet high and estimated to be 1,500 years old. Ironically, fire, which scarred the trunks of a few trees, saved 80–100 acres from the loggers' saws until the county purchased the land in 1924. Tanoak, bay, madrone, and buckeye trees abound. Redwood sorrel and trillium wildflowers are plentiful along the trails.

Several short trails have been built for hiking in the park, such as Creek and Huckleberry trails. Trails into adjacent parks can be added for more ambitious loops.

Redwood groves and undisturbed Pescadero Creek are the park's major assets. Once inside the redwood groves you become immersed in the quiet and gentle peacefulness that envelops the area like fog over the treetops. Fog deposits moisture on the leaves of the redwood trees, allowing for some 15 added inches of drip runoff during the rainless summer season.

Pescadero Creek is a winter spawning stream for steelhead trout. In the park the creek is dammed during summer for swimming. Summer temperatures remain cool because of the protective fog and the canopy formed by the redwood trees. Banana slugs can be found crawling along the paths near the streams.

Heritage Grove

This special park holding at the edge of Sam McDonald Park consists of an impressive 37-acre stand of first growth redwoods, spared by loggers. The site is on Alpine Road one mile east of Pescadero Road. As you drive up

128

narrow Alpine Road from Pescadero Road, it's easy to imagine the days when oxen pulled logs down narrow paths by the creekbeds.

After you park in the small lot upstream from the trees, walk the designated trail. You'll notice on some trees the lines of blue spray paint. These paint marks are from 1973 when the logging foreman went through the forest determining which trees would be cut and how. The saving of magnificent redwoods in this section came not a moment too soon. An aroused citizenry, alerted by one angry individual who saw the blue paint, argued that the cutting of these trees at this late date would be an atrocity. In an impressive grass roots conservation effort, citizens contributed half of the funds needed to buy the trees just as loggers' chain saws threatened to cut them.

There is a Lower and an Upper Grove in the park. From the Upper Grove you get a better perspective on the size of the giants, looking down to the creekbed, so be sure to walk up there. Tanoak, sword ferns, trillium and sorrel wildflowers, and diverse other plants thrive. The setting is an ideal redwood environment in a creekbed.

Portola State Park

This state-run redwood park lies at the end of twisting 3.6-mile Portola State Park Road off Alpine Road. The entrance is 7 miles from Skyline Boulevard (Highway 35) down Alpine Road and then Portola State Park Road. The park honors the great explorer, Gaspar de Portola, and provides 52 campsites for travelers who want to discover for themselves the redwood trees. Redwoods were first seen by Europeans when Portola's party passed along the coast in 1769. Campsites must be reserved through Ticketron. For information on the park call 415/948-9098.

On the self-guided .7-mile Sequoia Nature Trail you see, as expected, some magnificent examples of *Sequoia sempervirens*, including old giants who survived hundreds of years of brush fires that periodically surge through, clearing the forest floor. The "shell tree" is an intriguing example of the redwood's ability to survive. Fire hollowed out the interior of this tree, but some cambium remained intact under the bark and the tree survived, nurturing the needles with nutrients and moisture through this precarious remaining conduit.

Portola Park lands were first harvested by Chris Iverson, who split shakes. William Page set up a mill 1867–75 on Peters Creek and built Page Mill Road extending from here to the town of Mayfield, now part of Palo Alto. The Islam Shrine, a branch of the Masonic Lodge, bought the grounds as a picnic and recreation holding in 1924 and sold the 1,700 acres to the state in 1945.

Alpine Road from Skyline Boulevard to the park road is one of the loveliest drives on the peninsula. The vistas are both beautiful and instructive as you see juxtaposed the full range of plant communities in the region, including redwood forests and grasslands, oak woodlands and chaparral. Thick-leaved mule's ear, with its yellow compositae flowers, is an abundant wildflower along this road.

Butano State Park

Two routes lead you to Butano Park. As you approach the Cloverdale Road turnoff to Butano from Pescadero, you pass the Tom Phipps Ranch, where you can pick blackberries and olallieberries in season and purchase other fresh produce. The Dias Strawflower Farm, near the turnoff, is another major business. Cloverdale Road into Butano Park shows redwoods on the high ridges to the left, cattle ranches on the hillsides, artichoke fields on the valley floor, and some greenhouses for floriculture. The other approach to Butano is along Gazos Creek Road, a gravel road with rich stream bank vegetation of bay, buckeye, and alder trees.

Butano is an Indian word said to mean "a gathering place for friendly visits." The 2,200-acre park, in the redwood environment of the Santa Cruz Mountains, is an excellent place for hiking, camping, picnicking, and the study of nature. For information, phone 415/879-0173. Reservations to camp can be made through Ticketron.

Butano has 40 campsites, including 19 that are secluded and require a short walk in. One camp, Butano Trail Camp, accommodates backpackers who hike 5 miles up a 1,600-foot grade. This trail camp must be reserved in advance by contacting the park. Rangers at Butano sell firewood. Extensive trails, such as Doe Ridge and Jackson Flats, are a pleasure to hike, especially to enjoy the wealth of plant life. Alders, tanoak, buckeye and bay trees, plus sword ferns, blackberries, and trillium abound. The land was logged in the 1880s, but second growth redwoods and a varied hardwood forest remain.

At the park entrance you'll notice a long wooden flume, which may seem to benefit potential steelhead or salmon runs; actually, it channels water for farm irrigation below the park.

The Coast

From Pescadero through Año Nuevo the drive along Coast Highway 1 offers many pleasures, including several inviting beaches, the historic Pigeon Point Lighthouse, closely cropped fields of artichokes and brussels sprouts, and the most attractive range of coastal wildflowers on the entire peninsula coast, at Pebble Beach. Fill your gas tank before entering this rather secluded stretch because the only available gas is at Gazos Creek.

Pebble Beach

About a mile and a half south of Pescadero Beach, past artichoke fields and rugged coastal vistas, lies an unusual beach where offshore currents break up quartz rocks, then tumble and polish the stones, and finally deposit them on the shore. In the 19th century a major resort hotel hosted travelers who wished to spend their days digging for these attractive stones.

Access to Pebble Beach prompted a long and litigious struggle between landowner Loren Coburn and the public. The case reversed itself time and again in the courts and in the state legislature. Coburn charged people to visit this natural wonder on the beach and sometimes simply locked the gate to prevent them from entering. This was the first chapter in the long saga of struggle for public access to the coast. That drama continues to be written today by the California Coastal Commission, which voters mandated to manage coastal development with the public interest in mind.

You can still find lovely rocks here, but the 1980s' ethic makes it imperative that you take only memories or photos and leave only footprints so that later visitors may appreciate these stones also. The pebble beach lies on the north side of the parking lot and is accessible by stairs. It is remarkable that the pebble area is so localized, not more than 100 yards long. Pure quartz rocks and quartz mixed with different color impurities, producing what are called jasper and agates, are numerous. Fossils can be seen in the cliffs.

The south side of Pebble Beach offers a self-guided nature trail featuring the loveliest displays of spring wildflowers you are likely to find in a coastal bluff habitat. Fields of blue iris, seaside daisy, buttercup, plantain, blue-eyed grass, lupine, and the well-known poppy proliferate. Leaflets describing this rocky, coastal habitat can be found at the first marker on the trail or obtained from the County Beaches State Park headquarters in Half Moon Bay, 415/726-6238. This nature trail, extending south to Bean Hollow Beach, is one of the most interesting discoveries along the coast.

Bean Hollow

Pebble Beach is not a sandy beach, but suitable sand for child's play and sunning can be found just to the south at Arroyo de los Frijoles, which translates as "Bean Hollow." Wide patches of sand extend north and south from the parking lot, and there is some wind protection because of landforms on the north side.

Pigeon Point

To modern travelers Pigeon Point, another 3.5 miles south, looks photogenic, but to 19th-century sailors this jutting rocky outcrop was ominous. Several ships were wrecked here with substantial loss of life and goods.

The road to Pigeon Point passes several more Coastal Access points, greenhouses, and fields. The turnoff to Pigeon Point is a favorite informal camp for self-contained RVs.

The lighthouse building has a marker indicating that it was constructed in 1871. A plaque in the wall traces to 1872 the installation of the light, then of a Fresnel lens with 1,008 pieces of glass to magnify the light. Stop to look at this handsome white painted brick structure. It's an architectural gem.

A hostel run by American Youth Hostels (AYH) now occupies the buildings, as at the Montara Fog Signal Station and Lighthouse 28 miles north. The Coast Guard favors the hostel presence to keep down vandalism. Sleeping quarters are in cottages with the appealing names Dolphin, Seal, and Whale. Up to 40 people of all ages can stay here if they abide by the hostel code of behavior, which includes morning cleanup and an 11 P.M. curfew. Call 415/879-0633.

Pigeon Point was and is a site of enterprise. Portuguese whalers once set out from here in their boats in search of the migrating mammals. The sailors would row out in swift boats to harpoon their prey, though fully one-third of the harpooned whales sank rather than floated, making them impossible to recover.

Today the Pigeon Point Shellfish Company breeds oysters and clams in an ambitious sea farming operation. The tiny oysters are shipped throughout the world to be grown at different locations. This company also brings in oysters from Humboldt Bay to purge them in filtered sea water prior to sending them to market. On weekends the company sells oysters and cherrystone clams direct to visitors. If traffic is light and you can persuade the proprietor to show you around, a look at this operation is engrossing. Various strains of quick-growing and highly nutritious seaweed are raised to feed the oysters. Mexican and Filipino oyster farmers are trained here. Experiments are underway to raise new species of shellfish commercially.

Shipwrecks

Pigeon Point was named for the first substantial ship that hit the rocks here. In 1853 the *Carrier Pigeon* broke in two. The ship sent to salvage it, the *Seabird*, met the same fate and went aground at Año Nuevo.

The coal ship *Hellespont* ran aground in November 1868 with a major loss of life. Eleven crew members died; only eight were saved.

Shipwrecks have not been merely a 19th-century phenomenon on these shores. In August 1929, an oil tanker hit the steamer *San Juan* off Pigeon Point, taking 87 lives. All up and down the coast there are stories of shipwreck.

The next point south, Franklin Point, is named after an 1865 disaster when a clipper ship out of Baltimore, the *Sir John Franklin*, hit the rocks. The painful private tragedies that resulted from such a wreck could formerly be read on a marker stone, now stolen, which said:

> To the Memory of Edward Church of Baltimore, Md. Age 16 years, and the ten other seamen lost of Ship *Sir John Franklin* January 17, 1865.

In November 1886 the coal ship *Coya* sank at Año Nuevo. The cargo and 27 lives were lost. In April 1887 the *H. W. Seaver*, a sailing ship, wrecked.

The most spectacular of the coastside wrecks occurred farther north, at Half Moon Bay. In 1898 the three-masted *New York* ran aground in the breakers off Pillar Point, with so much cargo floating ashore that U.S. Customs sent its inspectors to Half Moon Bay to collect duties.

Part of the danger in shipping along here was the loading of

The Lighthouse at Pigeon Point

produce from the coast side without the benefit of a port. Roads were too poor, or nonexistent, to transport crates and sacks of produce to the market in San Francisco. At Pigeon Point, because of its high bluffs, produce and lumber could be slid out to ships on long cables, but the procedure was tricky and dangerous, due to the sometimes treacherous waves.

In 1868 Josiah Ames built a wharf 1,000 feet beyond the surf north of Half Moon Bay. William Waddell also built a wharf at Año Nuevo for lumber export. But perhaps the most fanciful effort was an immense chute built by Alexander Gordon from a bluff at Tunitas Creek. Produce and lumber could be slid down the chute onto waiting ships. Good connecting roads finally made the chutes and wharves obsolete, and gales eventually dismembered all of them. Not a remnant remains visible today.

Gazos Creek

Gazos Creek offers both beach access and an enterprise selling food, drink, and gas to the traveler on this remote coast. The Gazos Creek Beach House, 415/879-0125, provides libations at its luxurious high-ceilinged bar. Food in the restaurant ranges from omelets to fresh salmon dinners. A fireplace cheers the traveler in cold and rainy weather. Fill your gas tank here, if necessary.

Gazos Creek is a pleasant beach with a wide stretch of sand. With recent acquisitions, Año Nuevo Reserve now extends to Gazos Creek, two miles south of Pigeon Point. The creek is stocked with rainbow trout during the summer fishing season. Wild salmon and steelhead use this coastside stream to spawn, and yearling silver salmon have been planted in efforts to increase the run.

The pleasant road south from Gazos Creek to Año Nuevo takes you past high dunes, grazing lands, yellow bush lupine and goldfields wildflowers, artichoke fields, Christmas tree ranches, and on the ridges to the east, Monterey pine and eucalyptus forests.

Año Nuevo

For the appreciator of nature, Año Nuevo is the piece de resistance of the peninsula. The dramatic story is the saving of northern elephant seals, but there are also quieter aspects of nature equally interesting at this reserve.

In recent years interpretive work at Año Nuevo has become

more sophisticated as thousands of visitors descend annually, especially during the winter. A historic 1880s' dairy barn belonging to Flora Dickerman Steele has been restored as a staging area for tours. You can see the old milking stations and browse through nature exhibits.

Elephant seal viewing requires a reservation because the size of the animals makes humans and seals an explosive mix. Call the reserve to find which days guided hikes are available, December through March, 415/879-0227 or 415/879-0595. When you've picked a day, go to the nearest Ticketron outlet to get your tickets. Reservations are advised a month or more in advance. The Año Nuevo number can give you information on Ticketron locations. Some public transportation entities arrange blocks of tickets and provide excellent alternative bus transport to the site. Call SamTrans 415/348-SEAL or the Santa Cruz Metropolitan Transit 408/425-8600.

The entire reserve is closed roughly December through March except for the guided tours. During the rest of the year you are free to explore on your own. Call ahead to see if any naturalist-led tours are available currently to help you comprehend the diverse pleasures of this reserve. Among wildlife seen here are numerous bobcats, whose hairy scat is highly visible. Wild radish is one of the chief wildflowers flourishing at Año Nuevo in the spring. Bird life in all categories is abundant. But the first object of most people's attention here is the remarkable elephant seal.

Elephant Seals

One of the awesome human encounters with wildlife anywhere on the planet occurs each winter at Año Nuevo. There you can meet, close-up, three-ton bull elephant seals, their harems, and the baby seals born on the mainland.

Because public interest has become so widespread since the elephant seals expanded their range to give birth, rest, and mate on this mainland location, guided tours have been necessary. The tours protect people and seals from inadvertent or malicious encounters that could be dangerous. An aroused bull seal could snap off a human leg or crush a human with its weight if antagonized. Though the seals look cumbersome on land, they should be treated with much respect, because the bulls can move short distances at surprising speed, lurching forward.

The excitement at seeing these elephant seals comes from two awarenesses. First, there is the massive size and fearlessness of the creatures when encountered by mere man. Males grow to 16 feet and weigh three tons. And second, seeing these animals alive today is possible because of a notable conservation success of our time. They had been hunted almost to extinction for their blubber, which was used as a lamp fuel. As lists of endangered species grow longer, it is encouraging to learn that these northern elephant seals have made such a striking comeback. They are no longer in danger.

In 1800, before they were slaughtered wholesale, the mammoth creatures numbered in the hundreds of thousands. By 1869 the seals were hovering precariously above the abyss of extinction. By 1892 less than a hundred were known to exist, surviving on the Isle of Guadalupe off Baja California, Mexico. Formerly, their range had been all along the West Coast at selected jutting outposts of land. Gradually the elephant seals are reclaiming that former range.

After the U.S. and Mexico agreed jointly to protect the species, the elephant seals began to make a comeback. Today their numbers have climbed to 30,000.

A walk out to see the seals is a hefty hike, so wear good boots and clothing to protect yourself against rain and wind. A total of nearly 1,000 male and female seals can be found at Año Nuevo at the peak of the winter season.

The common name, elephant seal, arose because the extended noses of the bulls reminded early observers of elephants. The bulls have large canine teeth and powerful necks that can be extended quickly. Fights for territorial dominance can be extremely bloody encounters. Baby seals are sometimes crushed by the rapid movement of bulls through the harems to protect their territory from encroaching bulls.

Only limited knowledge exists concerning the habits of these largest of the pinniped (finlike feet) mammals. It is believed that the elephant seals spend most of the year at sea, coming ashore only in winter to give birth, mate, and molt their fur. Elephant seals can dive as deep as 1,000 feet. With their large eyes they search out fish as their food, feeding mainly on rays, skates, sharks, and ratfish, species seldom eaten by man.

Early in January the females arrive at Año Nuevo and their other Pacific breeding grounds. Within a week the female gives birth to a pup, usually one per mother. After nursing the pup for 27-29 days, the mother weans her baby abruptly by leaving it and returning to sea.

The females mate, sometimes several times, during the four or five days before returning to sea. By mid-March most of the adult seals have left the island to begin their nautical journeys.

An elephant seal at Año Nuevo

At Año Nuevo the huge pinnipeds look almost otherworldly as they sun themselves and snooze, blending into the dunes. Awakened males occasionally let out staccato grunts that sound like an auto engine turning over on a cold morning. A bull elephant seal, aware of your presence 30 feet away, will awaken for a few moments, open his languorous eyes, perhaps contentedly flip sand over its back, and then fall fearlessly back to sleep.

Indians and Dairy Ranchers

Indians populated Año Nuevo in large numbers, living off the shellfish and finfish easily obtained. Archeologists digging in the Indian garbage dumps, known as middens, have uncovered stone arrowheads and tools. The middens are located mainly near the point amidst sand dunes. Indians at Año Nuevo were also expert gatherers of seeds, grinding the seed into a meal that the Spanish called pinole. In the interpretive center you'll see a reed boat of the kind Indians used skillfully on ocean trips.

The first European who noticed this Indian bastion was navigator and mapmaker Sebastian Vizcaino, who named the point when he sailed by shortly after New Year's Day, 1603.

Not until the second half of the 19th century was white settlement here extensive. The Steele Brothers' dairy ranches are the main story. The Steeles controlled their own and 11 other dairy ranches. In the era when dairying first flourished, mountain lions and grizzly bears roamed Año Nuevo, hunting down young seals and sea elephants. The Steele Brothers' dairy empire was built at this foggy, wind-swept location against the advice of others, but the family knew the terrain, having already succeeded in the similar environment of Point Reyes. Isaac Steele started his ranch at Green Oaks in 1862, working with his cousin R. E. Steele.

The Steeles were Union sympathizers, partly because a brother was a general in the Union Army. From one day's milking they made a celebrated, 4,000-pound cheese, 20 feet in circumference. This was auctioned off in San Francisco at a dollar a pound to benefit the early version of the Red Cross, which attended the wounded of the Union Army.

Año Nuevo Island served as a fog signal station and later as a lighthouse to warn ships. The government bought the island in 1870 and installed the fog whistle in 1872. The lighthouse followed in 1890, operating until 1948 when an automatic offshore buoy replaced it. In 1958 the state of California acquired the property and named the University of California at Santa Cruz as its responsible lessee. Biologist Burney Le Boeuf has been one of the attentive researchers, especially regarding elephant seals. He and colleagues have recently put together a book well worth reading, called *The Natural History of Año Nuevo*, available at the reserve ranger station and some bookstores.

The interpretive program has developed specialized booklets on different aspects of Año Nuevo, such as geology, tracing the San Gregorio Fault that passes through the area. Such features as shifting sand dunes and varying ocean levels are part of the geologic dynamics active at all times. Volunteers from the Santa Cruz campus and community have done much to make the reserve accessible to the public in this era of lean budgets for nature studies.

Riding the Roaring Camp and Big Trees Narrow Gauge Railroad, Felton

Santa Cruz Mountain Country 8

Big Basin to Nisene Marks

T he Santa Cruz Mountains provide the lover of nature with a diverse, forested hiking and camping terrain, beginning with the first California state park, Big Basin, and stretching south to one of our least developed state parks, Forest of Nisene Marks, now recovered from logging scars to a lush, second-growth forest. A back road through the area, Highway 9 down the San Lorenzo River, takes you through the arts and crafts center of Boulder Creek and several small villages with a Scots flair, such as Ben Lomond, to another major park, Henry Cowell Redwoods State Park. Adjacent to Henry Cowell rests one of the few remaining historic railroad experiences available to the public, the Roaring Camp and Big Trees Narrow Gauge steam trains.

Once you begin to enjoy the trails of the Santa Cruz Mountains, an organization worth knowing about is the Santa Cruz Mountains Trails Association. Through them you can meet fellow hikers and participate in the extensive volunteer work that helps maintain the trails. Over 100,000 volunteer hours have been contributed by this organization to maintaining trails since their first Trail Day in 1969. They also sponsor a Clean-Up Day in the autumn. For information, contact Santa Cruz Mountains Trails Association, P.O. Box 276, Mountain View 94042.

A group with a special interest in advancing the appreciation of natural history in the region is the Santa Cruz Mountains Natural History Association, P.O. Box P-1, Felton 95018, 408/335-5858. This group enhances interpretive activities in the park by sponsoring campfire programs, training volunteers who lead

142

nature walks, arranging for the publication of nature literature, and maintaining the self-guided trails.

Big Basin Redwoods State Park

T his was the first state park and is, in many ways, the most significant of all the California state parks. The park was created in 1902 as a result of public outcry over the impending doom of virgin redwoods in this area. Much credit must go to Andrew Hill, a San Jose photographer, who spurred the movement. The park lies on ocean-facing slopes about 20 miles north of Santa Cruz. You can reach it via Highway 236. Phone 408/338-6132.

Legacy of Andrew Hill

Though no one man can be credited with founding the California State Park System, certainly one pioneer deserves special mention. That is Andrew P. Hill, photographer, painter, conservationist, propagandist.

An ugly incident at Felton in 1900 kindled Hill's rage. On assignment from a British publication, Hill went to the Felton area to photograph redwood trees. He felt the best specimens could be found there. But an irate landowner threw Hill off his land and screamed at him, "This is MY property. These are MY trees. No one can photograph them unless I say so."

As Hill waited at the depot for the train ride back to San Jose, he fumed, and suddenly an idea occurred to him. "The thought flashed through my mind that these trees, because of their size and antiquity, were among the natural wonders of the world," he later wrote. "They should be saved for posterity. Thus was born my idea of saving the redwoods."

Hill was tireless in this pursuit. He organized a meeting with David Starr Jordan of Stanford and representatives of other colleges and organizations, including the Sierra Club. Together they agreed to focus on the Big Basin rather than Felton area because property in Big Basin could be purchased more cheaply. The group formed a committee that went to survey Big Basin. Around a campfire one night on Sempervirens Creek they passed the hat, collecting the first $32 of the millions that would eventually be needed to save sizable chunks of redwood real estate.

At Big Basin you can hike or drive to the site, called Slippery Rock, opposite Sempervirens Falls, and read the marker that recalls this historic camp:

> The first state park. A group of conservationists led by Andrew P. Hill camped at the base of Slippery Rock on May 18, 1900, and formed the Sempervirens Club to preserve the redwoods of Big Basin. Their efforts resulted in deeding 3,800 acres of primeval forests to the state of California on September 20, 1902. This marked the beginning of the California State Park System.

Around 1900, not many people were attuned to the redwood trees as a finite resource, and Congress was not then interested in saving California redwoods. The Big Basin area was being logged rapidly, with the Big Basin Lumber Company shipping out 150 rail cars of lumber daily from its Boulder Creek Mill.

Partly because of a persuasive speech by the University of Santa Clara's Father Robert E. McKenna, the state legislature appropriated $250,000. With this money the first 3,800 acres were secured under the name California Redwood Park, which opened to campers in 1904. In 1927 the name was changed to Big Basin.

Over the years additional tracts of land have been acquired, and the process continues today. In 1916 Congress transferred 4,000 acres of federal land to the park. Through efforts of the Save the Redwoods League and the Sierra Club, another 3,400 acres were acquired in 1967. The movement's leader in the last decade has been Claude A. "Tony" Look, who manages the Sempervirens Fund, P.O. Box 1141, Los Altos 94022. Today the park encompasses 15,000 acres of diverse terrain, with current acquisitions including gradual turnover of the Waddell Creek lands provided by the generous Hoover family. At park headquarters the Sempervirens Room tells of this ongoing work and how interested members of the public can join the effort.

Early Big Basin

The white man was a greater appreciator of the Big Basin redwoods than were the earlier Indians. To the Indians the dark quiet of the redwoods was less hospitable than the open meadows and oak woodlands where their food of acorns, deer, berries, and seeds was more abundant. Indian trails crossed Big Basin as part

A western azalea at Big Basin

of annual migration patterns from the Santa Clara Valley to the coast for fishing.

The Portola expedition passed along the coast here in 1769, camping at the Waddell Creek watershed. Portola and his men were sick at the time, but recuperated quickly, so they called the area La Salud, "the health." They saw redwoods here, but the first reported comment by Europeans on redwoods occurred a few days earlier near the Pajaro River to the south.

Logging began in earnest in the 1860s. William Waddell, after whom the creek is named, built a substantial lumber mill and a wharf along the seacoast. Waddell's operations ceased when he was mauled by a grizzly bear about 1875 and died.

Several small timber claims were filed in the next decade in what was then called Big Gulch. These settlers lived by stripping tanoak bark, which was used in the leather-curing industry, and by splitting straight-grained redwood into roofing shakes to be sold in Santa Cruz and San Francisco. Typical of these small homesteads was the Tom Maddock cabin, now recalled by an inscription carved into a log at the homestead site, two miles north of park headquarters on the Opal Creek Trail. The Maddock family had a 100-acre homestead with orchards from 1882 to 1902.

From Park Headquarters

When you arrive, stop at park headquarters and pick up a free map. New maps will show changes in trails made after the severe damage of the winter storms in 1982. Finding good maps of Big Basin has long been a problem because the USGS topo map has been outdated and the park service maps have been woefully inadequate. A good map is available for a fee from the Bay Area Orienteering Club, 3151 Holyrood Dr., Oakland 94611.

At park headquarters an exceptional museum, called Nature Lodge, celebrates the park's history, flora, and fauna. The museum has excellent displays of stuffed birds, snakes, and mammals seen at the park. Campfire naturalist talks and nature hikes take place daily in summer. Camping is by reservation through Ticketron, except for several backpacking camps, which are reserved direct by calling the park. Campgrounds are situated right in the redwood trees.

The finest redwoods stand along the Redwood Nature Trail near park headquarters. This self-guided trail has the noblest specimens of redwoods on the peninsula. You make the acquaintance of the massive Santa Clara Tree and the Chimney Tree, whose entire core has been hollowed out by fire. Growth continues in the Chimney Tree because the cambium layer next to the bark was not damaged.

Redwoods have a capacity to inspire wonder, partly because of their age. At park headquarters stands a cross section of one tree that has been ring-dated as 2,200 years old. At the time of the Romans this was still a young tree. But the tree may in fact be countless eons older. Most redwoods sprout clonally from the roots of their parent tree rather than from seeds. The same tree may continue to live in this way for thousands upon thousands of years.

The other main plants around the headquarters and campgrounds are tanoak, Douglas fir, huckleberry, and western azalea. Huckleberries produce large amounts of food for mammals and birds in August. Azaleas perfume the air with their white blossoms in June.

At higher elevations and more open terrain the vegetation becomes increasingly diverse, with much oak and madrone. The book, *Plants of Big Basin Redwoods State Park*, available at headquarters, has excellent photos and brief descriptions of plants found throughout the Santa Cruz Mountains.

My recommendation for the choicest hiking among Big Basin's 60 miles of trails is the stretch from Berry Creek Falls to Silver Falls, which shows profuse wildflowers in spring and lovely waterfalls all year. Allow a half day from headquarters for a loop trip to this area. The Skyline-to-the-Sea Trail (discussed in detail in the Castle Rock Park write-up) threads through Big Basin to the ocean, allowing you to walk from the spine of the mountains to the sea. The trail ends at the most recent addition to Big Basin, the historic Rancho del Oso on Lower Waddell Creek.

Castle Rock State Park

High on the mountain ridges above Big Basin rests Castle Rock State Park, a special park for the hiker, backpacker, and rock climber. Castle Rock's parking lot, on Skyline Boulevard (Highway 35) three miles south of the junction with Highway 9, is also the start of the Skyline-to-the-Sea Trail, one of the most inspiring hikes on the peninsula.

Rock climbers like to scale the large sandstone rock near the parking lot. This eminently climbable rock gave the area its name. All sorts of rock scrambling and climbing can be practiced here and throughout the park.

From the parking lot a 3.5-mile hike leads to the campground. You can hike in and out easily on a day trip if not staying overnight, taking the Skyline-to-the-Sea Trail in and the Ridge Trail out, making a pleasant loop. You can also hike into the camp and continue, walking all the way to the sea.

The hike to the campground is one of the loveliest in the Santa Cruz Mountains. You pass several plant communities and witness compelling vistas of the mountains in all their wildness. First you pass through a redwood forest, with its cool, moist streamside aura, dark and peaceful, with some large madrone, tanoak, and bay trees scattered throughout. This jaunt ends with a view of Castle Rock Falls, which slip over sandstone with a sheer drop of several hundred feet. However awesome, this scene is only a prelude of vistas to come.

Next you walk through a chaparral plant community, with its

drier vegetation, exposed to the sun. "Chaparral" comes from the Spanish, *chaparra*, for small scrub oaks. Much manzanita, ceanothus, and chamise can be seen here. Red-tailed hawks wheel about in the sky, catching the thermal updraft of cliffs below you, looking for meals of mice and rabbits. In the spring there are wildflowers, such as Indian paintbrush. Panoramas of the mountains open up on the left as you hike along. You also pass many large sandstone outcroppings, including some carved by nature into caves, suitable shelter in a storm.

Finally you pass into an oak woodland plant community, where the trails are thick with leaf duff, soft to the feet. A range of oak species clusters here, including live, canyon, and black oaks. Buckeye trees make occasional appearances and some madrone thrive on these slopes.

Castle Rock Park would qualify as a wilderness, except that some old access roads pass across it. Hiking through here may provide many private pleasures. I recall a day when, as I rested on the Ridge Trail, the plaintive yipping of coyotes enveloped me. The pack sang not more than 100 yards away, giving me a half-hour concert.

Though the elevations here are not those of the Sierra Nevada, nevertheless the 2,645- to 3,215-foot heights may affect your breathing pattern. Allow a little easier walk than usual because of the slightly thinner air at this altitude. With so much to see, hiking should be considered an enjoyable and educational stroll rather than a marathon endurance test.

Both the Ridge and Skyline-to-the-Sea trails take you to the camp. Ridge Trail has some fine examples of oaks as you approach within a mile of the camp, but the major spectacle is a thick grove of young madrone trees. If you want to see lovely red-barked madrone in all their beauty, there is no finer place on the peninsula. Actually, this growth has now become somewhat too thick, dominating the countryside, because fires here have been controlled for the last 50 years. A healthy burn will someday clean out this forest floor.

The walk into Castle Rock campground has one disquieting aspect. Occasionally, you can hear gunshots from the Los Altos Rod and Gun Club, which owns property adjacent to the park.

Once you reach the campground, you begin to perceive that this is an extraordinary camp. First, it is only accessible to hikers or backpackers, which thins the crowd considerably. But the camp itself is luxurious, with picnic tables, fire pits, and toilets. Excellent water is available from a tap that reaches into a spring.

Though downed wood can't be gathered, bagged firewood can be bought. The camp fee itself is modest, but pack in extra money for firewood and a map of the area if you don't already have one. There is also a pay phone here to alert the outside world of your progress, an unusual amenity in the wilderness.

At Castle Rock campground the fine self-guided nature trail, the Danny Hanavan Trail, acquaints you with the flora.

Skyline-to-the-Sea Trail

The map to get for Castle Rock Park alone is the map for the first part of the Skyline-to-the-Sea Trail. The entire trail comes in two maps, with the second covering Big Basin. (Topo maps of the area from USGS are outdated now, with the new trails, and you'd have to get four topo maps to cover Castle Rock because of its location at the corners of the maps.) You can send ahead for the two-part maps with a stamped self-addressed envelope to the ranger at Castle Rock State Park, 15000 Skyline Boulevard, Los Gatos 95030. Phone 408/867-2952 for the current price and for camp reservations.

The map(s) can also be bought direct for the same price and a stamped self-addressed envelope from their producer, the Sempervirens Fund, P.O. Box 1141, Los Altos 94022.

For a full-blown walk of 37.5 miles from the Castle Rock skyline to the sea at Waddell Beach, allow four days and three overnights. This gives you some time to look at nature as well as make the walk.

The next stop after the Castle Rock trail camp is Saratoga Gap, which has a parking area that can be a starting or stopping point if you have two cars as shuttles. From Saratoga Gap you can walk toward Big Basin along a trail that parallels closely the highway, but the more scenic route is Toll Road Trail, which takes you away from the highway. These trails eventually join up 8 miles later. You must backtrack a mile along the trail by the highway to the camp at Waterman Gap if you take the Toll Road Trail.

The trail from Castle Rock to Big Basin will be improved eventually to eliminate one stretch through a subdivision. Call ahead to register for the next camp along the trail, near Waterman Gap, by contacting Big Basin Redwoods State Park, 408/338-6132.

From Waterman Gap the next leg of the trail takes you to China Grade in Big Basin, where vast views of the forests and ridges of Big Basin unfold. From China Grade you can glimpse the ocean that will wet your toes if you make the full walk through the Waddell Creek basin to the sea.

Much credit for the existence of the 37.5 mile Skyline-to-the-Sea Trail must go to the Sempervirens Fund, an organization vital today and well worth supporting. An impressive turnout of 2,500 volunteers came together in one day to help build the trail. Now there is a network of more than 80 miles of trails between and within Castle Rock and Big Basin parks. Contributions of money and labor to build trails can be granted to the Sempervirens Fund.

San Lorenzo River Valley

Highway 9, the San Lorenzo River basin road after leaving Highway 236, meanders through a scenic valley toward Santa Cruz. This is a more leisurely and rewarding drive than Highway 17 if you have the time. The area has many charming small towns whose bucolic serenity was disturbed somewhat by the severe floods of 1982, which cut the road, inundated numerous houses, and killed several persons.

Boulder Creek was once a booming lumber town and later became known as the Gateway to Big Basin. Today its three-block main street supports diverse enterprises from jewelry makers, whose wares are seen at Sadie's and the Blind Pilot, to organic food stores, such as The General Store. The Country Store sells antiques in the old International Order of Odd Fellows building, which dates from 1907. The artisans, entrepreneurs, and other folks who inhabit Boulder Creek live in rustic cottages set amidst the redwoods.

Scopazzi's restaurant on Big Basin Road in Boulder Creek, 408/338-4444, dates from 1904 and serves good food for the entire family.

Ben Lomond is a lovely small town, named after a similar site in Scotland. The people in the region celebrate with a Scottish Festival in July. Throughout the area antique stores flourish, such as Country Antiques and Lion's Lair in Ben Lomond. Many of the stores offer a free map on Santa Cruz County Antique Shops.

Felton

Felton is known for its covered bridge. Though the bridge is not marked and is no longer used, it has been designated a state historic landmark, with the commentary:

> Felton Covered Bridge. In 1891 a bridge to replace the one built across the San Lorenzo River at Felton in 1878 was needed and the

present bridge, one of the first covered bridges in Santa Cruz County, was built.

Turn west along the river on Covered Bridge Road off Graham Hill Road to see this tallest covered span of its kind in the country. The floor is 140 feet long and has a 20-foot wooden approach at each end. The bridge is 18 feet wide and 34 feet high at its peak, with vertical board-and-batten siding. Covered bridges were thought to be more durable than open spans, even in a mild climatic region such as California.

The approximately 2,700 acres of vineyards in Santa Cruz County before Prohibition now grow mainly Christmas trees and other crops. Only about 120 acres of vines remain, distributed among several small wineries.

The Felton-Empire Winery, 379 Felton-Empire Road near Felton, hosts weekend tastings on an attractive deck overlooking their 40-year-old Hallcrest vineyard of Riesling grapes and some Cabernet less visible behind the trees. Call ahead 408/335-3939 to be assured of a tasting. Try their White Riesling and Cabernet, made as full-bodied wines that benefit from bottle aging.

Tasting at the Felton Empire Winery

As you prowl about the back roads, the number of Scots names becomes apparent. Loch Lomond Recreation Area offers picnicking, plus trout fishing in the lake. Bonny Doon is a retreat favored by horse-riding, ranch-home families. Weatherly Castle, a private residence off Highway 9 at Ben Lomond, could pass for a Scots castle.

As might be expected in a region dominated by the redwood tree, numerous stores sell ornamental redwood limbs and burls, the gnarled buds whose grain is much admired by appreciators of fine wood. Sections of burls are often fashioned into attractive tables.

Roaring Camp and Big Trees Narrow Gauge Railroad

T he prospect of a ride on an authentic steam-powered train, with the locomotive belching steam and sounding whistles, tends to excite explorers of all ages. On the peninsula such a ride is possible near Felton on the Roaring Camp and Big Trees Narrow Gauge Railroad, one of the last steam-powered passenger trains still operating. The entrance is off Graham Hill Road just south of Mt. Hermon Road, 408/335-4484. You can also enter from the nearby parking lot of Henry Cowell State Park. If you plan to visit the train and Henry Cowell Park, go directly to the park and walk to the train.

The tracks twist around a five mile loop through redwood groves. Back in the 1880s lumberjacks and pioneers used the same train to make their livelihoods, hauling out lumber and shingles. During the hour-long trip you climb some of the steepest grades ever built for a railroad. Unfortunately, in 1976 vandals burned the extraordinary corkscrew trestle that enabled the train to gain altitude rapidly. An ingenious system of rail switchbacks now allows the train to traverse the steep grades.

At Bear Mountain, during the trip, you can get off the train for a picnic or a hike in the redwoods and then catch a later train back to depot headquarters. The conductor gives a competent commentary on the flora of the region during the stop and as the train moves. A stop in a "cathedral" of redwoods allows for a description of how new redwood trees sprout in a circle from the deceased mother tree.

Near where you board you can see the steam-powered sawmill that will mill the wood to rebuild the corkscrew trestle. In the spirit of the setting, meals of chuck wagon barbecued beef are served. Local musicians sing ballads of the lumbering West and other themes of country-and-western music.

Another popular ride is the Moonlight Steam Train Party, on Saturday nights in summer, with singing and dancing under the stars.

At Roaring Camp you can see a short covered bridge and visit a reconstructed 1880s' General Store that sells items from western garb to a complete line of books for the rail buff. Legend asserts that the name Roaring Camp had its origin in the Mexican impression that the American settlers here, who had a fondness for whiskey, created quite a roaring time.

The railroad is rich in legend and history. Riding it today can help you approximate the days when passengers from the East Bay, starting at Newark, could board a train and ride down the East Bay shore, across the Santa Clara Valley, then over the mountains, to resort pleasures here in the redwoods or beach attractions at Santa Cruz. These Picnic Trains or Suntan Specials are now gone forever, but the present Roaring Camp Railroad goes a long way to arouse nostalgia.

Five locomotives constitute the rail company's main holdings, ranging from the Kahuku, a 12-ton Baldwin locomotive from 1890, to the Dixiana, a 42-ton Shay locomotive from 1912.

Isaac Graham's Roaring Camp

The original logging settlement, near the present-day Roaring Camp, was founded by Isaac Graham, mountain man and nephew of Daniel Boone, in the 1830s. Graham plotted, along with John Fremont, to make California independent of Mexico.

In 1867 businessman Joseph Welch bought the property, partly to save it from logging. This was one of the first efforts in California to view redwoods as an attraction with a worth other than board feet of lumber. Welch fought bitterly the efforts to build a railroad to the area, but later reversed himself when it became apparent that the railroad could bring visitors to the scenic attraction of his trees, for which they were charged 25 cents.

Bret Harte's tale, "The Luck of Roaring Camp," takes an incident he learned about in an 1868 visit to this area and relocates it in the gold country of the Sierra Nevada two decades earlier.

Over the years the area was called Felton Big Trees and excursions to see the great redwoods became popular. The trees have attracted a roster of dignitaries, such as Presidents Benjamin Harrison and Theodore Roosevelt, King Kalakaua of Hawaii, and Prince Edward of England.

Henry Cowell Redwoods State Park

Henry Cowell is another of the majestic redwood parks in the Santa Cruz Mountains. Stately groves of the giant trees include many first growth specimens with clusters of redwood sorrel flowers around their bases. Fifteen miles of hiking trails await the traveler.

The main entrance to Henry Cowell Park is just south of Felton on State Route 9. This entrance puts you close to the Redwood Grove with its first-growth trees. The campground is on the east side of the park, accessible from Graham Hill Road. One hundred thirteen roomy campsites lie partly in a unique forest of ponderosa pine, which usually thrives in drier environments. The camp boasts an amenity rare among state parks, hot showers.

Redwood Grove, with its 29 numbered interpretive stations along a .8-mile loop trail, offers one of the outstanding nature walks on the peninsula. The walk begins near an attractive small Visitor Center devoted to nature exhibits and literature. Sword fern, oxalis, and ginger plants cover the forest floor. The first-growth redwoods are majestic and are named mainly after presidents. The tallest here is 51 feet in circumference and 285 feet high, even though a strong wind broke off another 75-foot top section. Small specimens of the inland giant redwood and the so-called dawn redwood have been planted at the end of the trail. Though these young trees are overpowered in the battle for light by the indigenous *Sequoia sempervirens*, you can look closely at the leaves to note family similarities and differences among the three.

The dawn redwood is a tree with a special modern story. Fossil remains in California indicated that there had been three species of redwoods in earlier eons. Besides the coast redwood, *Sequoia sempervirens*, and the inland giant redwood, *Sequoia gigantea*, there was a third tree, which scientists named *Metasequoia* or dawn redwood. This tree was thought to be extinct, but in 1944 botanists cataloguing plants in China discovered dawn redwoods there. Many have been planted in California from seed or shoots brought from China since the late 1940s.

The San Lorenzo River passes through Redwood Grove. In winter there is a spawning run of salmon and steelhead.

Henry Cowell Park was formed in 1953 when Samuel Cowell donated 1,600 acres of land to the state in memory of his father, Henry Cowell. That donation included the superlative stand of first growth redwoods. The county later added another 120 acres.

In 1976 a new 2,335-acre section of Henry Cowell Park opened on Ben Lomond Mountain. This is the Fall Creek unit of the park, west of Felton off Felton-Empire Road. The area was a busy limestone quarry from 1870 to 1925. Hiking trails open the Fall Creek unit to travelers.

Back-road Adventures

West from Felton the Felton-Empire Road, Ice Cream Grade, and then Martin Grade lead you to the community of Bonny Doon. Bonny Doon Grade takes you through redwood country down to the coastal shelf and Davenport, a historic and once-vital, small, seaside town.

During the 19th century Portuguese whalers set out from Davenport in small boats to harpoon the gray whales migrating south. This unique land-based whaling differed sharply from the typical sea whaling described in Herman Melville's *Moby Dick*. Today you can see the whales pass close to the shore in January, sometimes almost brushing the sand. The best vantage point is on bluffs high over the water, which falls off sharply to some depth here. The actual whaling site was at the beach on Davenport Landing Road.

When you come to this area, the central stop is the Davenport Cash Store, which has a restaurant, local pottery from the Big Creek Pottery Studio, and information on whale watching. On Coast Road, a quarter mile from the Cash Store, you can visit the Jim Lundberg Studios, internationally famous for Tiffany-style art glass. Lundberg's "seconds" are sold at his Mother's Day Spring Seconds Sale on the first two weekends in May and at a pre-Christmas sale in December.

Of the many small, back-country towns in the mountains, none is more historic than tiny Glenwood. There you'll find a marker, shielded by ceanothus bushes, a quarter mile up

Glenwood Drive from where it intersects Glenwood Cutoff. The marker tells this abbreviated tale:

> Historic town founded by Charles C. Martin, who came around the Horn in 1847, and his wife, Hannah Carver Martin, who crossed the Isthmus. First homesteaded area in 1851 and operated toll-gate and station for stage coaches crossing mountains. Later Martin developed a lumber mill, winery, store, and the Glenwood Resort Hotel.

For the next generation, whenever weather is a subject of discussion in the Santa Cruz Mountains, the big storms of winter 1982 will spring to mind. The first storm hit California on January 3 and deposited 23 inches of rain in 36 hours at some locations in these mountains. Hillsides became water-soaked, triggering many large earthslides. Water pressure deep inside lifted the land, which then slid along on slick sheets of clay. Twenty-one people died in Santa Cruz County, buried by mudslides or drowned in the floods. Two hundred twenty homes were destroyed and 8,000 were damaged. The dollar damage was set at roughly $250 million. The worst disaster of all here occurred at Love Creek, out of Ben Lomond, where a dozen people still lie buried beneath mudslides whose size staggers the imagination. Bean Creek Road from Scotts Valley to Glenwood Cutoff shows many slides that only another decade of vegetation growth will obliterate.

Forest of Nisene Marks State Park

Marked "undeveloped" on some maps, this 10,200-acre park offers a secluded hiking and backpacking experience, encompassing the complete drainage of Aptos and Hinckley creeks. The generous Marks family of Monterey bought this property and deeded it to the state in 1963 with the proviso that it be named after their mother, Nisene Marks.

You can reach the park from Aptos Creek in Aptos, just off Soquel Drive. The park land was clearcut of redwoods 1893–1925 by the Loma Prieta Lumber Company, but by now attractive, second-growth forests have arisen. Production of lumber was sufficient for Southern Pacific to lay a broad-gauge spur track here in 1884. The top of the park is a ridge at 2,600 feet, south of Loma

156

Prieta, one of the higher peninsula mountains, at 3,791 feet. You can walk about 30 miles of trails in Forest of Nisene Marks Park, including one along the railroad track leading back to Hoffman's Historic Site, the original frenetic logging site. Buildings at Hoffman's are now being reclaimed by forest.

Reservations for backpackers to stay at the West Ridge Trail Camp can be made with rangers at Henry Cowell Park near Felton, 408/335-5858.

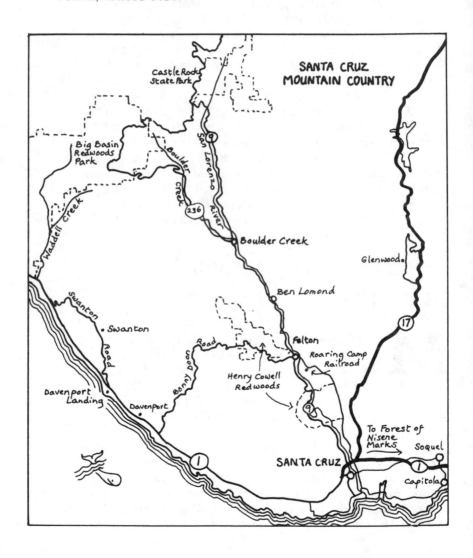

Nisene Marks Park has a special historical significance because near here, at Corralitos, the Portola expedition made European man's first contact with redwood trees. The party was walking north past the Pajaro Valley in 1769 on their quest for what mapmakers had indicated was an excellent bay. Diarist Crespi wrote:

> The scouts came back from exploring what had seemed to be pine trees, which they were not; but very straight, very thick trees of no small height, with a very slight short leaf; some said they were savins (cedars), but in my opinion they are not, the wood is red, and they are not junipers; they may be savins, who knows, but if so, they are not like any others we have seen elsewhere.

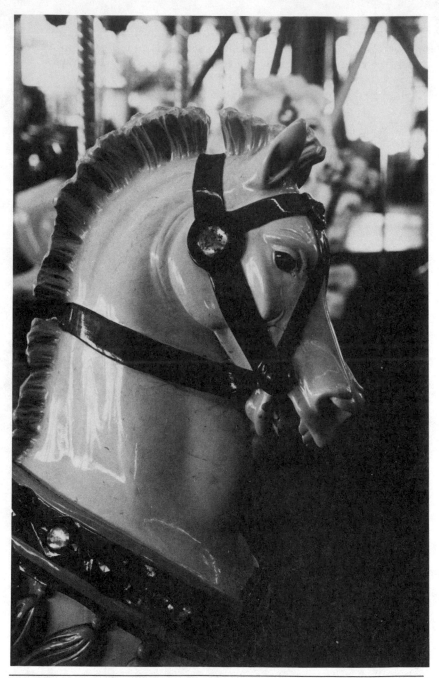

The historic carousel, Santa Cruz

The Santa Cruz Coast 9

Santa Cruz to Sunset Beach

C limate and seaside location have made the Santa Cruz coast an appreciated resort region since 1865, when John Leibrandt erected a few tents at the mouth of the San Lorenzo River to accommodate swimmers changing their clothes. The tourism pace picked up when the South Pacific Coast Railroad built a narrow gauge line in 1880 from Alviso to Santa Cruz, making the beach side easily accessible to San Francisco Bay Area residents.

Fueled by the early prosperity of lumber milling, lime mining for use in cement, leather tanning, and tourism, the region prospered, creating a legacy of lovely Victorian architecture from 1880–1900. By 1880 the easy lumber had been cut and the tanoak, whose bark was used for hide tanning, became more difficult to find. Tourism gradually rose in importance, but the earlier prosperity gradually diminished.

From the Depression to the 1960s Santa Cruz languished until a new vitality emerged with the opening of the University of California at Santa Cruz in 1965. Other factors in the renaissance included spillover prosperity in the mid-seventies from the Silicon Valley and a general reawakening of public appreciation for the Victorian past. Today Santa Cruz nourishes an art, craft, and culinary creativity unparalleled on the peninsula.

Santa Cruz lies on the sunny northern tip of Monterey Bay. Weather here compares favorably to that of Key West, Florida, with 300 sunny days a year and an average high temperature of 69 degrees F. Attractive beaches begin with sand in front of the Santa Cruz Boardwalk and extend all the way to Sunset Beach, west of Watsonville. Some beaches allow camping as well as sunning. The population mix includes retirees, university students and staff, craftspeople, artists, a cluster of professionals who have put

160

lifestyle ahead of career advancement and moved here, and the "just plain folks" who keep the community rolling along.

Entering Santa Cruz

The best overall information source after you arrive via Highway 17 from the Santa Clara Valley or Coast Highway 1, is the Santa Cruz County Convention and Visitors Bureau, P.O. Box 1476, Santa Cruz 95061, 408/423-6927. If you're walking, they're downtown in the civic auditorium at Church and Center streets. As you drive into town along Ocean Avenue, stop at their kiosk above Water Street for a map of the city and such specialized brochures as the *Victorian Walking Tour*.

Santa Cruz Boardwalk

Beach, boardwalk, and pier have been enduring attractions in Santa Cruz. While all the other Pacific Coast boardwalks have long since perished, the Santa Cruz Boardwalk continues to thrive. This is partly because entrance is free. You pay only for rides you wish to use or for meals at fast-food outlets. The Boardwalk is at 400 Beach Street, 408/423-5590, open daily in summer and weekends in winter.

The Santa Cruz Boardwalk was built in 1904, burned down in 1906, and rebuilt in 1907. Its large roller coaster, the Giant Dipper, is a classic wooden structure from 1924 that has carried 25 million riders on white-knuckle trips. The Giant Dipper was constructed in just 47 days at a cost of only 50,000 uninflated dollars. Proprietors pride themselves on the fact that not a single major accidental injury has occurred on this ride, which has a half-mile track length and a 55-MPH train speed. There are 18 other rides also, and the most recent addition has proven almost as popular as the Giant Dipper. That ride is the Logger's Revenge, which sends you hurtling down a watery flume.

The Boardwalk has kept up with the times in its three arcades, which present a cornucopia of computer games. Pac-Man and all his descendants can be brought onto screens by mesmerized patrons with fistfuls of quarters.

To see what bathing beauties of 1900 or Miss California of 1925 wore to this beach, peruse the photos at Hodgie's coffee shop. The beach in front of the Boardwalk offers a wide swath of clean sand for sunning.

The merry-go-round on the Boardwalk is a museum piece in itself. In 1911 a Danish woodcarver, Charles I. D. Loof, delivered the first merry-go-round with 70 hand-carved horses. That carousel still operates today, along with its original 342-piece Ruth band organ, built in 1894. Loof's horses are beautiful classics of carousel art, with long, flowing manes, jewel-studded saddles, muscular legs, and faces that express laughter at life. At this merry-go-round the riders actually reach for brass rings, which are then thrown through a clown's mouth, causing the clown to light up. Reaching for the brass ring may be only a metaphor until you see this authentic little touch on the Boardwalk.

The Boardwalk's Cocoanut Grove Ballroom, site of a flourishing big-band culture in the 1930s and forties, was restored in 1981 at a cost of $9.5 million. The Sun Room at the Cocoanut Grove opens to give an airy effect when weather permits. This is an elegant setting for popular Sunday brunches. The exterior of the building has been faithfully restored to its appearance when built in 1907, but the interior kitchens have been modernized to improve the restaurant offerings.

To some extent the big swing-band era of Tommy Dorsey has returned also, with monthly big-band dances that began again in 1977. Today's big band may be Les Brown or Del Courtney. Phone 408/423-2053 for current performances. The Dorsey brothers, Artie Shaw, and Benny Goodman all performed here in the past. Paul Whiteman and his 44-piece orchestra opened one of their performances here in the 1930s with a new composition, George Gershwin's "Rhapsody in Blue."

Over the decades different forms of amusement have flourished at the Boardwalk. From 1907 to the 1920s music dominated especially with bands in military garb offering outdoor concerts. From 1927 to 1945 a carnival air prevailed, with flying trapeze artists, distance underwater swimmers, comedians, and the slide-for-life feat that sent a daredevil down a cable from which he had to jump seconds before smashing into the pier. From 1947 to 1962 the Miss California Pageant held sway. In the 1950s and sixties bands were popular, and in the 1960s and seventies circus acts, such as the Flying Wallendas, made a comeback.

The Municipal Pier

West of the Boardwalk, the Municipal Pier offers a pleasant stroll, interesting shops, fish markets, seafood restaurants, and pier fishing or deep-sea fishing excursions. If you walk out on this mile-long pier, the longest on the Pacific Coast, you get plenty of bracing sea air and a splendid view looking back at Santa Cruz. Tables at the far end of the pier make a good picnic spot.

Those who drop their lines at the pier sometimes catch pilot perch or flounder. Crabbing with baited nets is popular at the far end. Several seafood restaurants serve up the local catch. Miramar is a good choice for red snapper or salmon, 408/423-4441. The fresh fish stores that sell direct from the boats display a wide range of catch, from shark to halibut. Stop in at Riva's to witness the bounty of the sea on display. Italians have been the major ethnic group in the Santa Cruz fisheries.

Lighthouse Point

An easy walk along a paved route, shared with roller skaters and bicyclists, takes you west from the pier to Lighthouse Point. Because the orientation of Santa Cruz is actually south rather than west, due to its location at the north edge of Monterey Bay, directions can seem confusing.

Surfers rank the waves at Lighthouse Point among the world's finest. Late winter toward the end of the storm season brings the strongest swells. Spectators get an excellent close-up view of surfers here because the unique topography of Lighthouse Point causes waves to run parallel to bluffs along the shore. This long surfing stretch, called Steamer Lane, serves as the arena for international surfing competitions.

A small museum in a replica of a lighthouse at Lighthouse Point informs you about the earlier lighthouse and about the eternal forces of beachside erosion. The lighthouse replica was erected by Chuck and Esther Abbott in memory of their son, who died in a surfing accident. Chuck Abbott was the primary figure inspiring the revitalized historic downtown and central residential area of Santa Cruz.

From Lighthouse Point you can continue to walk, bicycle, skate, or drive another 2 miles down West Cliff Drive on a paved path along the top of the bluffs to Natural Bridges State Beach.

Santa Cruz Mission

Santa Cruz first existed as a Franciscan mission, Mission La Exaltacion de la Santa Cruz. Today you can locate the old mission site from anywhere in Santa Cruz by looking for the dominant white spire of the later church, Holy Cross Church, on the same hilltop.

The mission period, 1769–1832, is an important part of the peninsula's heritage. Missions were the first permanent outposts of European culture in California. A mission allowed Spain to assert a right to ownership of the land by fact of occupation, requiring only the manpower of two padres and a few protective soldiers. Missions were intended to become self-sufficient after a few initial years of investment with outside supplies.

The priest's role was to Christianize and educate the natives, teaching them agriculture and other skills for a period of ten years. At that time the mission and all its improvements were to be turned over to the self-governing natives as Spanish subjects. If all worked according to plan, the Franciscans would have saved souls and the Spanish king would have controlled the land at minimal cost. The alliance between the two was seen as mutually beneficial.

But all did not work well, for a host of reasons, not the least of which was that European diseases, smallpox and tuberculosis, decimated the Indian population and rendered impossible any sustainable mission system.

By 1832 the entire California mission chain had reached relatively high levels of productivity, in spite of problems, and Santa Cruz experienced more problems than most missions. The padres demonstrated that cattle and sheep could be raised profitably for their hides, wool, and meat. An inventory of the missions in 1832 recorded 151,180 cattle and 137,969 sheep.

The influence of the missions on the modern peninsula is both obvious and subtle. The names and locations of major cities, such as Santa Cruz or Santa Clara, are those of the local mission. Roads such as El Camino Real, "The King's Way," are throwbacks to the mission times. The abundance of Spanish names on the landscape testifies to the mission era. A tradition of California hospitality and openness to the stranger started at the missions, which sustained travelers at no expense. Grain and vegetable farming, so important to California's $15-billion agricultural industry, began in the mission system as vast fields of wheat, barley, corn, beans, and peas. Mission-style architecture emphasized heavy walls, arched hallways, red semicircular roof tiles, and extensive overhangs to protect from sun and rain. This style has been perpetuated in many later peninsula structures, down to the latest tile-roofed housing development.

The mission system collapsed abruptly in 1832 when Mexico attained its independence from Spain. The Spanish Franciscans were ordered to depart from California, leaving the missionized Indians in a vacuum without support against the secular society. The Indians fled to the hills or died of disease as the missions disintegrated. Californios, the Spanish Mexicans who had migrated here or were born in California, eyed the rich and developed mission lands and herds with envy. Gradually, they assumed control over these properties. Strong families became wealthy from large land grants.

When Fermin Lasuen established the Santa Cruz Mission, 12th of 21 in the chain, the work of conversion and church building moved quickly at first. Grazing grass, berries, redwood and pine lumber, and water were plentiful. Vegetables thrived in the fertile soil. The mission reached a population of 430 neophytes, as the recently converted Indians were called.

The mission that Lasuen built in 1794 has vanished, a victim of secularization, earthquake, and neglect. But you can see a 2/3-scale replica of the structure, built in 1931, at 126 High Street, 408/426-5686.

A reliquary at the side of the mission contains vestments, missals, a baptismal font, a chalice, and altar statues said to be from the original mission.

Across the street from the back of the mission stands the Neary–Rodriguez adobe, a part of the original mission complex. This adobe, now owned by the California Department of Parks and Recreation, will eventually be restored as a site to interpret Santa Cruz history. Santa Cruz citizens celebrate their mission at the Mission Day Fiesta and Parade in September.

The Brancifortians

Though the Santa Cruz Mission began with promise, difficulties soon developed, reflecting sharply the tensions between mission and pueblo that plagued the entire mission system. When the pueblo of Branciforte was founded near the mission in 1797, the governor failed to observe a prudent law requiring that a pueblo be at least a league distant from a mission. The character of the Brancifortians was also a factor. Though the settlement was named after the king's viceroy in Mexico, some of those sent to California were low types who had spent time behind bars and had been given the option of serving their full term or migrating.

Predictable friction between neophytes and Brancifortians reached a high point in 1818 when the Argentine pirate, Hippolyte de Bouchard, was sighted off the coast. The governor, presuming that Bouchard would land and plunder Santa Cruz, ordered the padre to retreat with his charges to Santa Clara, which he did, leaving the Brancifortians in charge. Upon his return, the padre realized what a tactical mistake he had made. Bouchard had not landed, but the Brancifortians themselves had lain waste the mission. Among other atrocities, they drank all the accumulated sacramental wine. They savaged the sacred relics and plundered whatever was of value.

Historical Preservation in Santa Cruz

T his city should be saluted for doing what other communities have failed to do: preserve and enhance its historic downtown. To some extent Santa Cruz was the fortunate benefactor of its own middling prosperity 1930–60. There simply was not enough money to warrant bulldozing older commercial and residential structures in favor of some boosterish modernization. In the interim an appreciation of the past and its artifacts emerged.

Today it's a pleasure to walk down Pacific Avenue, the old main street, which has been turned into a walker's Garden Mall. Many interesting labeled trees and shrubs flourish along this mall, from magnolias to azaleas.

At the mall there are outdoor benches where you can eat a picnic lunch, perhaps supplied by Zoccoli's Deli or Kelly's Bakery. The central building is the yellowbrick Cooperhouse, which has shops and an outdoor sidewalk cafe with live music. Cooperhouse was originally the Santa Cruz courthouse, built in 1895 after fire ravaged the earlier courthouse. The building has been described architecturally as a type of Romanesque revival. After the county's needs outgrew the structure, it was auctioned off in 1971 and remodeled to house shops and restaurants. Three stories of shops make this one of the focal points for sale of gift and boutique items.

Cooperhouse is only the beginning of interest that Santa Cruz residents have shown in the town's proud architectural heritage. Next door to Cooperhouse is the Octagon, now site of the county historical museum, which hosts changing exhibits on the region and sells books on local history. The Octagon, built in 1882,

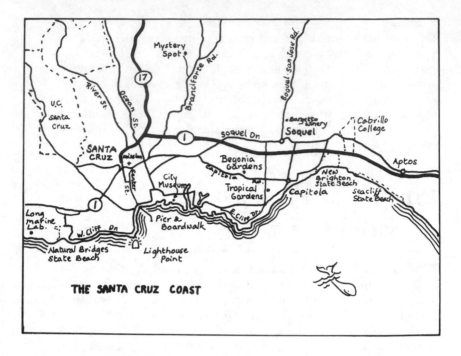

THE SANTA CRUZ COAST

was originally the Santa Cruz County Hall of Records. Octagon-shaped buildings were an architectural fad of the period.

Most of the architectural restoration has been focused on maintaining or restoring private homes constructed in the decades around the turn of the century. Loosely called Victorian, the architecture is eclectic. A free walking tour guide covering four areas is available from the Santa Cruz Convention and Visitors Bureau, at Church and Center streets in the civic auditorium, or from the city planning office across the street. Without the guide you might view a sample of houses by walking up and down residential Walnut Street and parallel streets for a few blocks from the mall. For a thorough look at historic houses, get John Chase's *The Sidewalk Companion to Santa Cruz Architecture*.

Restaurants occupy some of the restored buildings. For example, the Santa Cruz Hotel, at the corner of Cedar and Locust, is not a hotel, but an Italian-style eatery that has flourished since 1877, 408/423-1152. Try any of their lavishly portioned specialties, such as minestrone soup followed by roast beef. Upstairs is a new-style bar and grill for seafood and beef, 408/429-1000, called the Santa Cruz Bar and Grille. Consider their halibut or salmon. The two restaurants seem like new Santa Cruz building on and growing from old Santa Cruz.

Salz Leather Tannery

One Santa Cruz industry, which can be toured, ranks as a historic monument. That is the Salz Tannery, 1040 River Street, 408/423-1480, which dates from 1861, making it the oldest tannery in continuous operation in California. The peninsula was formerly a major tanning center, especially at Redwood City and San Jose as well as Santa Cruz. Tanoak in the hills was cut for the tannin in its bark, which was boiled out and used to cure hides by lengthy soaking.

Today Salz is the last of the region's leathermakers. A tour here is a nostalgic adventure, though the tanning technique has now changed. Call ahead for an appointment to make the one-hour tour, or just stop by to visit their extensive leather shop, which features all kinds of leather, leather working tools, finished leather goods, and free expert advice for the aspiring leatherworker. Booklets explain the historic and modern leather-tanning processes and the history of tanning in this region.

The major ingredients needed for tanning were all present historically in Santa Cruz: cattle hides were numerous; tannin from tanoak bark was plentiful; water to wash the hides was abundant; and a further ingredient, lime, used to clean the hides and remove the hair, was available. Today the processes have changed considerably, with chrome salts, for example, used in the tanning process.

Arts and Culture in Santa Cruz

The art, craft, and cultural life of Santa Cruz is vital and diverse, nurtured by the university audience and by the large percentage of culturally and environmentally aware people in the general populace. Bear Republic Theater is a lively group, performing at the Santa Cruz Art Center Theater, 408/472-1725. This is one of Santa Cruz's half dozen theater companies. Bear Republic puts on productions ranging from theatrical classics, such as G. B. Shaw's *Arms and the Man*, to their own fresh experimental works, such as *Signals* and *Wanderings*, with an emphasis on bringing theater to sectors of the population that would otherwise not experience it. Another half dozen theater companies also perform either here or at the university.

168

The Art Center itself, located at 1001 Center Street, is a remarkable story of true believers in a community artistic renaissance who put their sweat equity into creating a block-long combined workspace and showspace. Be sure to see this Art Center, 408/429-1609. Fabrics, jewelry, pottery, stained glass, blown glass, graphics, photography, and leatherwork are just a beginning list of the arts and crafts created and sold here by some 50 artisans.

India Joze cafe in the Art Center offers an interesting menu of Indian, Middle Eastern, and Indonesian fare, 408/427-3554. Try their gado gado, an Indonesian vegetable platter.

Typical of the zany but refreshing innovations in Santa Cruz is the annual Calamari Festival in August, instigated partly by Tom Brezsny, a partner of the India Joze cafe. At the cafe you can see postcards of calamari fashion, plus squid T-shirts. This is Santa Cruz's parallel to the Gilroy Garlic Festival. Squid also happens to be a relatively underfished sea bounty off Monterey.

Other art galleries in Santa Cruz flourish on the Pacific Garden Mall and on side streets, such as Locust, Church, and Maple. While strolling in this area, drop in at 1308 Pacific, a co-op of 25 artists and craftspeople. In 1981 a new Santa Cruz County Art Museum opened on the second floor of the public library, Church and Center streets. The museum features changing shows of major stature.

As you might suspect, Santa Cruz also has excellent bookstores. Two well-stocked stores on the mall, which carry books by local authors and volumes about the region, are Bookshop Santa Cruz and Plaza Books.

On a night out in Santa Cruz, when you want to listen to music, consider taking in The Catalyst, 1011 Pacific, 408/423-1336. The Catalyst is a cavernous, plant-filled, friendly, listening and meeting place. Some entertainers of national renown perform here. Kuumbwa Jazz, at 320 Cedar, 408/427-2227, also thrives in downtown Santa Cruz. In nearby Soquel a country music spot called O. T. Price's Music Hall, 3660 Soquel Drive, 408/476-3939, sponsors a local talent night every Wednesday. O. T. Price's is a dark, smoky, high-decibel, kick-up-your-heels establishment, where you'll see a sprinkling of cowboy hats. The monthly calendar put out by the convention and visitors bureau lists additional performances in Santa Cruz or nearby towns and colleges, with offerings from folk music to string quartets, often free.

University of California Santa Cruz Campus

T his campus, tucked among 2,000 acres of redwoods and rolling grasslands on the outskirts of town, consists of eight small colleges, each with its own architectural and thematic identity, emphasizing close relationships between the 6,000 students and 350 faculty. Seventy-five percent of all classes have 30 students or fewer. Seldom has an undergraduate university been so deliberately founded in the West, with such an optimum combination of architectural setting, academic planning, and capable student body.

The campus, which opened in 1965, starts at 1156 High Street, 408/429-0111. Self-guided tour maps are available at a kiosk a quarter mile into the grounds. Ask for the map showing you the walking trails on the university grounds. A free shuttle bus loops the grounds during the school year. The campus is interesting to visit for its architectural uniqueness and natural setting. The hills on which the university is sited also offer panoramic views of Santa Cruz and Monterey Bay.

Pause by the side of the road as you enter the grounds to note the old Cowell Ranch buildings from the limestone-mining and cattle-ranching days. These structures have been preserved rather than bulldozed, a brilliant architectural strategy, linking the present to the past. To the left, as you enter, the old Cowell horse barn now serves as the Barn Theater. Farther up the road to the left, the red cookhouse now lodges admissions. To the right, the stone foundation building that was a payhouse now quarters the student newspaper. The white frame building next to the stone structure, once a granary, is now a child-care center.

Architecture of the past, however, certainly did not influence the university buildings higher on the ridges. In fact, the eight colleges were all executed by different architects as strong individual statements rather than as a unified campus look. For example, hard-edged, white-planed, stucco Kresge College contrasts with boxy, brown-cedar–shingled, bright color–accented Oakes College. The best way to see the colleges is by parking and walking with a map.

The amphitheater, to which you must walk rather than drive, is an ingenious example of recycling. The mammoth main quarry, where limestone was dug out and processed to make lime for cement, was turned into an amphitheater of Olympian dimensions.

Of particular interest are the ambitious 17-acre Farm and four-acre Gardens, raising food and flowers. Inspired by the legendary, late Alan Chadwick and his organic gardening technique, which he called the French Intensive biodynamic method, thousands of students have participated in these projects beginning about 1970. All the produce is rich in nutriments and grown pesticide-free. Vegetables, fruit trees, and herbs, plus livestock and poultry, flourish here. You can eat some of this food at the Whole Earth Restaurant on campus, 408/426-8255. Nearby is the Bay Tree Bookstore, which displays some of the scholarly works produced by faculty.

Extensive flower gardens lie across from Stevenson College. Call 408/423-2043 for a tour. The Arboretum, on Empire Grade, has interesting collections of South African and Australian plants, plus California natives. Call 408/336-5310 for a tour.

The Santa Cruz Predatory Bird Research Group, which has a facility on the Farm, attempts to aid in the recovery of the wild population of West Coast peregrine falcons. Ten years ago the falcons were almost totally destroyed because of pesticide-induced eggshell thinning. Only two known pairs survived. The facility at Santa Cruz operates a captive breeding lab, rehabilitates injured birds, and develops wildlife-management strategies to save the falcons and California condors. For a tour call 408/429-2466.

While on campus, check out the current exhibits in the Eloise P. Smith and Sesnan art galleries, as well as in the McHenry Library. Phone ahead for art show information.

Nature Observation in Santa Cruz

Proximity to the riches of the sea, the presence of unusual phenomena such as overwintering butterflies, and an informed audience with strong environmental interests are some factors that have made Santa Cruz an important center for the observation and study of nature.

Skeleton of a blue whale, Long Marine Lab

Long Marine Laboratory

Anyone with an interest in seashore life will find that the Joseph M. Long Marine Laboratory provides welcome acquaintance with the fauna and flora of tide pools and nearby ocean currents. This marine research and instructional facility of the university sponsors intriguing exhibits of tide pools and aquaria with sea life. A hands-on tank allows you to touch creatures such as soft sea anemones and starfish. The 85-foot skeleton of a blue whale forms a prominent display. Long Marine Laboratory is next to Natural Bridges State Beach at the end of Delaware Street, 408/429-4087.

Natural Bridges State Park

Especially in autumn, Natural Bridges is a unique experience. The eucalyptus trees here are a major overwintering habitat for monarch butterflies. Some students of these insects believe this is the largest concentration of monarchs in the world. An experimental milkweed planting next to the ranger headquarters will help determine whether large numbers of monarchs would remain in the region all year if this plant, on which they lay eggs and feed, were more abundant here. A nature trail leading to the butterfly trees contains what the pamphlet describes as "islands of nature in an urban scene."

Walk to the beach to see the "bridge," or sandstone arch, that gives the park its name. Originally there were three bridges, as historical photos at the ranger headquarters attest. Around the turn of the century one of the bridges fell. During a storm in January 1980 a second bridge disintegrated. Locals now dub the area Fallen Arches.

The tide pools at Natural Bridges are rich in sea life. Guided tours of the tide pools are run by U.C. student-interns at the lowest tides. Ask the ranger for the brochure, *Natural Bridges Tide Pools*, a fine brief description of sea life.

Natural Bridges is at the far western end of West Cliff Drive, 408/423-4609. While at this end of town, if you have an entourage of children to feed, try the Upper Crust Pizza & Pasta, 2415 Mission Street, 408/423-9010. Some enthusiasts wager that this is the best pizza in Santa Cruz.

Santa Cruz City Museum

The other major nature center in Santa Cruz is the Santa Cruz City Museum, which now has a 90-foot concrete model of a gray whale on its grounds. The primary emphasis in this museum is natural history, with a relief map of Monterey Bay, exhibits on land and sea wildlife habitats, plus seasonal wildflower and fungus fairs. The museum is at 1305 East Cliff Drive, 408/429-3773.

Displays of local birds are another interesting feature at the museum. Birders also like to visit Neary Lagoon, Corcoran Lagoon, and Schwan Lake to see birds in abundance. The museum staff can assist you with directions and may suggest that you call the local Santa Cruz Bird Club to join one of their frequent outings, 408/475-9455.

Mystery Spot

This magnetic phenomenon is a circle, 150 feet in diameter, where gravity seems strangely defied. You have to walk at a slant to remain upright. You'll have to judge for yourself whether this is an actual phenomenon or a hokey put-on, but plenty of true believers can be found among bus loads of Japanese tourists, who consider this second only to the redwoods as a favorite destination in the Santa Cruz region. Mystery Spot is at 1953 Branciforte Drive in Santa Cruz, 408/423-8897.

Capitola-Soquel: Begonias, Orchids, Restaurants

Two unusual horticultural tours are available in these small towns southeast of Santa Cruz.

Begonias have been developed to a high art form at Antonelli's, 2545 Capitola Road, Capitola, 408/475-5222. The peak season for a visit is July–September. Begonias first came from Bolivia and Peru, but the efforts of generations of plant breeders have produced today's large, luscious flowers. The September Begonia Festival is Capitola's major annual celebration, complete with sand-sculpture contests at the beach and a floating parade of flower-covered boats down Soquel Creek. For information on the festival, call 408/475-6522.

The salubrious climate of Capitola makes the Shaffer Tropical Gardens a success. Orchids grown here have a worldwide reputation. Fuchsias and cymbidiums are also sold. These gardens are at 1220 41st Street, Capitola, 408/475-3100. In April you can see 75,000 orchids ready for national Mother's Day sales.

While in this area, try the elegant Shadowbrook Restaurant for lunch or dinner. Shadowbrook is in Capitola at Wharf and Capitola roads, 408/475-1511. Situated above Soquel Creek, the restaurant lies at the base of 3.5 hillside acres of fuchsias, ivy, and oak trees. A small funicular railway takes you down the steep hill to the restaurant, where several new rooms, such as the Garden Room and Greenhouse Room, have been added to the original 1920s' Swiss chalet-style structure of heavy beams with massive stone fireplaces. Prime rib is a specialty, along with steaks and seafood, plus the regional vegetable in season, which may be asparagus in June or broccoli in October. The restaurant also makes its own desserts, such as chocolate torte, and features wines of some small Santa Cruz vintners, such as Cabernet from Ken Burnap's Santa Cruz Mountains Winery.

Another unique dining and browsing experience is Greenhouse Restaurant at The Farm, 5555 Soquel Drive in Soquel, 408/476-5613. There you dine in a lovely garden greenhouse or in the Victorian front room of a real farmhouse on a working farm. Omelets, quiches, fresh fish, and homemade soups are offered on the menu. You can purchase produce and nursery plants from The Farm or antiques at an adjacent store.

Capitola today is a lively, artsy little beach town, with plenty of sand and crashing waves. The walk along the beach is called the Esplanade. Stop in at The Bandstand Restaurant to see photos of the old Capitola Hotel, built in 1895, burned in 1929. Resort activity flourished throughout this area in the 19th century, and most of the early homes were summer cottages. Two good examples of early board–and–batten cottages with carpenter gothic touches are at 106 and 108 Central. The grand houses of this town are along Grand Avenue and Prospect Drive.

Capitola Museum, just north of the railroad trestle along Capitola Avenue, has interesting artifacts from the town's early days, such as a picture window–sized painting of the town in 1884, plus plenty of information for the traveler.

Capitola's wharf is a pleasant place to walk. Some of the fortunate anglers here catch respectable-sized flounder, perch, and halibut. Built in 1857, the wharf was originally known as Soquel Landing and allowed the Pacific Steamship Company to load goods for the run up to San Francisco. Redwood and fir lumber, plus wheat and produce, were the main products shipped. The wharf later served the fishing industry. Today it is mainly a recreational wharf, recently refurbished and reopened in 1982. It was closed for repairs after a devastating storm in 1978 damaged it badly. Fishing, boat launching, a chowder bar, bait and tackle shop, public restrooms, and boat rentals are available at the wharf.

The Would–Be Capital

The name Capitola originated when a group of Soquel area landowners offered land to the state, hoping that the state capital would be founded here. The offer had little practical possibility, but the name Capitola stuck. Usage of the area as a summer resort was more plausible. Frederic A. Hihn, a wealthy lumber producer and real estate developer, raised the tent-city, camping status of the area, reflected in the name Camp Capitola, to a sumptuous resort with a 150-room hotel, called the Capitola Hotel.

One interesting part of the Capitola story occurred in 1895. Developer Hihn leased space at the end of the wharf to the Gerlach Wave Motor Company, which proceeded to lengthen and widen the wharf and construct a wave-powered electric generator. A *Sentinel* newspaper reporter mused, "There is certainly lots of water, and if the power expressed in the rise and fall of the tide can get into the wire, one of the great forces of the sea will be in harness." Citizens from Santa Cruz to Watsonville watched with anticipation as the motor was constructed through the winter and spring of 1896. The *Sentinel* reporter later that year noted with regret, "The Gerlach Wave Motor at Capitola does not allow itself to be disturbed by the waves."

A sturdy 1890s' commercial structure still stands in Capitola. At 201 Monterey Avenue, you'll find a plaque that reads:

> Camp Capitola's Superintendent's Office. California's first seaside resort community was established here in 1869 by Mr. F. A. Hihn. The grand opening was held on July 4, 1874, for the 15 acre resort, located in the present village and depot hill area. The superintendent's office, built from local redwood in the 1880s, served as the headquarters of Camp Capitola until 1930.

Bargetto Winery

The Bargetto Winery has an outdoor tasting room at 3535-A Main in Soquel, 408/475-2258.

This main winery in the Santa Cruz region was founded in 1933 by brothers Philip and John Bargetto. Philip migrated from Italy in 1887 with his father Giuseppe, a wine producer near Asti in the Piedmont region. Philip worked first for the Demas Winery in Mountain View. John migrated to the U.S. in 1909 and engaged in the produce business. At the repeal of Prohibition in 1933, the brothers were poised to enter the wine business. Today the winery is run by John's oldest son, Lawrence, and by Lawrence Bargetto's sons and nephews.

Though the winery has some acreage of grapes in the Santa Cruz area, they mainly purchase grapes from other regions, especially Santa Barbara County. Bargetto makes Chardonnay and Riesling in the whites, as well as a Chenin Blanc. Their reds include a Cabernet, Zinfandel, and a traditional Italian Barbera.

Santa Cruz Festivals

A year-round calendar of festivals greets natives and visitors in the Santa Cruz area. Nowhere on the peninsula is there a region with such a cohesive regional identity and such an ambitious schedule of festivals. The central information source is the Santa Cruz Convention and Visitors Bureau, 408/423-6927, which puts out a monthly calendar.

Some of the celebrations are the Film Festival in January; Kite Flying Contest in Capitola in March; Santa Cruz Art League show in March; Spring Fair on the banks of the San Lorenzo River in

176

Santa Cruz in May; University Open House in mid-May; Watsonville Antique Fly-in for vintage planes in May; Miss California Pageant in June; Santa Cruz Harbor Festival in June; Swanton Corn Roast in June; Portuguese Festival in June; various July 4th Independence Festivals in different cities; July Arts Fair in Felton; World Flying Disc (Frisbee) Championship in August; Cabrillo College's prestigious annual Music Festival in August; County Fair in September at Watsonville; Capitola's Begonia Festival in September; Santa Cruz Mission Day Fiesta in October; and the virtually universal open house among artists and craftspeople in the first two weeks of December.

Coastal Beaches

I n Santa Cruz County you can camp in the redwoods at Henry Cowell and Big Basin state parks or on the state beaches at New Brighton, Seacliff, or Sunset, making a wide range of camping experiences possible. For day use, the county has 29 miles of public access beaches.

New Brighton State Beach is near Capitola, four miles below

Sand people at New Brighton Beach

Santa Cruz. Attractive New Brighton has 115 campsites, some located right on the cliffs above the beach, and is open all year. Seacliff State Beach, farther south, has 26 full-service trailer hookups for RVs, recently rebuilt after storm damage, and 100 regular campsites. A pier leads out to a World War II, cement-hull ship. Sunset State Beach, a sand–dune beach four miles west of Watsonville off Coast Highway 1, has 90 developed campsites. Sunset is also open all year.

All these beaches are excellent for the full range of beach pleasures, such as sunning, walking, swimming, fishing, frisbee throwing, and picnics. The vegetation tends to be Monterey pine or eucalyptus on the bluffs, with some lovely Indian paintbrush and sticky monkey bush wildflowers on the hillsides, plus enough poison oak in some areas to be wary. These parks also offer the luxury of hot showers, rare among state park camps. Reservations are crucial for summer camping and can be made through Ticketron or direct by writing to California Department of Parks and Recreation, P.O. Box 2390, Sacramento 95811.

Manresa State Beach, north of Sunset Beach, is another attractive ocean setting, open for day use but not overnight stays. This is a good beach for a walk, picnic, or sunning.

Mission Santa Clara de Asis

Mission Santa Clara's Legacy 10

From Cattle to Quicksilver

Shortly after George Washington crossed the Delaware to do battle with the British in 1777, Padre Thomas de la Pena was planting a wooden cross on the banks of the Guadalupe River to establish Mission Santa Clara de Asis, honoring St. Clare of Assisi, the first Franciscan nun. Settlement of the fertile Santa Clara Valley began with the founding of the mission and the pueblo of San Jose.

Today you can get a sense of the mission by visiting the University of Santa Clara to see its replica of one of the later mission churches. Aside from scattered historic monuments in Santa Clara and San Jose, the best place to get a feel for the development of San Jose, especially as the 19th century progressed, is first in the downtown area at the Peralta Adobe, recording the Spanish–Mexican era, and at Pellier Historic Park, celebrating the development of fruit agriculture, especially the prune orchards. Then proceed to the San Jose Historical Museum, 16 acres of Kelley Park.

Finally, the prominence of an unusual metal, mercury, also called quicksilver, in the development of the region can't be overemphasized. You can visit the mercury mining area by driving south from San Jose to the remarkable New Almaden Museum, the New Almaden County Park, and the former mine manager's home, Casa Grande.

Mission Santa Clara de Asis

Threatment his mission was founded in 1777 as the eighth in the Franciscan chain. It is located on the campus of the present University of Santa Clara, off The Alameda in Santa Clara, 408/984-4545.

Based on the Franciscan padres' own measure of success, Santa Clara exceeded every other mission in California. That criterion was, of course, the number of heathens baptized into Christianity, and 8,536 Indians passed through these rites at Santa Clara between 1777 and 1832. In 1800 it was recorded there were 1,228 Indians associated with Mission Santa Clara. This was one of the largest concentrations of Indians in a mission at the time. Every Saturday 12 cattle were butchered for their food. Santa Clara also ranked fourth in total livestock among the missions in 1832.

The viceroy of Mexico envisioned Santa Clara as a perimeter supply post and fortification for Mission Dolores and Yerba Buena, the early name for the city of San Francisco. Santa Clara was to be the food producing unit that would help sustain the regional Spanish presence. In this task the mission succeeded, assisted by the fertility of the soil, cooperation of the Indians, and able leadership of gifted executives in the Franciscan order. The mission artisans were also well known, especially for their weaving.

On the campus today you see a 1929 replica of the fifth mission church, from 1825. Floods, earthquakes, fires, and inappropriate siting choices damaged the four earlier, smaller churches. Fragments of the original mission cross are preserved under glass in the current cross in front of the church. An adobe wall from the 1822 mission period remains, along with an adobe structure that now serves as the faculty club. These adobe structures are the oldest buildings on a college campus in the western United States. Behind the adobe wall are olive trees also from the 1820s. This peaceful, floriferous, enclosed area approximates for the visitor the calm, orderly garden compound of the early mission, with the pealing bells marking out the routine of the day. Bells from as early as 1798 still hang in the tower.

As you turn into the college and mission grounds a guard will give you a temporary sticker to make close-in parking easy. Ask also for a map of the mission grounds and campus. After you park, visit the church, the rose gardens to one side and the wisteria and banksia rose-covered arborway on the other side, where the adobe wall is also located. The grounds are well maintained, and the flowering purple wisteria and yellow banksia roses reach their peak in May, an ideal time to visit.

The paintings of Santa Clara Mission were much praised in the 19th century. Agustin Davila, a gifted professional painter from Mexico, was brought north to teach the Indians painting and to oversee painting the facade and ceiling of the 1825 church. The 1929 replica, built after a devastating fire leveled the earlier structure, repeats Davila's facade design, but in concrete rather than in paint. The interior of the church still includes a reredos and an early crucifix, plus a duplication of the Davila ceiling paintings. A plaque outside the church points out that this was the first California mission to honor a woman, something of particular interest in this era of the women's movement.

After Secularization, the church and grounds were eventually given to the Jesuits, who founded a college that became the University of Santa Clara.

One of the amenities fostered by the mission was a string of black willows planted on either side of The Alameda between the pueblo of San Jose and the mission. These trees, no longer standing, protected pedestrians from marauding, wild cattle. The padres also hoped that such an inviting, clearly marked road would guide the faithful to frequent worship. As the trees grew they provided welcome shade from the merciless sun of summer.

Mission Santa Clara's history includes the stories of several characters and eccentrics among its padres. One was Magin de Catala, who became known as "the Prophet." It is said that he correctly predicted the arrival of Americans, discovery of gold, loss of California by Spain, and destruction of San Francisco by the Earthquake of 1906. Another was Jose Viader, a priest who might have heard another calling as a wrestler. In 1814 the muscular Viader was attacked by an Indian brute named Marcelo, who had violence in his heart. Viader thrashed Marcelo and two accompanying henchmen. Chastized completely, Marcelo thereafter became one of the mission's faithful supporters.

DeSaisset Museum

The DeSaisset Museum on the University of Santa Clara campus contains artifacts and photos that tell part of the story of the restoration and generally describe the mission. Among the Indian, mission, and university memorabilia is a large photo of Chief Ynigo, 1760–1864, chief of a tribe that once lived near the present

Moffett Field. The museum also hosts changing art shows and displays works from its collection of historic and contemporary art. For current exhibits, call 408/984-4528.

University of Santa Clara

T he university was founded in 1851 by Rev. John Nobili, S.J., with $150 and 12 students. First classes were held in an abandoned adobe from the mission or in an adjoining grape arbor. Meals consisted of meat, soup, and vegetables, all cooked in one large iron pot.

The University of Santa Clara is the oldest institution of higher learning in California. But the school has extremely modern as well as historical architectural interest. Visit the Thomas E. Leavey Activities Center, a fabric roof–covered structure built in 1975. This is the largest air-supported fabric roof in the West. The same builder, New York engineer David Geiger, has covered the Bullock store in San Jose with this material. The largest such covering is the Silverdome in Pontiac, Michigan, which encloses 10 acres.

The Leavey Center consists of 65,000 square feet of Teflon-coated fiberglass kept inflated by four large fans that maintain a slight pressure of five pounds per square foot. Thick cables on the roof prevent the cover from blowing off. Revolving doors keep the structure air-pressure tight. Translucence of the fabric roof reduces the need for lighting the basketball courts and other athletic areas. A greenhouse effect created by the covering minimizes the requirements for additional heating, creating in fact an environment suitable for tropical plants that flourish at one end of the building. Energy savings in operation and the original savings in construction costs make this style of architecture most attractive.

The complex covered by the fabric roof includes a 5,000 seat basketball arena, handball and squash courts, two small volleyball and basketball courts, and locker rooms.

Earlier Mission Sites

 fter visiting the mission and campus, make a short drive to see an early adobe and the markers noting the first mission sites.

Near the university stands one of the oldest adobes in the Santa

Clara Valley. A marker at 3260 The Alameda, near Benton, tells the history of the building:

> Santa Clara Women's Club Adobe. This adobe, among the oldest in Santa Clara Valley, was one of several continuous rows of homes built in 1792–1800 as dwellings for Indian families of Mission Santa Clara. It links the Franciscan padre's labors with California of today.

The adobe itself is closed, but you can enter the grounds through the front gate to look at the gardens, which include a wisteria-covered pergola made from timbers salvaged after the original mission burned.

The first site of the Santa Clara Mission is near Central Expressway and De la Cruz Boulevard, where a marker mounted on steel poles next to the airport property tells the story:

> Mission Santa Clara de Thamien. The first mission in this valley, Mission Santa Clara de Thamien, was established at this site by Franciscan Padres Thomas de la Pena and Joseph Antonio Murguia, January 12, 1777. Here, at the Indian village of So-co-is-u-ka, they erected a cross and shelter for worship to bring Christianity to the Costanoan Indians.

However, the site experienced repeated flooding, so a second and finally a third site were chosen. A cross marking the second site can be found in a small garden, complete with wisteria and olive trees, at the corner of Martin Street and De la Cruz Boulevard.

Exploring the City of Santa Clara

Your best source of information when exploring this area is the Santa Clara Chamber of Commerce, Convention and Visitors Bureau, 1515 El Camino Real in Santa Clara, 408/296-6863.

Adjacent to this office, next to fountains and landscaped grounds at El Camino Real and Lincoln Street, stands a statue of Saint Clare, namesake of the city. The sculpture is by Ann Van Kleeck.

Next to the sculpture is an interesting historical marker. Santa Clara and San Jose vie with each other as cities with the densest number of historic sites in the peninsula region, and well they should. Santa Clara was the site of the mission and San Jose was the site of the pueblo, which was the first city in California. This

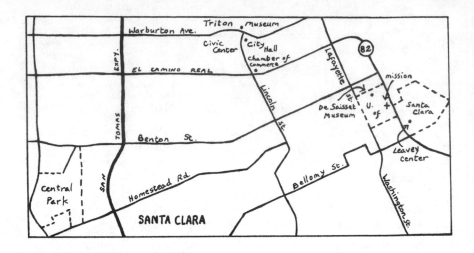

particular marker honors one of the more unusual incidents of the transition period from Mexican to American rule, the Battle of the Mustard Stalks.

Perhaps the most bizarre battle in California history was this so-called Battle of the Mustard Stalks in 1847. Tensions ran high in those years of 1846 and 1847 as an increasing flood of Americans entered California. Who would control the territory, eventually? The Battle of the Mustard Stalks was one expression of that tension. Historian Dorothy Regnery, in her excellent *The Battle of Santa Clara*, has tried to sift legend from fact in reconstructing the event.

This incident occurred on January 2, 1847, when 101 Americans faced about 250 native Mexican Californios. The Americans fortified the mission and blocked the road with trees from The Alameda. A small cannon was also brought into play, which fired one six-pound shot. The skirmishes took place in fields of head-high mustard with combatants at a fairly safe distance from each other. No one was killed or injured before the posturing was considered sufficient. The Americans agreed not to commit further depredations against Mexican life and property. The Mexicans submitted, tensions were somewhat released, and California plunged toward inevitable control by the United States, especially after the gold discovery in 1848 brought teeming numbers of Americans to California.

The marker recalls these events, as follows:

Santa Clara Campaign Treaty Site. After armed confrontation nearby on January 2, 1847, and a truce meeting the following day, Marine

Capt. Ward Marston, Commander of the U.S. Expeditionary Force, and Francisco Sanchez, leader of Mexican-Californian Ranchers, agreed to a treaty here on January 7. United States forces were to recognize rights of Californians and to end seizure of their personal property.

While exploring in this area, Central Park, 909 Kiely Boulevard, is a good place to picnic and relax. This park houses the International Swim Center, where several Olympic champions from the region have trained.

Triton Museum

Near the historical marker lies another testimony to the early life of this valley, the canvases of artist Theodore Wores depicting wildflower scenes and fruit orchards. Wores' paintings are a major resource of the Triton Museum at 1505 Warburton Avenue, 408/248-4585.

The Triton Museum also offers changing exhibits of folk art, contemporary paintings, and classic fine art. Be sure to see on the museum grounds the Jamison-Brown House, a well-preserved Victorian-era structure noted especially for the wood craftsmanship of its floors.

Seven acres of landscaped gardens at the Triton Museum feature an eclectic sculpture collection, with several sculptures of Sascha Schnittmann, most notably a reclining female figure called *Espoir* and a horse called the *Morgan Horse*. Further cultural offerings include theater performances, plus a juried spring show in varying media and an autumn ethnic art show.

Historic San Jose

I n November 1777, sixty-six soldiers, settlers, and family members were chosen from the Presidios at San Francisco and Monterey to found a new pueblo, San Jose de Guadalupe, at the south end of San Francisco Bay.

This pueblo was one of only three secular entities that would be founded in California during the Spanish era. The others were Los Angeles in 1781 and Branciforte, now part of Santa Cruz, in 1797. The rationale for pueblos was to boost food production that could sustain the presidios and missions, institutions with which the Spanish had much experience in settling new territories.

San Jose grew slowly. By 1841 the population had risen from

the original 66 to only about 300. Travelers commented that it was a small village with a few adobes and *palisada*, or tamped earth, houses. Life in San Jose was simple and primitive, yet the climate was attractive and retiring soldiers favored it for their homes. San Jose was a key point at the end of the immigrant trek from Sutter's Fort around the south end of San Francisco Bay, after the immigrants had crossed the Sierra Nevada. The Santa Clara Valley was often called the Valley of San Jose in those days. Later it received the affectionate name Valley of Heart's Delight because of the beauty of the fruit tree blossoms.

The San Jose Convention and Visitors Bureau, at El Paseo de San Antonio pedestrian mall and Market Street, 408/998-7000, between San Fernando and San Carlos streets, is a good information source for exploring San Jose. They can give you walking tour maps of the downtown and a "Country Crossroads" map useful for exploring rural Santa Clara and Santa Cruz counties. Park your car and walk in the compact downtown area.

Peralta Adobe

At 184 W. St. John Street, across Market Street from the convention and visitors bureau and a short walk north, you'll see the Peralta Adobe. The marker reads:

> The Luis Maria Peralta adobe. The last vestige of El Pueblo de San Jose de Guadalupe. This simple adobe was rehabilitated in the mid-19th century. It is believed to have been built before 1800 by Manuel Gonzalez, an Apache, who was one of the Pueblo Pobladores founders. It was later owned and occupied by Sgt. Peralta, pueblo Comisionado from 1807 to 1822, who also came to California with the Anza expedition in 1775–76.

When you enter the grounds, you'll see the adobe itself, whose empty interior can be viewed through barred windows. Other exhibits include a scale model of the original adobe complex and a detailed map of all early San Jose's adobes.

Luis Maria Peralta and his wife, Maria Loreto Alviso, populated the countryside with 17 children, a not uncommon number for the Californio families. As a reward for military service, Peralta was given one of the largest and most valuable Spanish land grants, Rancho San Antonio, 44,000 acres. When he died in 1851, Peralta's net worth exceeded a million uninflated dollars.

In the twilight of the adobe era, excitement ran high as the Mexican War with the United States broke out, in 1846. San Jose

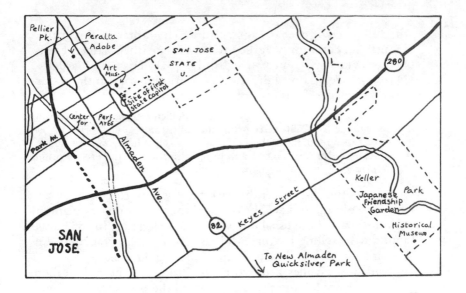

then had a public house and three or four small stores. Captain Thomas Fallon, whose later wooden house stands opposite the Peralta adobe, rode into town with his group of California Volunteers, captured the jail, and hoisted the American flag.

In the early years of the American period, San Jose enjoyed prominence as the first state capital. The presence of this original California legislative body, dubbed The Legislature of a Thousand Drinks, caused wild land speculation, but the capital was soon moved to Sacramento. A marker on the 100 block of Market, in City Plaza Park opposite the convention and visitors bureau, tells the story:

> Directly opposite this tablet was located the first State Capitol Building in which California's first Legislature assembled in December 1849. San Jose was the seat of government from 1849 to 1851.

Pellier Historical Park

The most sustained blood of economic life in this valley, before the recent electronics boom, was fruit agriculture, especially prunes. Pellier Historical Park, at Terraine and West St. James streets in San Jose, recognizes this contribution with plantings of prunes, pears, and other orchard crops, plus grapes, dedicated to individual pioneering agricultural families. The park is only a block from the Peralta Adobe.

This is the best place in the Santa Clara Valley to comprehend the full force of orchard agriculture. The father of this fruit industry is commonly agreed to be a Frenchman named Louis Pellier, whose portrait you see at this park. His City Gardens Nursery once occupied the site. A historical marker at the entrance to this small park tells his story:

> Site of City Gardens Nursery of Louis Pellier. Pellier, native of France, and founder of California's prune industry, came to California in 1849. In October 1850, he established a nursery called City Gardens. Here, aided by his brothers Pierre and Jean, he introduced the French prune, *Le Petit d'Argen*, during the winter of 1856–57.

Interpretive displays at the park convey with clarity the story of this agricultural drama. The demand for fruit was strong among gold miners, whose usual diet was meat and grains. In 1853 dried apples were selling for three dollars apiece in San Francisco. An orchard was a surer way to fortune than a gold mine.

Santa Clara Valley had two main virtues, climate and location. Until 1868 apples and pears dominated the orchard crops, but prunes then boomed. Up to 1870 this valley also led all other regions of California in wine production. The transcontinental railroad, completed in 1869, opened up new markets for all types of fruit production.

Prunes were cultivated between the first of March and mid-April. Harvesting began in mid-August. As part of the drying process, the prunes were dipped in boiling lye water, which checked the prune skin, hastened drying, and prevented fermentation. The prunes were then dipped in clear water and placed on trays to sun dry, or "cure," for 10 days. There were more than 50 canneries and packinghouses for prunes, which were the most easily preserved of all fruits.

At the peak of prune production, in 1929, there were over 267.7 square miles of prune orchards. The 1940s' population boom began the long, continuing destruction of orchards as subdivisions claimed the acreage.

Downtown San Jose

Today San Jose is California's fourth largest city, ranking after Los Angeles, San Diego, and San Francisco, and the 17th largest city in the country. The near coincidence of 1976 national and 1977 city bicentennials gave residents much to celebrate in recent years. At Bicentennial Plaza, Almaden

Boulevard and San Carlos Street, time capsules were buried, to be opened in 2000 and 2077. Citizens could include their comments for one dollar per page.

Much of modern downtown San Jose is now devoted to tall banking buildings with handsome landscaping, but there are three entities of interest to the general public.

The Romanesque-style post office building at 110 Market has become the San Jose Art Museum, 408/294-2787. Though much of earlier downtown San Jose has disappeared before the forces of modernization, this handsome old post office was saved. A marker at the site notes:

> United States Post Office. Constructed in 1892, this was the first federal building in San Jose. It served as U.S. Post Office from 1892 to 1923. Designed by Willoughby Edbrooke and constructed of locally quarried sandstone, this Romanesque style structure is the last of its kind on the West Coast.

If the building seems to you constructed of stone similar to that used for Stanford University's quadrangle buildings, your hunch is correct. The same quarry provided rock for both constructions. The museum features changing shows in most of its galleries and rotating materials from its permanent collection in one upstairs gallery. A gift shop exhibits crafts and a judicious selection of books about the region.

As a counterpoint to the Romanesque post office-art museum, walk past a host of banks to the corner of Almaden Boulevard and Park Avenue to see the San Jose Center for the Performing Arts. In front you'll find a characteristic marble Benny Bufano sculpture called *California Bear*. The center started shakily in 1972 with a roof cave-in, but has recovered to become a new focus of vitality in the downtown area.

Some interesting restaurants in downtown San Jose are clustered on two blocks of North San Pedro Street called San Pedro Square. Try the baby pork ribs at the Laundry Works, located in an old bakery and laundry at 87 San Pedro, 408/287-1447. Holding up the structure are huge beams, some 24 by 24 inches, museum pieces in themselves. The Old Spaghetti Factory at 51 San Pedro, 408/288-7488, has a decor of comfortable furniture and serves tasty pasta with clam and mizithra cheese sauce. At the Pacific Fish Company, 177 West Santa Clara, 408/298-7222, consider the trout or salmon.

The major annual festival in downtown San Jose occurs over the July Fourth weekend and is called the Great American Arts

Benny Bufano sculpture at the Performing Arts Center, San Jose

Festival. Food, arts and crafts, and live entertainers are featured in this two-day, multicultural event. With San Jose's rich ethnic mix, several other festivals can be enjoyed, such as Japanese Obon in July, Mexican Cinco de Mayo in May, and Italian Columbus Day in October. Call the convention and visitor bureau for details, 408/998-7000.

San Jose Historical Museum

Kelley Park, 150 acres of greenery two miles from downtown San Jose, includes the San Jose Historical Museum, which offers good access to the late-19th-century history of the region. The adjacent Japanese Friendship Garden is a setting for a tranquil walk. The museum and gardens are at 635 Phelan Street off Senter Road.

The San Jose Historical Museum is a 16-acre, open-air park at which 11 buildings reflecting the region's history, especially from the late 19th and early 20th centuries, have been gathered or re-created. The park has only existed since 1972, and backers hope that it will eventually house some 50 Santa Clara Valley historic structures, so membership is encouraged.

You enter through an old water tank, typical of those that supplied water and pressure at almost every farm and house in the early days of San Jose.

Start at the Pacific Hotel, the heart and headquarters of the museum, 408/287-2290. This structure reproduces the original hotel that stood at 74–80 South Market Street in the late 19th century. From here tours begin periodically to acquaint you with the other buildings. In the Pacific Hotel there are interesting displays on periods in Santa Clara Valley history, beginning with the Costanoan Indians, who lived from hunting, fishing, and acorn gathering. Here you can see an acorn granary used to store these fruits of the oak trees through the winter season.

The Mission/Pioneer-era displays show the land grants to specific Spanish families. Cattle were the main product until 1880, when fruit orchards began to dominate. Grain farming also flourished briefly, with wheat production peaking in 1874 and then rapidly declining. Frank Norris's novel, *The Octopus*, recounts this brief wheat boom. The orchard era was bound to be more enduring because of the combination of mild winters, brilliant spring and summer sunshine free of rain, and suitable soil for fruit crops.

A special exhibit features the famous San Jose man to whom we all owe a debt, Andrew Putnam Hill, painter and photographer, who started the Sempervirens Club and lobbied to save the Big Basin redwoods from logging. One of Hill's interesting paintings here shows The Alameda, the black willow-lined street that led off from the Santa Clara Mission.

Other exhibits at the Pacific Hotel include coverage of the New Almaden Quicksilver Mine, complete with a piece of red cinnabar rock, the mercury ore, and an example of the steep wooden steps up which laborers carried 200-pound baskets of the ore, mined deep in the ground.

The early bicycling era in San Jose is portrayed with several nostalgic examples of high wheelers. Also on the ground floor of the Pacific Hotel you see 19th century fashions.

Upstairs is the book collection, plus the written and photographic archival holdings of the San Jose Historical Museum. Call ahead to make an appointment, 408/287-2290, if you want to peruse this collection for some special interest.

From the Pacific Hotel you can make a self-guided tour or take a guided walk. Next door is the O'Brien's Candy Store, said to have been one of the best in the West in its day.

On the corner stands a replica of the humble beginnings of the Bank of America, first called the Bank of Italy when founded by A. P. Giannini, a native San Josean. The building reproduces the first out-of-town branch of the Bank of Italy.

Near the Bank of Italy stands a unique tour de force of city lighting, a re-creation of San Jose's unusual Electric Tower, built in 1888 of tubular wrought iron for $3,500. The original tower stood 237 feet above the intersection of Market and Santa Clara streets, until a windstorm blew it down in 1915. This re-creation is only half as large as the original, but still completely dominates the skyline. You can see one of the six original 4,000-candlepower arc lamps in the Pacific Hotel.

The Print Shop, formerly a residence built in 1884, offers a good selection of historical books and pamphlets on the Santa Clara Valley region. Look at the encyclopedic *San Jose: California's First City* by Don DeMers and Edwin Beilharz. Historic photos are reproduced and sold as postcards.

Nearby is a 1927 gas station from a time when America's romance with the automobile was totally euphoric and motor clubs were springing up everywhere as touring became the fad. This Associated Products gas station shows the fuel, oil, and tools of the day, complete with photos of the adventuresome going on their excursions. With the auto came a demand for better roads, and with the roads came a further commitment to the automobile. Today, when pollution, energy costs, and land use are major concerns, it's nostalgic to look back at the innocent first decade of this century, when the auto was pure fun.

The Thomas E. Gallup Dental Offices building shows something of the medical and dental practices of the valley in the 19th century. This office originally stood on Benton Street in Santa Clara. It was opened in the 1870s by Dr. Henry Hume Warburton and used continuously by medical providers until the 1950s.

The Dashaway Livery Stables reconstruct the trades of horseshoeing, blacksmithing, and harness making so essential to the era when horse, wagon, and stage were the main means of transportation.

All considered, the open-air museum is a worthy collection. Some of the buildings are reconstructions rather than originals, but without them San Jose would have few approximations of its early days.

Japanese Friendship Park

On lawns and tables outside the historical museum you can picnic or take a miniature train ride to a children's petting zoo and small amusement area called Happy Hollow.

But the main pleasure adjacent to the San Jose Historical Museum is the Japanese Friendship Garden, six acres of meditative, highly sculpted landscape with granite boulders, pools of Japanese carp (*koi*), laughing waterfalls, stone bridges, and carefully manicured bonsai plants. The koi are particularly beautiful, a rainbow moving through the water. A teahouse opens when visitors are numerous. The park is exceptionally well cared for, an encouraging experience in the post–Proposition 13 world of minimal park maintenance. If you want to be carried off in a tranquil, meditative state, commune with the surroundings at this Japanese Friendship Garden.

A block away, near South Tenth Street and Phelan Avenue, you can see another type of garden, the Mi Terra community food gardens, where skilled practitioners of the vegetable-raising arts grow food all year-round in this benign climate. This community garden invites an outsider to come and take a look around. As the name suggests, the roots of this garden are deep in the Mexican community of San Jose.

New Almaden Quicksilver Mine

F ew institutions in the San Jose region were more important to California and the nation than the New Almaden Quicksilver Mine, 11 miles south of San Jose on Almaden Road (G8). A marker near the mine reduction site on the right side of the road reads:

> New Almaden Mine. The Indians used pigment from this cinnabar hill for paint. Mercury was mined as early as 1845. The gold discovery made mercury indispensable, and the mine, the most productive in America, became world famous. It sold for $1,700,700 in 1864.

California's first mining dramas concerned quicksilver, or mercury, rather than gold. Before gold was discovered at Sutter's Mill on the American River, men were digging out cinnabar in these hills. In fact, this was occurring even while California was part of Mexico.

The mercury mines at New Almaden were not only the first,

Casa Grande, home of the mine manager, at the New Almaden quicksilver mines

but also the richest mines in California. Between 1845 and 1975 about 70 million uninflated dollars' worth of mercury were mined.

Political implications of this mine were also decisive, in two ways.

First, the presence of mercury in this new-world location ensured domestic control over California gold mining when substantial deep rock mining of gold in quartz-bearing veins occurred. The 49ers soon picked up all the gold nuggets in sight in Sierra Nevada streams, but the later discoveries of gold in quartz rock required that the rock be crushed, then mixed with mercury, which adhered to the gold but not to common ferrous metals. From this amalgam gold could be recovered by vaporizing the mercury, which was condensed again for reuse. No other technology was available for this procedure. The other major known source of mercury was the Almaden Mine in Spain, controlled by the Rothschilds of England. These foreign interests would have played a substantial role in controlling California and Nevada mining if mercury had not been discovered near San Jose.

Second, the New Almaden Mine was crucial in California's decision to side with the Union rather than the Confederacy in the Civil War. Title to New Almaden was shaky because, aside from the expected quarreling inspired by greed, the original mining claims failed to acknowledge that the lands had been deeded to another party earlier. After substantial investment had been made in the mine, this fact came to light. New York financiers who had an interest in the outcome asked President Abraham Lincoln to step in and invalidate the claim. All mining claims in California would have been shaky had such a decree been made, and California might well then have sided with the Confederacy. Lincoln wisely stayed out of the fray, and California remained with the Union.

The New Almaden story began when Andreas Castillero, a Mexican military captain with a knowledge of chemistry and geology, had Indians from Mission Santa Clara lead him to the cave from which they took red ore for ceremonial body painting. Castillero perceived in 1845 that the ore was indeed cinnabar, filed a claim, and began working the mine. Cinnabar must be crushed and roasted to release the mercury vapors, which can then be condensed. Castillero sold out to the Barron Forbes Co., which invested more capital in the operation. Under Forbes the New Almaden operation pushed forward, with the building of a Casa

Grande, still standing, as quarters for the mine manager. An Englishtown and Spanishtown were established for the miners. Litigation began when Forbes learned that Castillero had filed on land that had already been granted. In the end Forbes was forced to sell to the Quicksilver Mining Company, which operated the mines until the company went bankrupt in 1912.

New Almaden Today

Today there are two ways you can relive this historic time. Visit the outstanding New Almaden Mining Museum and walk the recently opened Almaden Quicksilver County Park, site of the mines.

The New Almaden Mining Museum at 21570 Almaden Road, 408/268-7869, is a notable private effort to sustain the historical story. The museum is half a mile down the road from the historic Casa Grande building, once the sumptuous quarters of the mine manager, now lifeless except for Opry House satirical entertainment on Friday and Saturday nights. The Barbary Coast Players put on these antics, 408/268-2492.

Constance Perham, an energetic appreciator of history, conceived of the New Almaden Museum at the age of 18, in 1926, and has been working to develop it since then. She personally leads tours, telling the story of mercury mining in its larger context of world history. The tour and artifacts in the museum are full of fascinating detail on the miners, including Mexican, Chinese, and Cornwall men. You see stamp mills used to crush the cinnabar, whaling try pots first used as primitive retorts, and the 76-pound flasks in which dense mercury was stored. Mercury's use through the ages is discussed, from the Romans, who combined mercury and sulphur to make a durable ink for their important documents, to the modern electronics manufacturer, who uses mercury in switches and lamps.

Constance Perham has also been a lifelong collector of California artifacts and has excellent displays on California Indians and such crucial earlier trades as blacksmithing.

The gift shop sells books, pieces of cinnabar, and fascinating artifacts from the early mining era, such as old canceled checks from the mining company in the 1860s.

The Almaden Quicksilver County Park lies above a maze of tunnels where workers went down to 2,400-foot depths to get the cinnabar ore. Most of the shafts have now been plugged up for safety reasons, keeping people out of the 110 miles of underground passages carved while mercury mining flourished, 1845–1975.

Since the Santa Clara County parks system bought the mine property, several miles of hiking and horseback riding trails have been built. You can walk past some of the closed shafts and see red tailing dumps, but the compact area of the major mining activity is closed off as dangerous. In future years there will be ambitious historical and nature interpretation at the park.

The most accessible entrance to the park, including picnic grounds, is off Mockingbird Hill Lane in a terrain of oak trees and grasslands. Equestrians share the trails with walkers. Get a map of the trails at the New Almaden Mining Museum.

Silicon Valley architecture, the Digital corporate headquarters

Silicon Valley

11

*Computers and
Other Attractions*

S ilicon Valley, so named because of the silicon wafers used
as chips in printed circuit boards in modern electronics,
spreads prosperously over the floor of the Santa Clara
Valley with spillover to such outlying regions as Gilroy. This is
Electronicsland USA, and it booms even when the rest of the
economy sags or the Japanese stand poised to swoop in with
competing products. Numerous Horatio Alger stories of American
entrepreneurship occur here as bright and hard-working people,
believing they have a better idea on the frontier of electronics,
leave the big company, start out modestly in their own garages,
and sell out for millions a couple of years later. The median family
income in the San Jose region is about $30,000, highest in the U.S.

Though the electronics companies are secretive and don't offer
tours of their assembly lines, you can make your own self-guided
tour of the corporate palace architecture that forms a new genre of
American building style. You can tour NASA-Ames, which has
played such an important role in space exploration. And you can
see the Sunnyvale Patent Information Clearinghouse, the only
such facility outside Washington, D. C.

The Foothill College Electronics Museum celebrates
Electronicsland, though with emphasis on earlier development of
the radio as much as on the recent computer explosion. The
Eastridge Shopping Center, largest enclosed shopping area in the
West, tells you a little about the lifestyle of the area. And four
major attractions interest millions of natives and visitors each year:
Marriott's Great America, the Rosicrucian Egyptian Museum,

Winchester Mystery House, and the open-air San Jose Flea
Market.

Appropriately enough, one of the major information places for
travelers in this region is on Technology Drive near the San Jose
Municipal Airport. This resource, called the San Jose/Santa Clara
Valley Visitor Information Center, is at 1762 Technology Drive,
408/298-0400. Not only are knowledgeable humans available to
give brochures and answer questions, but, symbolic of the Silicon
Valley, there is on duty, 24 hours a day, another entity bristling
with regional information. That entity is called PIC, short for
Public Information Computer.

High-Tech Industry

T he dazzling rapidity of development in pocket calculators
and home computers makes the electronic wonders of
only a decade ago now seem neanderthal. About 30
percent of the country's personal and business electronics
components are produced here in the Silicon Valley. Space and
military research also has been a major employer. Lockheed, with
20,000 people on its payroll, is the single largest employer.
Medical and genetic engineering is yet another dimension, with
companies such as Syntex. The acronymous titles of companies
with exs, ecs, ics, iks, onics, teks, tex, digi, bio, auto and other
euphonious, abstract syllables in their names give no clue as to
what they produce. Whatever they make, they are growing
dramatically. There were only 290,547 people in Santa Clara
County in 1940, but 1,295,071 were recorded in the 1980 census.
In the late, lamented orchard era culminating in 1940 there were
only 29,725 houses in the city of San Jose. In 1980 there were
213,197.

Generally, the Silicon Valley corporate world is highly
competitive and mobile, but with fewer bureaucratic structures
and more meritocracy than is found in other industries. The entire
industry is fueled by knowledge, making a continuing ability to
learn and grow a prerequisite for success.

The style of corporate management is best exemplified in the
corporate history of Hewlett-Packard Co. Careful and meticulous
hiring, generous employee profit sharing, informal rather than
highly hierarchical management techniques, and the creation of
pleasant, campuslike workplaces, often with flexible working
hours to accommodate employees, have characterized the HP

approach. When the semiconductor industry slumped in 1970 and there were widespread layoffs elsewhere, everyone at HP took a 10 percent pay cut and no one was fired. This bred loyalty to the company, which helped HP retain its employees over many years, with personnel seen as an important asset.

The secretive, competitive, and fast-breaking nature of Silicon Valley technology makes it difficult to tour the major companies. Other industries with more standardized production procedures, not at all mysterious, welcome you to tour, but not here, where corporate secrets are carefully guarded and espionage is widespread. A look at the buildings themselves, however, is well worthwhile.

Silicon Valley Architecture

The special architecture of Silicon Valley is open for all to see and will undoubtedly be viewed retrospectively as a major architectural style. You can drive by, and where the interior architectural features are interesting, you may be able to enter a building.

The basic elements of this style in its simplest and purest form can be seen at the Digital Equipment Corporation (DEC) building at 2525 Augustine Drive in Santa Clara. Designed in 1976, this structure is a clean, straightforward black box, as mathematically elegant as the computer products the company makes, with the visual plane interrupted only by the company logo. Surrounded by wide green lawns, the building looks like a black gem on a jeweler's green cloth.

The Dysan Corporation building, at Patrick Henry Drive and Bunker Hill Lane in Santa Clara, transforms the basic rectangle into a low-slung wedge-shaped Swiss cheese effect with several tiers of windows facing south to pick up the light and heat. An almost subterranean appearance of the structure is heightened by an encircling landscaped berm of earth. The need for a clean, well-lighted, and climate controlled environment in the Silicon Valley is a primary architectural parameter. The opulence of the interior at Dysan is difficult to penetrate because of corporate security, but to view the interior would give you some sense of the profitability of these enterprises. One large auditorium where I meet monthly with fellow users of my personal computer, the Osborne 1, has solid hardwood walls, desks with well-padded individual chairs, and a place to plug in each person's computer!

Qume Corporation's headquarters, 2350 Qume Drive in Santa

Clara, should definitely be seen inside and out. Qume's exterior is a red, white, and blue metal and glass facade, clean and simple. The glass is actually an insulating fiberglass that greatly decreases both the heating and cooling load. The interior is basically two boxes with a mall in between and a massive greenhouse with a humanized, parklike workspace containing plants and fountains.

The Alza Corporation Building at 950 Page Mill Road, near El Camino Real in Palo Alto, takes the basic rectangle of the DEC building and softens it with landscaping. The grass lawns in front and the oak and willow trees, white marble sculpture, and picnic tables in back are aspects of this architectural statement.

International Business Machines' (IBM) Santa Teresa Lab, 555 Bailey Avenue in San Jose, extends the vision of Silicon Valley geographically. The building is a streamlined, efficient structure, a kind of parallel to the corporate body.

After looking at several of these buildings, some common notes on the style of this architecture emerge. It is low-rise rather than high-rise, consisting usually of huge faces of glass on plain rectangular boxes. Shrubbery, trees, and lawns are essential to soften the stark lines and provide some balance to the glass, concrete, and steel. Lawns are so well kept they resemble Astroturf. The workplace is clean, well lit, and comfortable. Usually the worker has no distraction visually from the outdoors. Statuary, striking art, or an ambitious macrame hang on the wall behind a receptionist's massive desk as you enter the structure.

Many of the buildings have been constructed with a "tilt-up" technique, in which the concrete walls are poured on the ground and tilted up into place, then clipped onto the steel girders that give the building its structural rigidity. This has been the basic industrial building style in the Santa Clara Valley. The style is precise, neat, and restrained. Logos will not generally be named after a person, nor will they indicate what products are made. The architecture is as abstract as the acronymous names of the companies.

These buildings have spilled south from the first Varian and Hewlett-Packard structures in the Stanford Industrial Park, near the Stanford University campus.

Sunnyvale Patent Information Clearinghouse

This unusual adjunct of Silicon Valley is worth a visit. Here you will find the only subject-classified collection of U.S. patents outside Washington, D.C. You can research everything that has ever been patented, from patent #1 in 1790 to all patents issued as of last week, which meant 4.3 million as of 1982. Framed and on display is a copy of the first patent ever granted, celebrating that Samuel Hopkins of Philadelphia had a better idea for making pot and pearl ash, useful in soap manufacture. The clearinghouse was started in 1962 by a patent attorney, Jack Bohan, who foresaw the boom in patent interest in this area.

Patent attorneys, historians, small-time inventors, whiz kids, shade tree mechanics, and curious onlookers from the general public are all welcome. Patents are arranged by about 600 main categories, with 90,000 subcategories. Staff personnel will assist you in learning how to use the system or how to obtain information to apply for a patent, copyright, or trademark. A computer terminal hooked into 3,000 major data banks can also be used here to look up bibliographic information. The first $30 of computer use is free.

In 1980 the patent library received a large grant to expand its holdings and personnel as an inventor information resource center. Magazines and trade journals useful to inventors can be perused.

The Sunnyvale Patent Information Clearinghouse is located in Sunnyvale at the Raynor Activity Center, 1500 Partridge Avenue, Building 7. Call ahead for current hours, 408/738-5580. The existence of this patent center salutes the entrepreneurial energy, especially in electronics, for which Silicon Valley is world famous.

NASA-Ames Research Center

The NASA facility at Moffett Field engages in a range of flight research programs in aircraft design, life sciences, and aerodynamics. The spectrum of research suggested by the NASA title, National Aeronautics and Space Administration, might lead the average taxpayer to feel that all this effort goes into rather exotic space-oriented studies. Not so, however: some of these studies vitally interest the average member of the flying public. In 1982, for example, NASA began an ambitious study of civil aviation flight safety that will last through the 1980s. The study will define the human factor in air safety, such as the pilot and control tower relationships on which every airline passenger depends. A new center for this research includes two simulators and a mock Air Traffic Control Facility. Since human error accounts for 60 to 80 percent of airline-flight accidents, the causes of those errors, as pilots and controllers interact with weather and equipment, can all be tested, with the hope that lessons learned

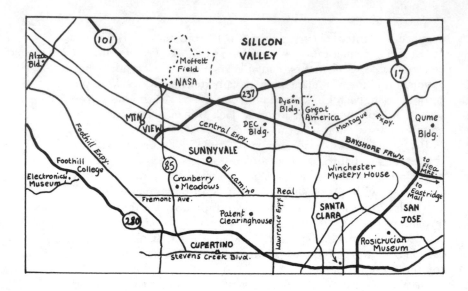

here can help set policies leading to safer commercial airline flights.

NASA-Ames can be toured by adults and children fourth grade and older. Call for details on making an appointment, 415/965-6497. The tour includes a film and talk, followed by selected stops at the wind tunnel, flight-simulation facility, centrifuge, and hangar housing experimental aircraft.

The massive dirigible hangars at the Moffett Field installation provoke wonder among natives and travelers speeding down Bayshore Freeway 101. The largest hangar, built in 1933, housed the giant lighter-than-air dirigible, the U.S.S. *Macon*. Just eight days before the Sunnyvale installation was to be dedicated as the Sunnyvale Naval Air Station, Rear Adm. William A. Moffett, champion of lighter-than-air craft, perished when the *Macon*'s sister ship, the U.S.S. *Akron*, went down in a storm off the New Jersey coast with a loss of 73 crewmen. The Sunnyvale installation was dedicated to this guiding light of the dirigible vision. Hope persisted that the *Macon* would live a long and useful life. The 785-foot dirigible was large enough to function as a flying aircraft carrier, housing five Sparrow Hawk fighter planes, which could be launched from the dirigible and then retrieved in midair by an ingenious trapeze mechanism. But after 16 months of service, the *Macon* met the same fate as its sister ship, going down in a February storm off Point Sur. The hangar for the *Macon* was 1,133 feet long, 308 feet wide, and 198 feet high, so large that clouds would form on the inside. All the Moffett hangars now house military antisubmarine aircraft.

An open house on one weekend each spring or summer gives the public a chance to see the Moffett Field facility and witness performances by precision flight-demonstration teams. Call Moffett Field for time and details, 415/966-5976. To get there, take the Bayshore Freeway 101 exit in Mountain View labeled Moffett.

Historic Sunnyvale and Mountain View

The most prominent residents in these parts during the late 19th century were Martin Murphy Jr. and his clan, California-Irish gentry well portrayed in Kevin Starr's *Americans and the California Dream*. The Murphy story unfolds for you at the Sunnyvale Historical Museum, in Martin Murphy Jr. Park, corner of California and Sunnyvale avenues, 408/749-0220. The park has ample lawns and picnic areas under pepper, oak, and eucalyptus trees, a good site for a rest and picnic while exploring. An annual summer barbecue sponsored by the historical association recalls a tradition of feasting started by the Murphys.

A historical marker in front of the museum synopsizes the story of Murphy and his first house, now gone:

> Home of Martin Murphy Jr. Martin Murphy Jr. arrived in California in 1844 in the first wagon train to cross the Sierra Nevada. The founder of Sunnyvale, he constructed here his house of prefabricated lumber, brought around the Horn in 1849. Members of the Murphy family lived here continuously until 1953, when the property was acquired by the city of Sunnyvale.

The oldest remaining house in the Sunnyvale area is called Cranberry Meadows, 1234 Cranberry Avenue, and dates from 1862. This white board house, with an adjacent tank tower, was formerly known as the Wright Ranch House, after a grain farmer.

Sunnyvale's 20-acre Community Center, at 550 East Remington Drive, 408/738-5521, includes a Creative Arts Center Gallery that shows local artists in all media and a Performing Arts Center used for theater, dance, and concerts. The Art Affair Festival each May is a major selling occasion for artists.

Sunnyvale's neighboring city is Mountain View. Storekeeper Jacob Shumway, looking across the valley to the mountains in the 1850s, is said to have bestowed the name Mountain View. The clarity of the air in the 1850s is matched today only on certain crisp winter days after rain has cleared the skies of smog.

Castro Street has always been the historic heart of Mountain View. Its architecture is not stunning, but the blend of ethnic restaurants gives Castro Street a special vitality. No less than 17 restaurants flourish here between Central Expressway and California Avenue, including Mexican, Japanese, Indonesian, and Chinese. At these kinds of restaurants thousands of Silicon Valley technical workers eat lunch. Try the tasty homemade creations, which may be radish green soup, broccoli quiche, and corn bread at The Gourmet Soup, 102 Castro, 415/961-4139. The merchants of Castro Street, from the appliance dealer to the music store, have competed successfully against shopping centers because of a steady tradition of knowledgeable and competent service.

Another good lunch spot, typical of the area, is the cluster of small fast-food booths with various ethnic specialties at the Old Mill, 2540 California Avenue. At this dining area, called the French Quarter, try the moussaka and the feta salad from Zorba's and perhaps a rum ball for dessert from Salim Mourad's Lebanese Bakery. The enclosed shopping center has a good bookstore-coffee house, Upstart Crow, and another store unique to the region and typical of the Silicon Valley, called Computer Capers, 415/941-1360. This store, first of its kind on the peninsula, is not a conventional computer store selling hardware and software, but a user center where you rent time hourly on a computer of your choice or receive instruction on computer use.

Foothill College Electronics Museum

Some Silicon Valley leaders envision a new museum devoted to the valley's main industry, but that has not yet been realized. Your best opportunity to view something of Silicon Valley's development is at the Foothill College Electronics Museum, which has been strongest in historic development of the radio prior to the microprocessor breakthroughs for computers in the 1970s. Holdings of the museum include ancient radio tubes and spark transmitters. Hands-on experiences give you a chance to interact with the exhibits.

The major contributor celebrated here is Lee De Forest, who concocted the first electronic tube to amplify sound, making possible the radio. The first West Coast radio station was Dr. Herrold's KQW in San Jose, started in 1912.

In recent years electronic circuits and computers have received more emphasis here, so Foothill may well become the museum of the modern electronics age in Silicon Valley.

Foothill College Electronics Museum is at 12345 South El Monte Avenue in Los Altos Hills on the Foothill Community College campus, 415/948-8590. Take the Foothill exit from Highway 280.

Shopping Center Country

Nowhere in America is the shopping center a more dominant feature of life than in the Silicon Valley. At least 135 shopping centers flourish here. Together they cover an area over three miles square and perform functions far broader than traditional shopping. At these centers people get married, have dinner, groom the dog, see movies, watch movies being made, such as Robert Redford's *The Candidate*, and even attend the symphony.

Shopping centers have become small communities unto themselves and have contributed strongly to the dispersed feeling of San Jose rather than the centralized focus typical of other cities. The explorer looking for a central city focus will be disappointed, perhaps unaware that shopping centers militate against the prospects.

Eastridge is the premier example of the phenomenon of the shopping center. Many people visit Eastridge not to shop, but simply for the adventure of going there, a secure place with plenty of activity and free parking. Eastridge is off Tully Road in San Jose, east of Bayshore Freeway 101. This complex, largest enclosed shopping center in the West, consists of 160 shops, 8 banks, 4 major department stores, and 14 restaurants. Eastridge even publishes a monthly newsletter of activities. The San Jose Symphony Orchestra performs here on the open mall.

Marriott's Great America

Great America, northern California's major amusement park, excites the white-knuckle enthusiast with the best thrills modern technology can offer. The Tidal Wave,

Eastridge, the largest enclosed shopping center in the West

Demon, Sky Whirl, and Willard's Whizzer are bound to please the connoisseur of stomach-wrenching and vertigo-inspiring rides.

When you look at a map, Great America, including the mammoth parking lot, occupies almost a town-sized area adjacent to Santa Clara. Eighty-six acres of family-oriented entertainment cluster around the landmark carousel, Columbia, whose 103 prancing animals evoke a nostalgic, earlier America.

Constant performances by brass bands, trained dolphins, and Americana theater groups entertain the visitor, who is met by Warner Brothers characters, such as Bugs Bunny and Wile E. Coyote. There is a notable American effort at superlatives, with the Pictorium movie theater's screen billed as the world's largest. You can operate your own race car on the Barney Oldfield Speedway.

Five areas of America's past have been chosen as themes in the park: Yankee Harbor is a simulated New England fishing village; the Great Midwestern Livestock Exposition and County Fair celebrates mid-America; Yukon Territory suggests a wild Alaska; Hometown Square approximates the nostalgic image of a rural town in the 1920s; Orleans Place offers the public's expected image of the Old South.

Marriott's Great America is located at Great America Parkway, off Bayshore Freeway 101 in Santa Clara. Open daily in summer, weekends in winter, 408/988-1776.

The Rosicrucian Egyptian Museum

A one-of-a-kind historical and spiritual experience awaits the explorer at the Rosicrucian Egyptian Museum, Park and Naglee avenues in San Jose, 408/287-9171.

Rosicrucians, known as "The Ancient, Mystical Order Rosae Crucis," operate here a free Egyptian Museum, Planetarium, and Science Museum. The assembled ancient Near Eastern artifacts are stunning in their range and uniqueness.

This worldwide fraternal and educational order of men and women attempts to cultivate learning about man and nature that first flourished around 1400 B.C. The organization encourages individuals to develop their own personal philosophies based on these knowledges and insights, which have ramifications in metaphysics, mysticism, philosophy, psychology, parapsychology, and science. Any pedagogic or propagandistic efforts at the museum are extremely low-key, almost as if the ancient artifacts should speak for themselves.

The Rosicrucians feel that American thinkers such as Benjamin Franklin and Thomas Jefferson have been continuers and broadeners of the original insights. The organization sees itself not as a religion but as an educational group whose teachings are compatible with a variety of religions.

From the world headquarters here in San Jose, the order distributes materials to some 250,000 active members worldwide and prints its documents in 11 languages, from such widely used languages as Spanish to such narrowly defined tongues as Dutch. Each year approximately 3 million instructional packets go forth from the San Jose headquarters to inquirers all over the world.

The Rosicrucian Egyptian Museum is also San Jose's largest tourist attraction, drawing half a million people annually. Holdings include the largest collection on the West Coast of Egyptian, Babylonian, and Assyrian artifacts. Human and animal mummies, metal tools, alabaster jars, stone jewelry, and Coptic fabric fragments are just a beginning inventory of the artifacts, all originals unless otherwise noted. The structure in which these treasures rest is patterned after Egyptian architectural designs. The facade, for example, is a reproduction of the Avenue of Ram Sphinxes from the Karnak Temple at Thebes.

A walk-in tomb, a composite re-creation of tombs dating from about 2000 B.C., is a highlight of the museum. The tomb re-creation is the only one of its kind in the U.S. and includes a replica of the sarcophagus of King Tutankhamun.

Perhaps most fascinating in the entire museum experience are exhibits about the wondrous early discoveries in mathematics and the initial efforts to form a written language, both of which underlie all later achievements of civilized man.

Within the museum an Art Gallery features changing single-artist exhibits of modern regional artists. Adjacent to the museum is a Planetarium and Science Museum. Call ahead to check on times for various astronomy shows.

Winchester Mystery House

Sarah Winchester's house is a tour de force, usually portrayed as a monument to her fears rather than to her eccentricity. The 160-room Victorian house, gardens, and historical museum of Winchester rifle paraphernalia are located at

Sarah Winchester's house, San Jose

525 Winchester Boulevard between Stevens Creek Boulevard and Highway 280 in San Jose. Call 408/247-2101 for current hours open and entrance fees.

For some 38 years between 1884 and 1922 Sarah Winchester kept a small army of workers adding onto the eight-room farmhouse she purchased when she moved to San Jose. She devoted five million uninflated dollars to the project. As the heiress to the fortune made from the Winchester repeating rifle, the "gun that won the West," Sarah had an income of about $1,000 per day and a fortune of around $20 million at her disposal. She died in 1922 at age 83.

It is difficult to separate fact from gossip when investigating Sarah Pardee Winchester and her motives. Evidently she was deeply disturbed by the death of her month-old daughter, Annie, and later the death by tuberculosis of her husband, William Wirt Winchester. Some say she consulted a spiritualist in Boston, who confirmed her fears that the spirits of those killed by the Winchester rifle were angry and would haunt her. It is said that the medium suggested to Sarah that she move west and begin building a house to appease the spirits. Only by continuing to build could she ward off the imminence of her own death. Others believe that her physician, not a medium, simply suggested she take up a diversionary hobby, such as building a house without an architect, and that this hobby became a passion for Sarah Winchester.

To those who view Sarah Winchester as a spiritualist possessed, she left some evidence. The house is filled with the superstitious number 13. There are 13 bathrooms. Rooms have 13 windows. Staircases have 13 steps. Closets have 13 coat hooks. Two enigmatic thoughts adorning stained glass windows are, "Wide unclasp the tables of their thoughts" and "These same thoughts people this little world." Emblems on some fireplaces are said to be upside down deliberately to confuse the spirits.

Yet there is also the mark of a playful and somewhat comic improviser on a grand scale. Sarah Winchester eschewed blueprints. She would review progress on the house each day and make rough sketches with the manager of her workers about what should be done next. If there were errors, they were either left or ripped out. The quality of the work done at the house is impressive throughout, from the parquet floors of rare hardwoods to the leaded glass doors and windows. An appreciator of Victorian detail will find much to admire here in the 47 fireplaces, 2,000 doors, 10,000 windows, and 52 skylights. But the lack of an overall design makes the house an oddity rather than an architectural masterpiece. The house, however, was sufficiently sturdy to withstand the 1906 Earthquake with little damage.

Sarah was also a clever improviser of household systems. She devised burglar-proof windows, watering systems that carried the waste water from plants on the second floor to plants in the garden, switches that could be pressed to flip on gas lamps in a room, and a servant intercom system. The house had complete heating, lighting, and sewer systems that were far advanced for their day.

Though never a fraternizer in her community, Sarah Winchester was known for her charitable donations to local hospitals and orphanages as well as to individuals in need. She was interested in art, science, and music and was a gifted organist. She enjoyed entertaining young children, especially little girls who played on the house's magnificent organ.

San Jose Flea Market

On a typical Saturday or Sunday 50,000–75,000 people gather at the year-round San Jose Flea Market, 12000 Berryessa Road, 408/289-1550.

The scene amounts to a thousand garage sales, a hundred farmers' markets, and a county fair all together, with a full spectrum of Silicon Valley residents in attendance. For a small fee, anyone can offer his or her recyclables at one of the 1,800 booths in the 40-acre complex. Live music entertains the explorer. Children can enjoy the giant slide, merry-go-round, and kiddie cars.

The Lick Observatory atop Mt. Hamilton

Above the Valley

12

The West and East Foothills

T he foothills above the Santa Clara (Silicon) Valley have attractive hiking parks. Duveneck, Monte Bello, Fremont Older, Sanborn–Skyline, and Villa Montalvo are the names of the major parks and open spaces on the west side of the valley as you move south along the flanks of the Santa Cruz Mountains. On the west side there are pleasant small towns to explore, such as Saratoga with its gardens, Los Gatos with its Old Town, Campbell with its theater and night life, and Cupertino with De Anza College, known for its California History Center and Flint Auditorium. The major east-side parks are Levin, Alum Rock, and Grant, with the Lick Observatory as the main attraction to visit.

Managing the Public Land

T wo government entities have responsibility for administering these parks. Both are good sources of information, such as trail maps.

The first is the County of Santa Clara, Parks and Recreation Department, 298 Garden Hill Drive, Los Gatos 95030, 408/358-3741. Altogether there are 29 units in the county park system, with some of the most prominent falling in this area, namely Sanborn–Skyline, Villa Montalvo, Levin, and Grant parks. Write or call them to receive a complete map of all the county parks and more detailed maps of individual parks that may interest you.

The second entity administering some public lands is called the Midpeninsula Regional Open Space District (MROSD), 375 Distel Circle, Suite D-1, Los Altos 94022, 415/965-4717. After explosive growth of peninsula population levels in the 1950s and sixties threatened the quality of life beyond a tolerable level, citizen support grew for more protection of open space, whether agricultural land or natural scenic space. Preserving open space promised other benefits also, such as erosion and flood control by absorbing ground water rather than sending it cascading into sewer systems. The voting electorate in a portion of Santa Clara County approved creating a new parks-acquiring entity, MROSD, giving it limited power of eminent domain and some funding from property tax assessments. A portion of San Mateo County did likewise in 1976. By 1982 MROSD controlled some 12,000 acres. The MROSD also organizes guided hikes in nature areas, introducing you to the geology, flora, fauna, and human history of the region.

As you proceed south along the foothills on the western side of the valley, here are the major parks you encounter.

Duveneck Windmill Pasture Preserve

These 761 acres of virgin oak and grass hillsides in the foothills above Los Altos have become a vast park with trails and a protected watershed, the legacy of Frank and Josephine Duveneck.

Reach the park by taking Moody Road a mile west from Highway 280 past Foothill College. Turn left onto Rhus Ridge Road and proceed a twisting mile until you see a small parking area, room for about five cars, and a gate with the sign Preserve Open Until Dusk. Park here and begin the walk.

The trail up to the high pasturelands is a steep grade, shared with equestrians, through bay, buckeye, and live oak forests. Many other types of vegetation, from toyon to sword ferns, thrive here because the twisting folds of land provide changing orientations toward sun exposure and wide variations in the amount of water the ground holds. Stay on the main path, ignoring side paths, as you climb to the top.

When you reach the high grasslands, views of the valley stretch out as engaging panoramas. The distinct wilderness feeling, despite proximity to an urban area, is one of the pleasures here. To reach the aging windmill, take the middle left of the four trails, walk a quarter mile, and look to your right. The historic metallic windmill, with its disabled blade on the ground, will appear in a shallow valley. Next to the windmill is a good picnic site under the oak trees.

Walk-in camping is sometimes allowed near the windmill, with a reservation and permit from 415/948-4690, but no fires are allowed because of the high fire danger in summer.

The land is part of Hidden Villa Ranch, whose other acreage is not yet a park freely open to the public. Hidden Villa has been a working farm, a youth hostel, site of the west coast's first interracial summer camps, and an elaborate open air classroom for generations of schoolchildren.

The Duvenecks rank as remarkable people. Josephine was born into the Bostonian Whitney family, attended Radcliffe and Oxford, and decided on a literary career. She married Frank, who had been born in Florence, Italy, son of painter Frank Duveneck. Together they set up a new life for themselves in the West. Eventually Josephine plunged her energy into organization work rather than writing. In the 1920s she served on the Palo Alto City Council and founded a progressive grade school, among other things. She was active after World War II in defusing acrimony toward Japanese Americans returning from internment. Frank Duveneck is an engineer and physicist who taught at Stanford and invented an x-ray apparatus. Later in life, as an avid gardener, he developed a strain of high-yield corn at Hidden Villa.

Monte Bello Ridge Open Space

This holding consists of 3,160 acres of rolling grasslands and canyon forests with access on Page Mill Road a mile west from Skyline Boulevard. The parking lot for Monte Bello lies opposite the lot for Los Trancos, the open space celebrating earthquake geology along the San Andreas Fault. Both reserves can be visited in an afternoon.

The view a quarter mile down the Stevens Creek Nature Trail directly out from the parking lot at Monte Bello presents a classic peninsula landscape of gently rolling hillside grasslands, clusters of

218

live oaks in the moister runoff gullies, and redwood trees in the distance. The view is uninterrupted by artifacts indicating human presence.

Ambitious hikers with a two car shuttle can walk 8.1 miles from here to Saratoga Gap. The .5-mile Canyon Trail is a less demanding outing. Wildflowers flourish on these grasslands in spring and wildlife thrives here, with coyote, bobcat, and blacktail deer tracks showing abundantly. Be sure to bring your own water because there is none in the park.

Rangers at a National Fish and Wildlife Service bird banding station at Monte Bello net and tag birds to study their migration patterns.

Fremont Older Open Space Preserve

T hese 734 acres include the home of crusading newspaperman Fremont Older and his wife, Cora Baggerly Older. The main access to this Older–Seven Springs property is at the end of Prospect Road off Saratoga–Sunnyvale Road. Gentle trails are easy to walk here through forests, chaparral, open hayfields, and apricot orchards.

After you park your car, walk into the preserve up the main road. You will see a trail marked Regnart Road cutting off to the right, which takes you through a creekside bay tree forest and ancient walnut orchard to a large hayfield. If you stay on the main road rather than take this Regnart Road shortcut, you will reach the hayfield also, after passing the stately gray-shingled home of Fremont Older and elaborate hillside rock gardens with flowers spilling over the side.

Beyond the hayfield you can walk the Seven Springs Loop Trail, with views of more orchards.

Sanborn–Skyline County Park

A bove Saratoga you can visit the 2,856 hilly acres of Sanborn Park. There are 37 walk-in campsites, an ample grassy hillside with picnic tables, and 16.3 miles of hiking trails. The terrain is richly diverse, ranging from grasslands to second-growth redwood forests.

To reach Sanborn Park, follow Highway 9 west 2 miles from Saratoga, then turn onto Sanborn Road and continue another mile until you see signs. This road passes through one of the lovelier big-leaf maple forests on the peninsula.

At park headquarters pick up the nature guide for the 1.25 mile, self-guided nature trail. The ranger office, 408/867-6940, is in the estate manor, built in 1912.

The elevation of Sanborn Park is high, from 1,500 to 3,000 feet, with the crest extending to Castle Rock Park, where you can join the Skyline-to-the-Sea Trail if you are ambitious. Views from the top of the 2.25-mile hike up to Skyline Boulevard are generally good, though sometimes hazy. Rock outcroppings both here and at Castle Rock are popular with rock climbers and scramblers.

Sanborn Hostel

A rough-hewn log house on the park property, constructed in 1908 during a brief era of back-to-nature architectural fancy, now serves as one of the network of 200 hostels in the U.S. Hostel tends to have the word "Youth" in front of it in Europe, but travelers of all ages, including families, are welcome here. Hostel style requires that you participate in the cleanup of the facility. For reservations write or call Sanborn Park Hostel, 15808 Sanborn Road, Saratoga 95070, 408/867-3993.

Villa Montalvo

This substantial, 175-acre estate, park, and cultural center, a fitting memorial to James Duval Phelan, can be entered half a mile from Saratoga down the Saratoga-Los Gatos Road by turning right onto Montalvo Road.

Montalvo was one of the final great estates built in California prior to World War I. The grounds and Italian Renaissance villa were built at the order of James Phelan, who had been for three terms mayor of San Francisco. Phelan's father was an Irish immigrant who came to San Francisco during the Gold Rush and amassed a fortune in banking, trade, and merchanting.

James Phelan's first love had always been the literary and artistic life that he forsook to participate in family banking and real estate businesses. Throughout his life Phelan liked to surround himself with artists and writers, supporting them financially and

A buckeye in bloom

buying their works to adorn his house. Novelist Gertrude Atherton was his constant companion in his later years.

In 1911 Phelan began the work of building Montalvo, naming it after the 16th-century Spanish writer in whose work the word California first appears. Ordonez de Montalvo used the word California in his *Sergas de Esplandian*, imagining California as a country west of the Indies, near the Terrestrial Paradise, rich in gold and precious stones, of great beauty and fertility of soil. The country was populated by Amazons, who rode red griffins when they went to war and slew all male prisoners they took in battle.

An inscription carved on the vaulting Ionic columns that support the structure reads:

Know Ordonez de Montalvo's fame. Did he not see in fantasy our California grow out of old Spain; conferred her name, foretold her gold; a paradise for eager eyes; his dream came true for me and you.

The grounds and house reflect a serenity of spirit found in classic Italy and Spain in their most prosperous times. Phelan brought the massive front door from Spain, plus objects of antiquity from Greece and Pompeii, Italy. Statuary and carefully tended gardens lend elegance to the setting.

Phelan purchased the acreage in the Saratoga foothills and arranged the timing of construction so that the Panama Pacific Exposition of 1915 would be the debut of Montalvo. Architect William Curlett was given the design assignment, which was completed by his son, Alex, and partner Charles Gottschalk. John McLaren, of Golden Gate Park fame, laid out the gardens.

In 1914 Phelan was elected U.S. senator from California. A Democrat, he served until the Republican landslide of Warren Harding swept him out in 1921.

After Phelan died in 1930, part of his will bequeathed money to run Montalvo as a place where artists, writers, and musicians could carry on their work. Today that function continues at Montalvo, with resident practitioners of the arts and with many programs and shows on cultural subjects. Call for current offerings, 408/867-3421. The first floor of the house is now an art gallery with monthly changes in shows. Senator Phelan's original carriage house has been converted into a theater.

The 170 acres of grounds beyond those immediately around the house are maintained as a public arboretum by the Santa Clara County Parks Department. Walks here include an extensive nature trail with 22 numbered stations that help acquaint you with California native plants. An especially large range of plants is available because of the altitude changes and different exposures, which determine habitats. There are half a dozen different oak species, for example. The area is also an official bird and wildlife sanctuary. Picnicking and pets are not allowed at Villa Montalvo. Plan your picnic for nearby Wildwood Park, a mile away.

Saratoga

W hen you begin exploring the small towns of the foothills beyond the parks, none is more intriguing or historic than Saratoga. Several aspects of Saratoga's past are gathered and commemorated on a plaque at the junction of Highways 9 and 85. The marker, in a white stucco arch next to the fire station, recounts the historical record with cryptic brevity:

> Saratoga. Formerly Tollgate, McCartysville, Banks Mills. Anza exploring party passed through March 25, 1776. Lumbering in mountains, which began in 1847 and continued many years, brought first settlers 1850. Among other industries formed were a lime quarry 1850s, grist mill 1854, tannery 1863, paper mill 1868, and pasteboard mill 1870. Pacific Congress Springs popular resort 1866–1942. Pioneered in fruit industry. Blossom Festivals began in 1900.

Your first stop here should be two buildings a quarter mile down Saratoga-Los Gatos Road toward Los Gatos. One is a historic 1904 storefront that now serves as the Saratoga Historical Museum, 408/867-4311. There you can get a free historical walking tour map of the town and see some intriguing exhibits, such as a "home life in the past" display case containing a razor strop and a charcoal clothes iron. Next door is a cottage from 1864 built for a blacksmith named McWilliams. This house is now the Saratoga Chamber of Commerce, 408/867-0753, which has information on the major festivals here each spring and summer: the Blossom Festival in April, the Rotary Art Festival in May, and the Antique Fair in July.

In the early days Congress Springs was a select resort where well-to-do families drank and bathed in the mineral waters. The name Saratoga was legally promulgated in 1865 because water from the mineral springs, located a mile above the town, resembled chemically the waters at Congress Springs in Saratoga, New York.

Many of the historic structures can be seen while walking on Big Basin Way and parallel Oak Street in the vicinity of Third Street. The Cloud/Smith General Store at 14503 Big Basin Way dates from 1884. Today it is Maddalena's Tea Shop, a popular, small outdoor cafe and rest stop. A dozen other small restaurants, shops, art stores, and antique traders can be found in the vicinity.

One local house that is well preserved, retaining much of its original appearance, is the John Henry House, 14630 Big Basin Way, built in 1869. Henry was an engineer of the Saratoga Paper Mill. Today the Henry House serves as an architect's offices.

One house not on the walking tour map is the James P. Springer House, 20770 Wildwood Way, the oldest house in town. To get there walk from Big Basin across the creek at Fourth Street and make two rights. This structure was a prefab house, built in New England, then shipped around the Horn and erected here at the early date of 1851. The house itself is a modest dwelling, but when you imagine the rustic state of the territory in 1851, the house's continued existence is impressive.

Aside from its history and browsable downtown, Saratoga is also famous for several major gardens.

Saratoga Community Garden

These are among the most advanced community gardens on the peninsula, producing food, flowers, and livestock.

To reach the gardens, turn onto Odd Fellows Road parallel to San Marcos Road at 19500 Fruitvale Avenue. Follow the signs to the gardens, park near the old dairy barn, and walk up to the gardens.

Operated by a nonprofit corporation dedicated to teaching and demonstrating bio-intensive gardening and the importance of harmonious ecological relationships between people and nature, the gardens have flourished since they were founded by a group of citizens in 1972. A 10-acre site is leased from the Independent Order of Odd Fellows for one dollar per year and financed by private contributions and the city of Saratoga.

Here you can see cultivation of flowers, herbs, vegetables, fruit trees and shrubs, native plants, and drought-resistant ornamentals, plus demonstrations of composting, intensive gardening techniques, and companion planting. All insect controls used here involve strategies other than toxic chemicals. Animals appropriate for some urban situations, such as rabbits, laying chickens, and goats, are housed here.

Sunday tours are generally given at 2 P.M. Guided tours at other times are sometimes possible by calling 408/354-8648. Classes are available to acquaint you with organic gardening techniques. Memberships and donations to the garden are encouraged, starting at $15 per year. The mailing address is Saratoga Community Garden, P.O. Box 756, Saratoga 95070. For a free map of the gardens, send them a stamped, self-addressed envelope.

The vegetable gardens are at the crest of the hill. There you can see wide beds of food plants growing year round. In winter, cabbage family and leaf crops predominate. In summer, there is a cornucopia of more diverse vegetables. Many good food-gardening practices, such as mulching to save moisture and reduce weeds or netting to cover seedlings from damage by birds, are demonstrated here. Even in the quiet time of winter and early spring, the greenhouses are fascinating to walk through to see the new seedlings being prepared for future planting.

The gardens serve as a valuable educational resource for local schools and for people interested in a summer program of gardening, crafts, natural history, and ecology. The Odd Fellows once used the land as a self-sustaining farm.

Hakone Gardens

The Hakone Gardens are authentic Japanese gardens and houses at 21000 Big Basin Way, 408/867-3468.

The site was purchased by Mrs. Isabel Stine in 1918. With an architect and skilled craftsmen from Japan she built the main house and guest house in the Japanese style, without nails. The gardens were designed and executed by one of the emperor's former gardeners, Ihara. Hakone recalls the name of a resort in the Fuji-Hakone National Park on the island of Honshu.

Today the property, owned by the city of Saratoga and operated as a public park, provides a meditative Japanese-style landscape, emphasizing harmony, tranquility, and reverence, a counterpoint to the frenetic world of Silicon Valley. Here you'll find dwarf pines and maples, boulders artfully placed, and quiet ponds filled with koi.

Saso Herb Garden

The Saso Herb Garden, 14625 Fruitvale Avenue, is a good place to see and buy hundreds of different herbs. The Sasos grow and use their herbs for culinary, medicinal, olfactory, and decorative purposes. Herbs thrive on an acre of carefully planted ground that was opened for public viewing 15 years ago. Each autumn a Fall Harvest Fair amounts to an open house where visitors drink herb teas and learn about uses of herbs. Phone for that date and other ongoing educational workshops, 408/867-0307.

Louis and Virginia Saso have been the resident experts for the past 25 years. They have amassed one of the largest collections of different herbs in the U.S. and also have many examples of each type, such as 50 different sages and thymes. A small vegetable garden shows how herbs can be interplanted as companions for vegetables. Throughout spring and summer, workshops discuss the culture and use of herbs, growing flowers for drying, blending potpourri, and creating unusual herb wreaths. Some Saso favorites for herb teas are lemon verbena, lemon grass, apple mint, comfrey, and chamomile.

Los Gatos

This small town in the foothills west of San Jose is a quiet and cultured retreat known for its attractive stores, antique shops, small restaurants, artists, and craftspeople. Experience Los Gatos by walking North Santa Cruz Avenue between Main Street and the Saratoga–Los Gatos Road.

While here, be sure to visit the Los Gatos Museum, housed in a Spanish-style structure at 4 Tait Street. This excellent small museum has rotating exhibits on history, nature, and fine art. Phone ahead for current hours, 408/354-2646.

Louis and Virginia Saso of the Saso Herb Garden, Saratoga

The Old Town development at 50 University Avenue recycles the town's earlier elementary school into an attractive complex of shops and restaurants, such as The Indian Store, featuring American Indian artifacts, and Mud In Your Eye, containing one of the peninsula's largest selections of hand-thrown, high-temperature–fired stoneware pottery. During summer there are outdoor concerts and art shows here. Theaterwest drama group flourishes in Old Town, emphasizing classic 20th-century dramas, comedies, and musicals. Call 408/395-5434 for current performances.

Restaurants to consider include Noodle Palace, 140 North Santa Cruz Avenue, 408/354-0555. If undecided, try the half spaghetti–half ravioli. Decor is eclectic Americana antiques, such as the wood-bladed fan recycled from the former San Jose post office. Steamers Seafood Cafe, at 40 North Santa Cruz, 408/395-3474, is a pleasant outdoor wine and seafood restaurant specializing in fresh oysters and charcoal-broiled fresh fish. For a lively evening of music, stop by Mountain Charley's Saloon, upstairs at 15 North Santa Cruz, 408/354-2510. The name honors an early builder of the turnpike over the mountains.

Los Gatos took its name from the numerous wildcats that inhabited the district when Jose Hernandez came here in 1838. Legend says that the Hernandez family set out to find an ideal home site in these hills. They found it when they encountered wildcats because they knew that wildcats would only flourish where water was present year round. The town was not always called Los Gatos, however. A historical marker north of East Main Street recalls an early citizen and his enterprise:

> Forbes Flour Mill. This is all that remains of the four-story stone flour mill built in 1854 by James Alexander Forbes. The town that grew around this building was first called Forbes Mill, then Forbestown, and finally Los Gatos.

The Fiesta de Los Gatos in August is the major annual festival here. Live entertainment, antiques, arts and crafts booths, wine tasting, and a barbecue are some of the activities. Call the Los Gatos Chamber of Commerce, 408/354-9300, for details.

Cupertino

Father Pedro Font of the de Anza expedition named this area of foothills west of San Jose, Arroyo San Jose de Cupertino, after his patron and recently canonized Saint Guiseppe of Copertino, Italy. Font praised the Cupertino area as having good firewood and water, but he saw no immediate plans for a settlement. The first substantial settler was Captain Elisha Stevens, who farmed here after leading a party of settlers successfully over the Sierra Nevada in 1844.

By the 1890s vineyards were prominent, but they were wiped out by the phylloxera root louse about 1895. Apricots, French prunes, cherries, and pears became the dominant crops until real estate development boomed after World War II. In 1955 the town incorporated to preserve its autonomy as neighboring towns edged closer.

Cupertino has its share of progressive electronics firms, especially the world headquarters of Apple Computers, which was operating out of an inventor's garage as recently as 1975. Cupertino has helped put Silicon Valley on the cutting edge of the world's computer development. Measurex is a well-known name and a major employer here. Zilog is famous for its industry-standard Z80 microprocessor, the heart of many personal computers.

In town, Vallco Fashion Park is the major shopping and office center, located at Highway 280 and Wolfe Road. Stop by the Vallco Park to see theme presentations of farming, harvesting, vineyard, and electronics history in the area.

Houlihan's Old Place is a lively establishment for listening to music, dancing, meeting people, and dining on specialties from trout almondine to teriyaki swordfish. Houlihan's is open nightly at Orchard Valley Marketplace off Highway 280 on Stevens Creek Boulevard, 408/725-0515.

The major annual celebration in Cupertino is the late July–early August Art and Wine Festival.

De Anza College

De Anza Community College at 21250 Stevens Creek Boulevard is a major resource in Cupertino for peninsulans. The general information number is 408/996-4567.

The name recalls the impressive leader who brought a band of Spanish settlers from the town of Alamos in the state of Sonora, Mexico. De Anza guided these people to the peninsula region in 1776 to help establish the San Francisco settlement associated with Mission Dolores. He accomplished this mammoth trek without loss of life.

De Anza College makes its contribution to the general community in several ways. Le Petit Trianon is the name given to an 1890s' building by Willis Polk in the Louis XIV tradition. This edifice, on the campus, now houses the California History Center, 408/996-4712. Le Petit Trianon is a valuable resource for anyone perusing regional or statewide California history. A changing exhibit on historical subjects keeps the research resources before the public.

The Calvin C. Flint Center for the Performing Arts is an excellent auditorium in which the San Jose and San Francisco symphonies perform. Ballet and folk dancers, entertainers, and various lecturers also use the Flint Center. Phone 408/257-9555 to receive a free listing of upcoming events.

The Environmental Study Area is a 1.5-acre site for the study of native California plants and animals. A well-labeled nature trail acquaints you with California vegetation. Conducted tours are also available, 408/996-4525.

Helen Euphrat Gallery on the campus has interesting exhibits of student artists and other regional painters, 408/996-4836.

Minolta Planetarium presents educational programs and astronomy events called "cosmic concerts," rock shows using lasers, 408/996-4814.

The annual De Anza Days in early June offer a good opportunity to make the acquaintance of this town and its community college.

Campbell

L ike the waterfront warehouses and wharves at the ailing Port of San Francisco, the fruit packing sheds of the Santa Clara Valley are mainly museum pieces. However, in Campbell, a town in the foothills west of San Jose, an exception can be found. As it is fashionable to have advertising offices on a pier in San Francisco or a shop in the Pier 39 complex, similarly, The Factory in Campbell has recycled a fruit-packing plant into a chic ambiance for offices, restaurants, and shops. The Factory is an echo of Ghirardelli Square in San Francisco or Vintage 1870 in the Napa Valley, but with more emphasis on offices than on shops.

These sheds at 93 South Central Avenue were once operated by Sunsweet for prune drying and shipping. Separate parts of the brick, wood, and corrugated metal complex, with the old machinery of pulleys, wheels, and cogs still displayed, are called the Box Plant, Drying Shed, and Sorting Shed. Among the interesting shops is Earth Antiques. A dinner favorite is the Black Kettle's stuffed prawns or prime rib, 408/374-9610.

Two lively, light-entertainment theaters flourish in Campbell. The Gaslighter Theater, also a beer and wine bar at 400 East Campbell Avenue, 408/866-1408, specializes in melodramas with plenty of booing and hissing audience participation. King Dodo Playhouse, 176 East Campbell Avenue, 408/266-6060, features modern comedies.

Ed R. Levin County Park

On the east side of the Santa Clara Valley this 1,544-acre park in the hills above Milpitas honors a local politician. Levin offers good springtime hiking and picnicking sites, especially around Sandy Wool Lake, before the summer sun dries out the grasses. Row and sail boats are allowed on the lake, and children enjoy the developed playgrounds at the Elms Picnic Ground near the base of the lake.

Part of the park is devoted to a golf course, but the unusual activity here is year-round hang gliding, from 960-foot Vista Point. Monument Peak Road and Sierra Trail are a good 3.2-mile hike to an elevation of 2,594 feet with a sweeping look at the East Bay.

The park can be reached via Calaveras Road east from Highway 680, 408/262-6980.

Alum Rock Park

You enter Alum Rock Park, San Jose's distinguished city park in the east foothills, along Penetencia Creek Road, which boasts some of the loveliest native sycamore trees in the region. Here the trees flourish because their roots are able to tap ground water in the dry season. In winter the bark has an engaging, gray-dappled look, and in summer the full leaves of the trees provide welcome shade.

The entrance to Alum Rock Park takes you under a stone archway that was an aqueduct built in the 19th century when the mineral waters of Alum Rock were famous for their health-giving qualities. A notable resort once flourished here.

Proceed up the Alum Rock Falls Road to the visitor center.

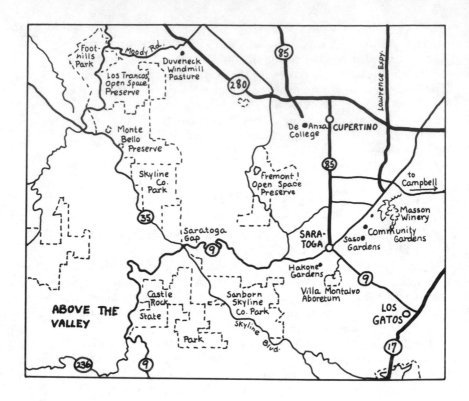

There you can get a good map of the fine biking and hiking trails. A brief orientation to the region at the visitor center is in both Spanish and English, an index of the flourishing Spanish-language culture of the San Jose region. A three-dimensional topographic map shows the park's terrain. The visitor center itself is set amidst fine specimens of coast live oaks alongside Penetencia Creek, which flows strongly in winter. Hills across the road from the visitor center are thick with sage, a chaparral community plant whose pungent aroma is unmistakable when a sprig is crushed in the hand. Some local people use the sage, steeped as a tea, for reputed medicinal benefits, especially to lower high blood pressure.

Plenty of picnic grounds and a developed children's playground are other pleasures of this park. From near the visitor center you can hike into the back country to see the falls and springs that once made Alum Rock a well-known name among the health spa enthusiasts.

If you drive back into San Jose from Alum Rock and feel hungry, stop at one of the many sit-down delicatessens that dot San Jose. Try Aiello's at 2854 Alum Rock Avenue and ask for Tony's Special sandwich or a plate of lasagna.

Joseph D. Grant County Park

This 9,522-acre former cattle ranch on Mt. Hamilton Road is destined eventually to be one of the most significant parks for Santa Clara Valley residents.

Opened in April 1978, this park benefits from a lively group of volunteers, called the Friends of Grant Ranch Park, who assist rangers in developing the area. The land was first used as a cattle ranch in the 1880s. Now the main ranch house, near where Quimby Road intersects with Mt. Hamilton Road, serves as a nature interpretive and visitor center. Ample, spacious picnic sites with tables can be found here. Campsites will eventually be installed along these western foothills of Mt. Hamilton. Twenty-two miles of hiking trails are now shared by walkers and horseback riders.

At the visitor center-ranch house a display board acquaints you with the native and European grasses locked in combat for dominance of these hillsides. Many interesting natural history exhibits can be seen at the visitor center, including live gopher snakes, king snakes, and rattlesnakes; stuffed birds from towhees to the large raptors that float on thermal updrafts; an aquarium with the bass and trout found in lakes here; a stuffed mountain lion; and skulls of a lesser-known animal introduced to this region, wild pigs.

A complete description of trails can be obtained at the visitor center. Ask for the *Grant Park Loop Trails* brochure.

For a good short hike, try the one-mile Barn Trail Loop, which is on level ground. Yerba Buena Loop Trail is also short, but more hilly. Bass Lake Trail is a half day outing that can take you up and across Mt. Hamilton Road and then back along Yerba Buena Trail to the visitor center.

Fishermen meet some success at catching largemouth bass and bluegill in four lakes on the property.

Lick Observatory

During the Gold Rush, James Lick came to San Francisco with $30,000 and parlayed it into a fortune. The real estate tycoon then decided to spend a chunk of his accumulated fortune on an astronomy observatory, resulting in the impressive Lick Observatory, with its 120-inch telescope, and Mt. Hamilton Observing Station on Mt. Hamilton Road, southeast of San Jose. The road is 23 miles from San Jose winding to the summit of 4,209-foot Mt. Hamilton. Phone 408/274-5061 for current tour schedules.

Lick Observatory has been operated by the University of California since 1888. Since 1965 the Santa Cruz campus's astronomy department has supervised use of the 120-inch reflector telescope, which attracts astronomers from all over the world.

Lick is recognized as the world's second most powerful observatory, surpassed only by the 200-inch Hale Observatory on Mt. Palomar in southern California. James Lick's original mandate bristled with eccentricity. He believed that the telescope should "prove or disprove the existence of animals on the moon." Some notable advances have been made here, including the first photo of the Milky Way. One of Lick's main uses has been in observing infrared wavelengths.

Lick's telescope is an extraordinary astronomical tool, but its effectiveness has been diminished in recent years. Telescopes need a dark night sky background, but the night sky over San Jose becomes brighter each year due to increasing urbanization. A new adjunct site for future astronomical work has been chosen on Junipero Serra Peak to the south in the Los Padres National Forest.

Visitors can view the telescope from the Lick Observatory Visitor Gallery, and in summer the observatory sometimes operates a Summer Visitor Program on Friday nights, allowing the public to look through the 36-inch telescope. The show consists of a lecture by a Lick astronomer and then a viewing of an astronomical object, such as a star cluster or gaseous nebula. The program is free, but tickets must be reserved. Call ahead to make arrangements.

The winding drive up Mt. Hamilton Road to the Lick Observatory should be savored as one of the most engaging outings on the peninsula. After passing the Grant Ranch/Park headquarters, you climb up steep switchbacks, with the white Lick domes bobbing up occasionally before you. Bucolic views unfold of lower grassy ranchlands and, finally, stunning views of the entire South Bay. Scenic cameos include the subtle blue leaves of blue oak groves, the pale gray foliage of digger pine clusters, the deep red bark of large madrones, and the abundant wildflowers of spring or the sere golden grasslands of summer.

Cabernet sauvignon grapes in the Santa Clara wine county

The Santa Clara Wine Country

13

North and South Valley Wineries

The wine industry in the Santa Clara Valley presents a microcosm of the entire California viticultural story, including early moments of historic importance to California wine development, the most inventive contemporary technology in the wine-making arts, the most pedigreed varietal grapes, the friendly and unpretentious "country wine" world of the bulk jug, the emergence of the multinational corporation buying up California wineries, and the challenging land use choices that have squeezed most of the vineyards from Santa Clara to the more southerly valleys of Monterey and San Benito.

The Santa Clara region has a moderate climate ventilated constantly by ocean breezes, making it an optimal place for varietal grape culture, based on the "heat summation" tables drawn up by enologists at the University of California, Davis. The tables add the mean temperature for days during the growing season to compute the total amount of heat on the grapes. Pockets in Santa Clara are good for the major red grapes, such as Cabernet and Zinfandel, and for the preferred white grapes, Chardonnay and Riesling.

The wine world of the Santa Clara Valley is easily accessible. Tasting rooms and touring opportunities are numerous and friendly. Charles Sullivan's book on the history of the Santa Clara wine country, *Like Modern Edens*, provides engrossing background. The book can be purchased from De Anza College's California History Center (see Index for writeup on them).

Basically there are two wine areas in the valley. The northern wine region nestles under Mt. Hamilton and around Saratoga/Los

Gatos. The southern wine area extends from Morgan Hill to Gilroy, then out the Hecker Pass (Highway 152).

North Valley Wine Country

A s you travel across the recently urbanized north Santa Clara Valley, it becomes apparent that people now thrive on acreage where grapes and other crops once grew abundantly. The first subdivision of large ranchos began in the 1880s when middle class city folks moved down from San Francisco and out from San Jose. People were drawn by the satisfying seasonal rhythms of grape and other fruit cultivation, the high yield expected per acre, the certainty of an expanding market because railroads could haul the fruit, and the attractive surroundings, especially in the spring blossom time.

An ideal climate promoted population growth, which eventually crowded out agriculture when electronics and defense industries opened major employment opportunities after World War II. There were 8,000 acres of vines in Santa Clara County in 1940, 6,500 in 1950, 3,500 in 1960, 2,500 in 1970, and there are about 1,500 today. The population in that time has jumped from less than 200,000 to over a million.

The resolution of this population story, looked at from the narrow perspective of wine production, is not entirely unhappy. The main producers of wine in the northern part of the valley have maintained their ancestral hearths here, but have found excellent new territory for grape growing farther south, in Monterey and San Benito counties.

The north valley's first wine producers were the Franciscan fathers who planted at Mission Santa Clara in the late 1700s. The so-called "mission" grape was generally thought adequate for sacramental requirements but of meager interest to secular people with purely gustatory concerns. Pioneers such as Etienne Thee, Charles Lefranc, and Paul Masson gathered cuttings from the standard noble grape varieties of Europe and planted them here in the decades after the Gold Rush.

Mirassou

The Mirassou Winery at 3000 Aborn Road in San Jose, accessible from the east exit of Capitol Expressway off Freeway 101, should be a first stop for the wine explorer. Phone 408/274-4000. The winery, open for touring and tasting, is in the lush foothills of the

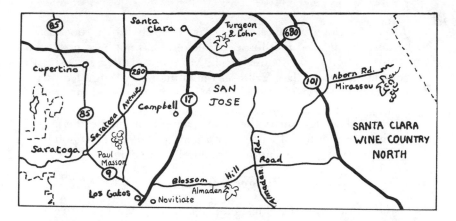

Evergreen area of east San Jose. Around the winery you'll see 22 acres of Cabernet grapes, replanted in 1973.

Mirassou is a family operation, but on a medium-size scale of 350,000 cases per year. Great-great-grandfather Pierre Pellier came from France during the Gold Rush, but he wisely foresaw that lasting fortunes were more readily available in agriculture. His vineyards dated from 1854. Pellier's daughter married into a neighboring wine family, that of Pierre Mirassou, which began the family name. Four Mirassou brothers and a brother-in-law, the fifth generation of a California wine making family, now manage the operation. The Mirassous sold wine in bulk to other producers for four generations. In 1966 they began bottling under their own name.

A beginner should try their accessible, slightly sweet Monterey Riesling. Among their noted varietals are Monterey Johannisberg Riesling, Monterey White Burgundy (Pinot Blanc), and their Brut Champagne. Mirassou's most select batches of certain varietals are bottled under a Harvest Reserve designation, with Zinfandel and Chardonnay among the most successful.

The Mirassous do a great deal to involve the public in their winery, starting with the hospitable tasting room and tours. They have a Cask and Candlelight Tasting in May, Grape Run athletic event in June, Vintage Festival in September, and Holiday Festival in December. Gourmet lunches and dinners are open to the public, plus classes on introduction to California wine and use of wine in cooking.

Part of the Mirassou success can be attributed to their innovative attitude. They were the first bottler to use the word Monterey on their labels, recognizing the major new grape growing area around Soledad, south of the Santa Clara Valley.

238

(Monterey County grapes can be planted on their own rootstock because the dreaded root louse, phylloxera, has not been present in Monterey soil.) Like Paul Masson, Mirassou planted extensively outside the Santa Clara Valley as the human wave engulfed their vineyards from 1950 to 1975. The Mirassous pioneered mechanical picking and field crushing of grapes. In operation the mechanical picker shakes vigorously the vines, trained on overhead wires, causing bunches to fall when they are mature. Peter Mirassou has been a primary proponent of mechanical harvesting.

Turgeon and Lohr

Just as Mirassou is the oldest family-run winery, so the Turgeon and Lohr Winery must take the prize as the most vigorous new winery in this northern region. Their tasting room and winery is at 1000 Lenzen Avenue in San Jose, 408/288-5057. Starting in 1971, Bernard Turgeon and Jerome Lohr planted 280 acres of vineyards near Greenfield in Monterey County, where they were among the pioneers. Grapes are field-crushed in tanker trucks and brought to the winery for processing. Try their Pinot Blanc or Chenin Blanc under the J. Lohr label.

The winery is located in the old Fredericksburg beer brewery, dating from 1869.

Almaden

The giants of Santa Clara wine are Paul Masson and Almaden. Almaden is the larger of the two, producing 12 million cases per year, but Paul Masson has been the more effective exporter. These giants are in turn dwarfed in the overall California wine picture by Gallo, United Vintners, and Franzia. Both Paul Masson and Almaden were sold to large corporate holdings, Almaden to National Distillers and Chemicals in 1967 and Paul Masson to the House of Seagrams in 1944.

Almaden has no tasting or sales room in the Santa Clara Valley, but it has a huge bottling facility with tours at 1530 Blossom Hill Road in San Jose, 408/269-1312. This is a large industrial operation rather than a place organized for visitors, so don't be alarmed by the Pinkerton guard asking your name and taking your license number. Tours are given, but phone for current times, 408/269-1312.

A bronze plaque at the entrance tells their story. In 1852, at this property, Charles Lefranc made the first commercial planting of grapes in California. He brought cuttings of the main varietals from Europe around the Horn. What you see on the tour is the original Almaden cellar of Etienne Thee, Lefranc's father-in-law, plus the old house on the property, now called the 1852 Club, and the immense storage and bottling operations that handle Almaden wine.

The nearest Almaden tasting room is at 890 Pacheco Pass Road where Highway 156 meets Highway 152. The major Almaden grape planting is in the San Benito Valley, southeast of the Santa Clara Valley, where they have 4,281 acres. This is the largest contiguous holding of vines in the world owned by a winery. They also have 2,104 acres in Monterey County.

The most select Almaden wines are bottled under their Charles Lefranc label. Try their Charles Lefranc Cabernet, Pinot St. George, or Fume Blanc (Sauvignon Blanc).

Paul Masson

The Paul Masson Champagne and Wine Cellars at 13150 Saratoga Road in Saratoga, 408/257-7800, are a major touring and tasting stop for thousands of people. You ascend a spiral staircase into the winery, passing a history-of-wine mosaic by Jose Moya del Pino. The mosaic overlooks a spiral fountain that suggests the effervescence of champagne. In the lobby you see a collection of wine containers and glassware ranging from ancient Greek to 19th century European. A narrated slide show then introduces the legendary man from Burgundy, Paul Masson. Educated at the Sorbonne, Masson made his way to California to seek his fortune. He was fortunate enough to marry the daughter of a winemaker. Masson eventually controlled what became Almaden Vineyards, the oldest continuing producer of wine in California, begun in 1852 by Etienne Thee and his son-in-law, Charles Lefranc. Lefranc, Paul Masson's father-in-law, planted the original vines that became the seed of both the Paul Masson and Almaden wine empires of today.

By 1892, Masson perfected a champagne that won the highest award at the Paris Exposition of 1900. Masson is portrayed in the show as a slightly overweight bonvivant, a gay blade early in life and a rakish fellow later, an impeccable dresser in his bowler hat and cravat, with silk waistcoat and striped pants. He was a companion of beautiful women, such as actress Anna Held. The actress took a bath in champagne on one occasion at Paul Masson's mountaintop chateau. When the press of the day sustained itself by covering the caper in detail, Masson was quick

A vineyard above Saratoga

to point out that she had bathed, remember this, in *Paul Masson* champagne.

Both this traditional pride in the wine and push behind the product assert themselves in the Masson winery tour. The tour is most enlightening on weekdays when the commercial activities are vigorous and the human crush less devastating. It is self-guided, with the aid of a wand that activates recordings spaced strategically along a walkway above the wine-making and bottling operations. Several 40,000-gallon blending tanks and some 5,000,000 bottles of champagne aging are awesome to consider.

Winemaker Joe Stillman chooses the best Paul Masson wine for their Pinnacles Selection label. The vineyards lie just below Monterey County's Pinnacles National Monument, a lovely scenic area, especially in spring. Try the Paul Masson Pinnacles Selection Chenin Blanc or their Brut Champagne.

Paul Masson Music at the Vineyards

At the tasting room you can also obtain information and get on the mailing list for popular Paul Masson musical events, which have become a major summer cultural happening on the peninsula. The 25th of these summer series of programs took place in 1982 with much celebration. There are concerts of classical music, known as the Music at the Vineyards, and a more contemporary jazz and folk series, Vintage Sounds. Both take place at the historic Masson hilltop winery, La Cresta, a few miles west of Saratoga. This hilltop winery is otherwise closed to the public. Intermission at these events amounts to a tasting of Paul Masson champagnes and wines. George Shearing, Dave Brubeck, Ray Charles, and many other celebrated musicians have entertained here in recent seasons.

For information, phone 408/725–4275 or write to Paul Masson Concerts, P.O. Box 1852, Saratoga 95070.

Novitiate

Another readily accessible winery in the northern area around Los Gatos/Saratoga is Novitiate, at the end of College Avenue in Los Gatos, 408/354–6471.

When the Jesuit order founded the Novitiate Winery in the 1880s, the purpose was to provide a steady supply of sacramental wines and assure a means of support for young men studying for ordination. Brother Louis Olivier, himself a vintner before hearing the call, returned to his native Montpelier region of Italy to secure the first vine cuttings. Today about 40 percent of the production goes to sacramental wines, and the rest competes for the California consumer market. Catholic religious orders producing wine in California, such as the Christian Brothers in Napa and the Jesuits here, are taxed the same as their commercial competitors and obtain no advantage because of a special legal status.

Novitiate runs a hospitable and intimate tasting room in a decorous stone cellar, which appeals to travelers who prefer to avoid the larger scale touring/tasting situation at nearby Paul Masson. Such niceties as breadsticks to clear the palate and water to wash the glass between tastings are marks of the Novitiate style. Try their Cabernet or Black Muscat dessert wine. Some of the Novitiate grapes come from property they own in the Central Valley.

The Miniaturists

Aside from these major touring and tasting opportunities, there are also the miniaturists, who produce small amounts of outstanding and expensive wines and are open by appointment.

Foremost among these is Ridge Winery, at 17100 Monte Bello Road, near the top of a long grade. Ridge winemaker Paul Draper makes wines "in the simplest and most natural way, consistent with good modern winery practice." Try any of their Cabernets or Zinfandels. The view from Ridge is impressive and the road is long, so bring a picnic lunch and phone ahead 408/867-3233 for an appointment, usually for a Saturday.

Other miniaturists sell their wine direct or through a few encyclopedic bottle shops, such as Beltramo's, 1540 El Camino Real in Menlo Park. Labels to look for include Pendleton, Calera, Martin Ray, David Bruce, Roudon-Smith, and Congress Springs.

South Valley Wineries

The other Santa Clara wine country lies in the southern part of the county, extending from Morgan Hill to Gilroy and onto the Hecker Pass Road (Highway 152) toward Watsonville. The wineries here have their own special style and vitality. Though there is one major national brand producer, San Martin, most of the wineries have more of a down-home "country" wine atmosphere as family-run operations. Nowhere in California is there a wine country more characterized by

family-style ownership, where you are likely to meet the
proprietors themselves in the tasting room. The wine-making
families in this area have often been bottling for several
generations. Some have emphasized wines sold in large jugs, but
the recent trend is toward more varietal wine in corked fifths, sold
in the premium wine market.

Most of the wineries are open for tasting at all times, though
the smaller ones may only open for tasting on the weekend,
depending on family availability. Tours are informal and usually
offered only if an appointment has been made in advance.

By far the most bucolic road remaining through the valley as
you drive south is Santa Teresa Boulevard from Bailey Road south
to Morgan Hill. Santa Teresa's main attraction is its continuing

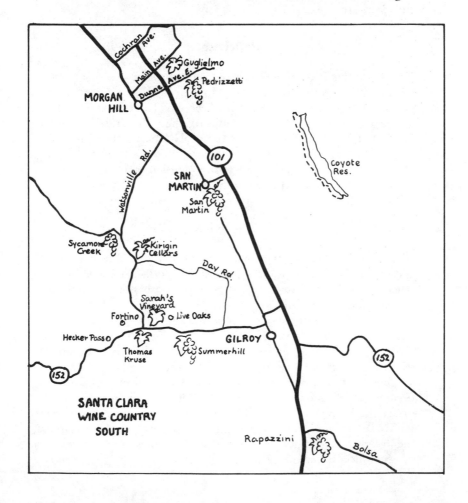

abundance of blossoms from orchard and nut trees, which delight the visitor from February through April. A traveler to the Santa Clara Valley might read about the legendary yield of prunes for which the valley was famous and yet pass through on Freeway 101 and see only a few fruit trees. The absence of fruit trees today might render suspect the claim that the Sunsweet plant in Campbell was once the largest packer of dried fruit on the globe. A drive down Santa Teresa, however, still lends some credibility to this past agricultural golden age. The wine country in the south valley has been spared the "subdivisionitis" that has afflicted winemakers in the north valley around Mt. Hamilton and Saratoga/Los Gatos.

As you approach Morgan Hill, there are three wineries within the town area.

Pedrizzetti

Ed and Phyllis Pedrizzetti's Winery is on the east side of Freeway 101 at 1645 San Pedro Avenue, Morgan Hill, 408/779-7389. However, the tasting room is on Freeway 101 just north of Cochran Avenue, where you should try their Zinfandel, Petite Sirah, and Barbera. The Pedrizzetti family has run the winery since 1945. Like many wine people here, they are from Italy, and have planted much acreage in Italian grape varietals. Tours of the winery can be arranged by appointment.

Guglielmo

The Guglielmo family winery is 1.5 miles east of Freeway 101 at 1480 East Main Street in Morgan Hill, 408/779-2145. The brown stucco winery in its setting of vineyards is a handsome sight on the east side of the valley.

Emilio Guglielmo started the winery in 1925 after arriving in the U.S. in 1908. Today Emilio's son George and grandsons George Jr. and Gene run the wine-making operation and manage the family's 125 acres of grapes, making them the largest of these south county–family wine operations. Because Emilio had many French as well as Italian customers, for decades the wine was sold under the French version of his name, Emile's. But recently the family returned to the original full family name of the patriarch as the designation. Under the Emilio Guglielmo estate label, try their dry Semillon Blanc or Grignolino Rose.

San Martin

Three miles south of Morgan Hill, the San Martin Winery opens wide its doors to the visitor. The main tasting room functions at the home winery in San Martin on the east side of the Monterey Highway, a quarter mile south of San Martin Avenue, 408/683-2672. Two other tasting locations are San Martin Cellars, corner of Highway 25 and Freeway 101, Gilroy, 408/842-7741, and San Martin Cellars, 1110 San Pedro Avenue, Morgan Hill, 408/779-8424.

The winery was begun by the Filice family, valley growers since 1892, but control passed in the 1970s to an outside corporation with vast plantings in Monterey County. Norton Simon, Inc., bought San Martin in 1977, a change of ownership following the customary pattern of contemporary wine economics.

Winemaker Ed Friedrich guided the development of San Martin until 1982, emphasizing low-alcohol "soft" wines favored in his native Germany, where the treasured Rieslings of the Rheingau and Mosel are often lower in alcohol than California wines. Friedrich maintained that alcohol actually masked taste. He aimed at what he saw as fruitier, fuller bouquet wines with a soft taste in the mouth. Among their soft wines try the San Martin Riesling or Chenin Blanc. Among their regular wines, try the Cabernet or Chardonnay.

(The emphasis on "light" wines, meaning low-alcohol wines, has caught the fancy of some weightwatchers, who realize that alcohol means calories. Many companies are coming into the market with so-called light wines. Light is not exactly the same as soft, which is a taste sensation rather than a calorie count. Consumers should know that light wines are usually finished quite dry, while soft wines may have a residual sweetness. The calories of residual sugar, added to the calories of alcohol, may result in soft wines with a higher caloric level than regular wines.)

Live Oak

Out of Gilroy, take the Hecker Pass Road (Highway 152) to encounter a dense cluster of wineries.

The first of these is Live Oak Winery, run by Peter Scagliotti, 4.5 miles from Gilroy at 3875 Hecker Pass Road, 408/842-2401. The Scagliotti family has made wine here since Peter's father,

Eduardo, started in 1912. He settled here because the green hillsides around Gilroy reminded him of his native countryside near Naples. Try their Grenache Rose or Premium Burgundy, a blend. Peter is a living history of this wine region and has many tales to tell and maxims such as "Fine wines are like nice people."

Summerhill

The Summerhill Winery is next as you continue down the Hecker Pass Road, at 3920, 408/842-3032. Summerhill took over the former Bertero Winery here in 1980, with the stated goal of "pleasant and affordable wines." Try their Fume Blanc or Grignolino Rose. The company is the only California winery with Aleatico grapes, an Italian grape that originated on the Isle of Elba. This Aleatico wine is like an after-dinner liqueur.

Angelo Bertero, the former winery owner, opened the modern tasting room on the property in 1973. The Berteros had been working the vineyards since 1917. Angelo saw the winery through Prohibition, when only sacramental wines could be made and tough, thick-skinned grapes, such as Zinfandel, Carignane, and Grenache, could be shipped without breaking to home winemakers. These amateurs were allowed to produce 50 gallons per year for family consumption. Summerhill has changed the wine character from heavier bodied Barberas to lighter styled wines for more contemporary drinking tastes.

Deborah Dodd Johnson organizes Sunday brunches at the winery.

Sarah's Vineyard

One of the newcomers in the Hecker Pass is Sarah's Vineyard, at 4005 Hecker Pass Road, 408/842-4278. Established in 1978, the winery concentrates on Chardonnay, Cabernet, and Zinfandel. Marilyn Otteman and her son Clark manage the winery, aiming for a full bodied Chardonnay in the French style. Most of their grapes are purchased, except for a 7.5-acre planting of Chardonnay they have made at the winery. Call ahead to make an appointment for tasting.

Kruse

Across the road from the intersection of Hecker Pass and Watsonville roads is the house and winery of Thomas Kruse, 4390 Hecker Pass Road, 408/842-7016. Kruse, a native of Chicago, graduate of Northwestern University, and former financial analyst, took up wine making as a hobby and soon found that his hobby took over his life. Finally, he founded the winery in 1971. Kruse makes some interesting specialties, such as Zinfandel Rose. The winery is a small, cobwebbed shed of a building, actually an old winery building from the turn of the century that had been abandoned. Kruse ages his wine in 50-gallon barrels and conducts experiments. Try his Zinfandel or Cabernet.

Kruse favors a European-style production system in California. He would like to see some 2,000 or more small producers come onto the scene, and to some extent that is happening. Today there are close to 500 bonded wineries in the state, while in 1970 there were only about 240.

Kruse is an individualist, with a sense of humor. He changed the name of his Gilroy Red and White in 1982 to Trickledown Red and White in honor of President Reagan. "I want to be a trickler rather than a tricklee," says Kruse. In the past he has enlivened the south valley in the autumn with his barefoot grape stomping contest. Now the other family wineries participate in the autumn grape stomp and also hold a spring barbecue. Both events are open to the public. Contact any of these family wineries for details.

Fortino

Half a mile west on Highway 152 and across the road lies Ernest Fortino's Winery, 4525 Hecker Pass Road, 408/842-3305. Ernie and Marie—no one stands on formality here—may be operating the tasting room as you arrive. In 1970 they bought the old Cassa Brothers Winery and 30 acres of surrounding vines. Ernie is a native of southern Italy with a long wine-making tradition in his family, though he admits that the primitive circumstances of his wine making in Italy make the Hecker Pass operations look opulent by comparison. Try his Petite Syrah (his preferred spelling) or Charbono, which have won a slew of medals, as he regales you with tales of his boyhood in Calabria.

Two picnic tables amidst the vines near the tasting room are available to travelers.

Hecker Pass

Last of the wineries along this route is named, appropriately, Hecker Pass. The winery is located at 4605 Hecker Pass Road, 408/842-8755. Friendly Mario Fortino, whose brother has the

Fortino Winery, owns this establishment. Try his Petite Sirah or Zinfandel. Both are made with Santa Clara Valley grapes from the Gilroy area. The winery has 60 acres in nearby holdings. Mario has built an attractive picnic area with several tables near the entrance to the winery, across the driveway from the vines.

Across the road from the winery stand fields of the strangest agricultural crop on the peninsula, prickly pear cactus. Candy is made from the red fruit of the cactus.

Sycamore Creek

Shortly after the turn of the century this winery on Uvas Road, off Watsonville Road, was started as the Marchetti Winery. Like many other wineries in this region, it was effectively shut down by Prohibition. New owners emerged in 1976 in the persons of Terry and Mary Kay Parks, who renamed the winery Sycamore Creek. Today they make about 3,000 cases per year. Try their Zinfandel or Cabernet, from grapes grown right around their handsome house in the vineyards. The address is 12775 Uvas Road out of Morgan Hill, 408/779-4738.

Kirigin

Turning north from Hecker Pass Road to Watsonville Road, you pass through attractive rolling hill country with grape vines, orchards, and nut trees. The valley was aptly named with the Spanish word for grapes, uvas. Kirigin Cellars, which took over the third-generation Bonesio Winery, lies at 11550 Watsonville Road, 408/847-8827.

Winemaker Nikola Kirigin-Chargin is a Croatian who brought new vigor to this winery and its 50 acres of surrounding grapes. Kirigin favors varietals with 100 percent of the stated varietal grape rather than a judicious blend. Try his Sauvignon Vert or his family wine, a proprietary blend called Opal Rose. He also makes a small amount of a sweet sipping wine, called Malvasia Bianca. Kirigin hosts a summer concert and barbecue at the winery each June. The winery stands on the historic Solis Rancho grant, with the oldest part of the existing building dating from 1827.

Kirigin Cellars has another tasting room on Freeway 101, at 19500 Monterey Road in Morgan Hill, 408/779-5478.

Rapazzini

Surely the most resilient winery in the region is that of the Jon and Sandra Rapazzini family. The winery has arisen phoenixlike from the ashes of a devastating fire in 1980. Try their Cabernet or Zinfandel, produced from grapes bought in choice locations from Mendocino to San Luis Obispo. The winery is at 4350 Monterey Road (Freeway 101) south of Gilroy, 408/842-5649.

Wine Events

Various festivals during the year, involving individual wineries or towns, are open to the public. These include an annual Summer Wine Seminar in August, plus wine as part of annual city festivals in Los Gatos, Sunnyvale, Mountain View, and Campbell. For current information send a stamped, self-addressed envelope to Santa Clara Valley Wine Growers Association, P.O. Box 1192, Morgan Hill 95037.

A group called Friends of the Winemakers, P.O. Box 543, Los Gatos 95039, 408/354-6471, meets eight or nine times per year to discuss wine making and the history of wine in the valley.

WINO is a tasting group that invites new members, 408/255-4084.

Aside from the Santa Clara Valley wineries, touring and tasting are possible on the peninsula at Bargetto in Soquel, Felton-Empire in Felton, and Obester in Half Moon Bay. (See the Index for writeups on them.)

Americans still drink more soft drinks than coffee, more coffee than beer, and more beer than wine. But 1980 was a milestone year for the wine industry because in that year Americans, for the first time, drank more wine than hard liquor. On a per-capita basis this great leap forward amounts only to an average yearly consumption of two gallons. That's about a tenth of the wine consumption of the average Frenchman.

An orchard in early spring, with mustard

The South Valley

14

Gilroy to Watsonville

T he loss of farmland to urbanization, especially in the Santa Clara Valley, is part of a dramatic national trend that now concerns many citizens. Farmland and allied greenbelts produce a portion of our food, catch and supply high quality water, absorb rain runoff to prevent flooding, provide a rich habitat for a range of plants, birds, and animals, and generally give us imaginative room to wander in as we cope with the pressures of urbanized life. The appreciation of farmlands as a visual amenity, an uncluttered landscape, is certainly an important factor. But as energy prices climb, the fundamental value of peninsula farmlands rises as a close-to-consumer source of our daily food. Food grown close to the point of consumption can be fresh and can bypass the energy-intensive costs of transport and processing.

Between 1949 and 1979, about 190,000 acres of Bay Area farmlands went into urban development. A third of all cropland on the valley floors has now disappeared on the peninsula. San Mateo County lost 18,326 acres of cropland to urbanization, but Santa Clara County lost 121,538 acres to the same creeping development. In the northern part of the valley only sparse islands of farmlands, about 10,000 total acres, remain around Sunnyvale, Los Gatos, the Evergreen section of east San Jose, and the relatively large croplands west of Milpitas. In the south valley, however, agriculture feels less pressure. Fifty-five thousand acres are planted to tomatoes, cucumbers, bell peppers, fruit and nut orchards, and lettuce. This is one of only two areas in California where cherries grow well.

In the southern part of the Santa Clara Valley, legendary productivity persists for orchard agriculture and other farming crops. Gilroy celebrates each summer with its Garlic Festival. Not to be outdone, Morgan Hill hosts a Mushroom Festival. Watsonville has the densest cluster of U-pick farms, offering everything from apples to olallieberries, and also hosts the most countrified county fair on the peninsula.

In addition to agriculture, two special parks can be found in this region. Henry Coe State Park occupies the eastern heights of the valley and has recently been expanded to an immense, 70,000-acre size, though some of the acreage has not yet been opened for public use. Henry Coe, mainly a hiking and backpacking park, is now second only to Anza Borrego Desert Park in acreage among California state parks. Mt. Madonna County Park, on the west slopes of the valley, offers ample redwood forests and some of the loveliest car-camping, hiking, and picnicking destinations on the peninsula.

A private museum and restaurant worth visiting in the area is the Flying Lady, near Morgan Hill, where an extensive collection of carriages, cars, airplanes, and model airplanes greets the traveler.

Farmer Direct Produce

Peninsula residents eat better because of local farms. Food for local consumption can be picked riper and have better taste and nutritional quality than food shipped long distances. Cherries, apricots, plums, pears, strawberries, grapes, peppers, onions, and tomatoes are some of the peninsula crops.

Though the soil is extremely rich on the peninsula, sometimes going down 14 feet, farming here enjoys one unique benefit, the climate, which can't be duplicated exactly elsewhere. The growing season is long, moderated by sea air. Summers are warm but not devastatingly hot, moderated by the influence of coastal fog. Cool, moist fog covers the coast almost every summer day. Climates in the valleys on the east side of the Santa Cruz Mountains are warm, but not withering in their heat in summer, and cool, but not extraordinarily frosty, in winter. This is the secret to growing such a diverse range of crops.

If you want to explore the countryside, buy the freshest produce, and meet actual farmers in Santa Clara and Santa Cruz counties, get the useful free brochure called *County Crossroads* by sending a stamped self-addressed envelope to County Crossroads, 1368 North Fourth Street, San Jose 95112. (There is also a separate, state-run, farmer-direct marketing organization that provides a similar booklet and information, but it's less specialized on the local scene. Call 800/952-5272 for the free list they've compiled on farms dealing directly with consumers.) The excellent *County Crossroads* brochure lists 50 commodities from almonds and apples through walnuts and wool and indicates where they can be purchased. A helpful Fresh Produce Calendar alerts you to what is in season. For example, blackberries can be harvested in June and July.

The listings themselves describe what the farmers offer. Some farms offer their foods prepicked and prepackaged, others allow you to pick your own. Sample listings are not always complete. For example, one farm I visited specializes in apples and apple juice, but I found they also offered berries and much other produce. Here is their listing, typical of what you find in the brochure:

> Gizdich Ranch, 408/722-1056. Apples at 55 Peckham Road, Watsonville. Red and Golden Delicious, Pippins, McIntosh, Prime Gold. Fresh natural apple juice. Tours by appointment. Open September to December 31.

Not all the listings require that you go into the country to buy direct from farmers. For example, here is a Farmers' Market listing for Santa Cruz:

> Monterey Bay Area Certified Farmers' Market. 17th Avenue and Capitola Road, Santa Cruz, at Live Oak School. Open Saturdays only 9 A.M. to 12 noon. June thru October. More than 29 farmers from Coastal and Valley Farms offering a wide range of vegetables, fruit, eggs, honey, and cut flowers. Excellent values and selection. Bulk purchases for canning, drying.

Many of the listings offer the lowest possible price because the farms are U-pick. Here is one such listing:

> BFB Ranch/Gurnee's Lakeside Farms, 408/722-1135. 600 Amesti Road, Watsonville. Olallie, Boysen, and Raspberries. Strawberries, Red Currants, and Persimmons. U-pick. Bring containers. Open May thru November, Tuesday thru Saturday, 8 to 5. Closed Monday.

This listing map is fascinating to browse as you contemplate future forays into the countryside. You can get Christmas trees at the Partridge Ranch in Saratoga, sausage at Neto Sausage in Santa Clara, cherries at the Saso Stand on Monterey Road. Those farms that are certified as organic growers, using no chemical fertilizers or pesticides, are so labeled.

Looking to the future, it is even possible to tour a farm specializing in the highly touted bean whose oil, it is said, will have so many far-reaching applications, partly as a replacement for whale oil. That bean is the jojoba (ho-ho'-ba). The farm is:

> Mathison Jojoba Plantation, 408/842-2782, 3350 Leavesley Road, Gilroy. Jojoba seeds. Jojoba oil products; cosmetics and motor oil. Jojoba nuts and seeds from early producing plants. Open all year. Tours.

All these farms, whether traditional or innovative, provide an opportunity for the city dweller to witness the process of food growing, the basic biological mystery and drama on which our lives depend.

The hillside grazing lands are also extremely productive, about three times as lavish in their grass production as the rest of California's hillsides. Especially near the coast in San Mateo County, the fog keeps grasses growing for an extremely long period of the summer.

Anderson Lake County Park

As you move south in the valley, the experience of farms, towns, and public parks mixes together. Anderson Lake County Park is a 2,031-acre park surrounding a large man-made body of water (Anderson Reservoir) in the hills east of Morgan Hill, accessible via East Dunne Avenue or Coyote Road. The grass and chaparral land around the reservoir offers a springtime encounter with wildflowers and lush, green grazing lands after the winter rains. Boating and fishing for bass, catfish, and crappies are popular in the reservoir. Picnic areas are located on the grounds below the dam and on East Dunne Avenue at a site called Wood Chopper Picnic Area. The view from the dam is the best available panorama of south county croplands. In July you can look down on numerous drying racks of apricots.

Henry W. Coe State Park

This 70,000-acre hiking and backpacking park in the hills east of Morgan Hill offers an exceptional outing in spring, when the wildflowers are blooming and the hills are green. In summer the park can be quite hot, dusty, and dry, though still enjoyable, especially since it is so little used. In autumn, the black oak and big leaf maple leaves turn shades of yellow and red as the weather once again becomes cooler.

Headquarters of Henry Coe Park, a former cattle ranch

Henry Coe was a cattle rancher who began homesteading here in 1883 with his brother, Charles. His daughter, Sada Sutcliff Coe, gave the ranch, called The Pine Ridge Ranch, to the state in 1953.

The feeling of the park is one of wide-open hilly grasslands, dotted with oak trees and pines at the higher elevations, bathed in sunshine, in contrast to the dark, cool redwood parks.

Two special botanical features can be observed at Henry Coe: exceptionally large manzanitas resemble trees rather than shrubs at Manzanita Point; and a botanical "island" of ponderosa pine thrives here, as well as at scattered Santa Cruz mountain locations, such as Henry Cowell Park, far from the nearest major stands 100 miles east in the Sierra Nevada.

Henry W. Coe State Park is at the end of a narrow, 14-mile road that zigzags into the hills from Morgan Hill. Allow plenty of time when driving East Dunne Avenue to see the dense forests of blue oak, black oak, live oak, and buckeye along the roadside.

Almost 100 miles of trails, mainly old cattle-ranch roads but some footpaths, await you in the park. The recent acquisitions that have more than doubled the park's size will result in many, many miles of additional trails. The size of the park on the next generation of available maps will surprise many visitors.

Seven backpacker camps stretch out at varying distances from the ranch/park headquarters. Be sure to carry water when camping here. Near headquarters there is also a small, primitive, drive-in camp with shade ramadas for 20 car camper groups. Backpacking camps operate on a first-come basis, but in practice camping pressure has been light. Eight "environmental campsites," the state parks' new concept of hike-in camps, can be reserved through Ticketron. Call the park at 408/779-2728 for current camping arrangements.

At headquarters you'll find two major structures, the historic home of the Coes, now a residence for the ranger, and a new nature and history interpretive center built in the same style. There you can get a trail map and review possible loop trails, running from one to 21.4 miles. The easiest walk is a short distance to a monument dedicated to Henry Coe, sited at the highest point in the park. From this vantage point a full view of Monterey Bay unfolds on clear days.

Displays at the interpretive center acquaint you with dramas in nature here, such as the efforts of a bobcat to catch ground squirrels. A particularly complete loose-leaf binder of wildflowers describes the spring annuals found on these lands. Exhibits on ranch life show much of the furniture that the Coes brought carefully from New England. The clothing that cowboys wore, the seasonal branding and hay gathering months, and even the occasional picnic social or hoedown dance are described. The Coes became skilled at living off the land, eating miner's lettuce and watercress in spring, making elderberry pastries in summer, gathering pine nuts in autumn, and searching out mushrooms in winter. They brewed eucalyptus-leaf tea for colds and drank yerba buena-leaf tea as a tonic.

Morgan Hill

The house to see in Morgan Hill is Villa Mira Monte, a turn-of-the-century Victorian built for rancher Hiram Morgan Hill. The house is still a private residence at 17860 Monterey Road. The town is named after a person rather than after a hill, as many travelers mistakenly assume.

Martin Murphy, co-leader of the first party of immigrants that opened the Truckee Pass across the Sierra Nevada, acquired 9,000-acre Rancho Ojo de Agua de la Coche here in 1845. The property had been in the hands of the Mexican Hernandez family. In 1846 Murphy moved to the Hernandez adobe on El Camino

Real. By 1870, Murphy's seven sons and daughters had acquired more than 70,000 acres, extending from Sunnyvale to Gilroy. They gained a reputation as generous people.

In 1851 the youngest son, Daniel, married Maria Fisher, heiress to the neighboring 19,000-acre Rancho Laguna Seca. Daniel and Maria's daughter, Diana, secretly married a dashing San Franciscan named Hiram Morgan Hill, in 1882.

Diana and Hiram built the Villa Mira Monte near the railroad stop. The railroad called the stop Morgan Hill's Ranch, and later, Morgan Hill. The house is built of redwood hauled from the Hecker Pass.

Morgan Hill is known for its mushroom production. In recent years the town has held a full-blown Mushroom Mardi Gras Festival each May, honoring the lowly fungus in all kinds of culinary efforts. Art displays and entertainment add to the carnival atmosphere surrounding the event. For details contact the Morgan Hill Chamber of Commerce, 408/779-9444.

Two restaurants to consider are the Morgan House, 275 East Dunne Avenue, for prime rib or veal scallopini, 408/779-6306, and Mathews Country Manor, 65 West Main Street, located in an old converted house, which features broiled peppercorn steaks and prawns cooked in beer batter, 408/779-6776.

Wagons to Wings Museum

A unique collection of winged and wheeled transportation can be seen at the Flying Lady Museum and Restaurant in Morgan Hill. The eclectic holding, called Wagons to Wings, has been assembled by Irv and Jan Perch over decades. The collection is open free to the public, but you might want to include a meal at the restaurant, which offers fixed-price, multicourse meals and a view of the adjacent golf course. To see the extravaganza, take Tennant Avenue off Highway 101 east from Morgan Hill and turn south on Foothill Road, following the signs.

When you reach the grounds, you first pass a rusty collection of 19th-century agricultural equipment along the road. Then you walk through a dusty barn full of carriages and wagons, housing everything from a U.S. Mail wagon to a hearse, a water tank wagon to fancy carriages.

After that, you visit a metallic airplane hangar that encloses a collection of old airplanes and automobiles. Here you see, among many other planes and cars, a 1930 Ford Tri-Motor with a 77 foot wingspan, 12-passenger capacity, and price tag when built of (only) $47,000. This plane helped start coast-to-coast passenger service. Among other planes here are a 1927 De Haviland Gypsy Moth monoplane that set speed records in flights from Europe to Australia. The vehicle collection is also intriguing, including everything from old Model T's to chic Packards of the 1940s.

The nostalgic, tour-de-force, airplane motif continues at the restaurant, which is an optional visit. Outside you're greeted by a barker selling tapes of early radio music. To the left, as you enter, glance over at the carved heads of W. C. Fields and other notables. You dine under actual airplanes or replicas of airplanes, such as a 1909 Beriot, first plane to cross the English Channel. Smaller model airplanes on a continuous overhead track circle during your meal. Smoked salmon or roast duck are excellent entrees for the elaborate dinners, with reservations advised, 408/779-4136.

Gilroy

S outh from Morgan Hill lies another small agricultural town, Gilroy.

The town owes its name to John Gilroy, an alias for John Cameron, who came to these parts in 1813 after taking French leave from an English trading vessel in Monterey. Cameron was a rugged and enterprising Scotsman who soon acquired a share of Rancho San Ysidro by marrying Clara Ortega, a daughter in the Ygnacio Ortega family. Gilroy had the distinction of being the first English-speaking settler in California. After the American takeover of California in 1848, land ownership was no longer restricted to Mexican citizens, and Gilroy's influence increased.

The early history of the area is told at the Gilroy Museum, 195 Fifth Street, where old photos portray the 19th-century residents. An unusual building is the old Gilroy City Hall, Sixth and Monterey streets, a Flemish-style stone structure dating from 1906.

Gilroy's Garlic Festival

The most famous farm and food festival in the peninsula region is the annual Gilroy Garlic Festival, held each year in late July or early August. For information, write to Garlic Festival, P.O. Box 2311, Gilroy 95020, phone 408/842-1625. The festival is held in Christmas Hill Park, a 36-acre site that allows plenty of breathing space.

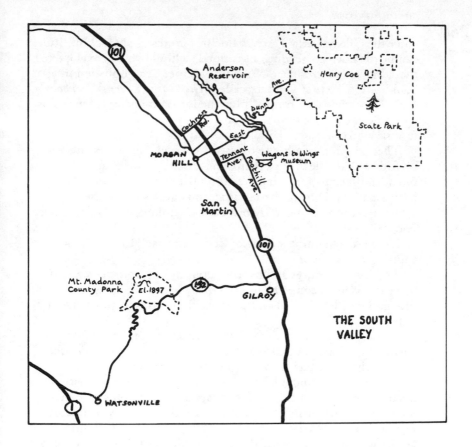

The following text labels appear on the map:

101

Anderson
Reservoir

Henry Coe

Cochran Rd.

Dunne Ave.

East

State Park

MORGAN
HILL

Tennant
Ave.

Foothill Ave.

Wagons to Wings
museum

San
Martin

101

Mt. Madonna
County Park

El. 1897

152

GILROY

THE SOUTH
VALLEY

1

WATSONVILLE

Basis of the festival is the garlic bulb, which grows to perfection in the climate of this area. The region around Gilroy produces about 90 percent of the U.S. supply of garlic. Humorist Will Rogers once remarked, "Gilroy is the only town in America where you could marinate a steak by hanging it out on the clothesline." Gilroy calls itself, in the American tradition of reaching for superlatives, the Garlic Capital of the World.

If you are among those who rank garlic high in the culinary hierarchy, this festival is an extraordinary event. About 60,000 people attend the festival now, though it only began in 1979. The heart of this festival is the serious eating of garlicky foods. Gourmet Alley features local chefs performing culinary magic over large fire pits in full view of the spectators. Garlic calamari is a festival specialty. Local vegetables, mushrooms, and fish caught off the California coast can be found in different garlic dishes.

Amateur cooks with a passionate commitment to garlic can

enter the Gilroy Garlic Festival Recipe Contest and Cookoff. Rules can be obtained by sending a stamped, self-addressed envelope to the address listed earlier. Winning recipes are published in a cookbook. The first volume, called *The Garlic Lover's Cookbook*, with 200 garlic-laced recipes, plus the lore and history of garlic, is available for $6.95 plus $1.50 for postage and handling from the festival address.

The trappings of a harvest festival beyond culinary events can be found in the beauty pageant, barn dance, golf tournament, musical offerings, bicycle race, 10,000-meter run, and theater performances. During the festival you can also tour the major garlic-processing plants of McCormick/Schilling and Golden West Foods.

Here are a few notes on the "stinking rose" for all garlic appreciators to savor:

The U.S. produces 150 million pounds of garlic per year, 90 percent of which comes from the Gilroy area. About two-thirds of that garlic is dehydrated and processed into flakes, powders, and salts.

France, Italy, Greece, and Spain are known for their use of garlic in cooking, but China, Korea, and Brazil each consume more garlic per capita than those European countries.

Garlic has been popular for some time. The earliest written documents, Sanskrit from 5,000 years ago, mention garlic. The Sumerians used garlic, and workers on the great pyramids of Egypt were fed garlic to increase their strength and stamina. Garlic was entombed with King Tutankhamun. Roman soldiers ate garlic, supposedly to increase their strength and courage in battle.

The medicinal claims for garlic are numerous and the subject of ongoing clinical verification. Some reports cite it as lowering cholesterol, preventing heart disease, reducing harmful bacterial levels, and even assisting the body in expelling accumulated heavy metals.

There are 300 or more varieties of garlic around the world, but only two predominate in California. Early, or California, garlic is white and is harvested May–June; late, or pink, garlic follows in three to five weeks. The early variety has a slightly rounder, flatter bulb, and the late variety has a pink skin.

Garlic is planted from late September to November from individual cloves, sprouting in three to five weeks, then growing through the winter and spring except when dormant at times of extreme cold. After the tops die back in late spring, the bulbs are harvested, cured in the sun, and packed.

Mt. Madonna County Park

From Gilroy, the road west on Highway 152 (Hecker Pass Road) to Mt. Madonna Park presents one of the inviting rural settings of Santa Clara County. Country-style family wineries, such as Live Oak, invite tasting and lingering, as detailed in chapter 13. Huge eucalyptus trees from plantings 80 years ago line the roads. And an unusual agricultural crop, prickly pear cactus, called *nopalo* in Mexico, grows in commercial fields. The cactus buds are harvested when the seeds have set and swollen in a soft fruit. This fruit becomes a kind of jam candy much prized in Mexico and among Mexican Americans.

Rustic Mt. Madonna Park, 408/842-2341, invites campers and hikers to explore its 3,056 acres of redwood forests, plus mixed forests thick with tanoak. Huge madrone trees show a red bark that glints handsomely in the sun. California bay tree leaves have a fragrance, similar to European bay, that delights the cook. When crushed fresh, the leaves are perfume to the nostrils of the hiker.

Mt. Madonna's campgrounds are often less crowded than Big Basin's. Excellent trails here have but one limitation, an occasional steepness that may discourage the novice walker. Start with the fairly level, half-mile trail beginning from the Giant Twins, two redwood trees that happily survived the loggers' insatiable saws. This trail winds down a slight slope and then angles back to the road, acquainting you with the full range of Mt. Madonna's flora. Deep in the redwood grove along the trail, you see good illustrations of how clusters of young redwoods sprout from the tree's roots after the dominant mother redwood has been logged off. The wondrous quiet of a redwood forest and the luminous filtered light streaming through the delicate redwood leaves are both present here. In the mixed forests of bay, tanoak, madrone, and some coast live oak the early morning hiker will encounter numerous varied thrushes saluting the awakening day.

After the Giant Twins walk, consider another easily negotiated warm-up hike from near the ranger station/visitor center to the home of cattle and lumber baron Henry Miller. This is not the writer Henry Miller, but another man who was equally well known in his world of substantial movers and shakers in late-19th-century California. Henry Miller and partner Charles Lux once controlled over a million acres of land and a million head of cattle.

Santa Clara County purchased the Miller estate for a park in 1927. Italian woodcutters employed by Miller had called the area

The Giant Twins redwoods at Mt. Madonna Park

Mt. Madonna, and the name stuck. Today his former summer house is a ruin, but the elaborate foundation of sandstone, mined on the property, suggests the former splendors of the estate. A half-mile nature trail starting at the Miller house acquaints you with the flora of the area and includes one intriguing stop, the stick home of a wood rat, a secretive mammal seldom seen because of its nocturnal habits.

If you find these modest beginner's trails well within your competence, graduate to the lovely but steeper walk along the Spring Lake Trail, descending through a redwood forest with many luxurious sword ferns to Spring Lake, a small pond created from a dammed creek drainage. Rangers open the dam's gate every winter for the excessive runoff of heavy rains and then close it again in spring to fill the pond before stocking it with trout. The return walk up Blackhawk Trail, a fire road of long, steep ascent, offers a glimpse at one of the extraordinary adaptations possible in nature. Bay trees, which normally sprawl, can be seen growing almost vertically, like conifers, in a life and death battle for light, meaning survival. Allow four hours for the Spring Lake–Blackhawk walk.

The most ambitious hikers will want to take the Merry-Go-Round Trail that skirts the perimeter of the park. Winter is an especially congenial time to hike here, when the sky is bright and clear, the air cleaned by rains, and the cycle of vegetative growth spurred anew by the presence of life-sustaining moisture.

Watsonville

West from the Hecker Pass lies Watsonville, a town in the Pajaro River drainage of Santa Cruz County. It is a charming small town with its own proud traditions. Stop by the Watsonville Chamber of Commerce at 444 Main Street, 408/724-3849, and ask for the *Walking and Driving Tour* pamphlet, which alerts you to the considerable Victorian heritage of the area, including the Tuttle House at 723 Eastlake Avenue, built in 1899.

The town plaza at Watsonville is a friendly meeting place, reminiscent of small-town plazas in the Midwest, the hearts of stable and enduring communities. In Watsonville, English- and Spanish-speaking residents rest in the plaza, all out enjoying the sun. The William Volck Memorial Museum, 261 East Beach

Street, describes the quiet, dependable growth and prosperity of Watsonville, based on agriculture.

Two annual celebrations of note here are the Antique Fly-In in May and the Santa Cruz County Fair in September.

The Antique Fly-In brings over 50 ancient planes and thousands of visitors to the Watsonville Municipal Airport for the Memorial Day weekend. Collecting and maintaining the planes hovers between a passion and an addiction for aficionados. Jack Landage won the award in 1982 for the longest flight, over 2,000 miles from Calgary, Alberta. Landage's plane was an open-cockpit, 1940 Waco biplane, and it was a chilly ride. Temperatures in the three-day flight didn't rise to 40 degrees until he reached Red Bluff in northern California. The 1982 celebration at Watsonville marked the 18th annual Antique Fly-In. Precision flying teams, partying, food, crafts, and entertainers are all part of this Watsonville happening.

The annual Santa Cruz County Fair, in September, offers a more rural feeling than other county fairs on the peninsula. Fairgrounds are four miles from Watsonville on Highway 152. Over 700 entries can be expected in apple competition, signaling the importance of apples to the local agricultural economy. Flower displays are also exceptional, including those done by children without adult supervision. A large horse show combines parading of horses for appearance with rodeo skills performed by local talent. Livestock judging is competitive, especially in sheep and goats. For the traveler, the pleasures of this agricultural county fair can continue year round when exploring the farms of the region that sell direct to consumers, with some even allowing you to pick your own, as indicated earlier. The Watsonville Chamber of Commerce is another source for the excellent brochure, *County Crossroads*, listing farms you can visit and buy direct from in Santa Cruz and Santa Clara counties.

Information Sources
For Natives and Visitors

In the three county area there are four major information sources useful to natives and visitors who wish to explore the region. They are especially helpful for rapidly changing information, such as the price of admission, the current offerings of a theater group, etc. They are:

San Mateo County Convention and Visitors Bureau
888 Airport Boulevard
Burlingame, CA 94010
415/347-7004

Santa Cruz County Convention and Visitors Bureau
P.O. Box 1476
Santa Cruz, CA 95061
408/423-6927

Santa Clara Convention and Visitors Bureau
1515 El Camino Real
Santa Clara, CA 95050
408/296-6863

San Jose Convention and Visitors Bureau
El Paseo de San Antonio
San Jose, CA 95113
408/998-7000

Index and List
of Peninsula Resources

Besides the individual items that serve as an index, these lists also include several generic subjects. With the lists you can guide yourself quickly to information in the book on peninsula resources, such as:

Architectural walking tours
Backpacking parks
Beaches
Books about the Peninsula
Camping parks
Festivals
Gardens and Nurseries
Museums
Nature trails, self-guided
Parks
Restaurants
Wineries

276

The Author

Lee Foster is a veteran writer/photographer whose work has been published widely in magazines and in ten previous books of travel, fiction, health, and how-to. Besides travel writing, his other main subject is food gardening and the ecological good life. On that subject he is the author of a recent book, *Backyard Farming* (Chronicle). Lee's interest in the peninsula began in 1965 when he came to the area from the midwest to do graduate work in literature at Stanford. Since then he has been a continuing resident of the Bay Area. He takes particular pleasure in exploring the world of nature and the story of human history on the peninsula.

Other California Guides from:

PRESIDIO PRESS

☐ MAKING THE MOST OF MARIN $7.95
    Patricia Arrigoni; photographs by Michael Bry
    Across the Golden Gate Bridge to beautiful Marin
    County—an insider's guide.

☐ MAKING THE MOST OF SONOMA $8.95
    Don Edwards
    An insider's guide to the land and people of
    Sonoma County.

☐ MAKING THE MOST OF THE MONTEREY $5.95
    PENINSULA AND BIG SUR
    Maxine Knox and Mary Rodriguez

☐ THE MONEYWISE GUIDE TO CALIFORNIA $9.95
    Plus Reno, Las Vegas, the Grand Canyon, and
    Baja California
    Vicki León

☐ THE CHINESE RESTAURANT EXPERIENCE: $6.95
    The Best of the Bay Area
    Jennie Low and Diane Yee

    And from Margot Patterson Doss—A series of walking
  guides by San Francisco's well-known walker/writer/teacher:

☐ BAY AREA AT YOUR FEET $7.95

☐ GOLDEN GATE PARK AT YOUR FEET $4.95

☐ THERE, THERE: EAST SAN FRANCISCO BAY $6.95
    AT YOUR FEET

☐ A WALKER'S YEARBOOK: FIFTY-TWO WALKS $8.95
    IN THE SAN FRANCISCO BAY AREA

Available at your favorite bookstore, or order from Presidio Press,
P.O. Box 892CR, Novato, CA 949480892; telephone: (415) 883-1373.
When ordering, please include $1.75 for shipping and handling
(California residents add appropriate sales tax).
Presidio Press honors Master Charge, Visa, and American Express.
Include card number and expiration date.